AF778062

In Pursuit of Justice

In Pursuit of Justice

A. Shakoor Manraj, Q. C.,

Barrister-at-Law

NDueCzon Publishing Group ♦

Tampa, FL

NdueCzon

A. Shakoor Manraj, Q.C.
1021 SW 100 Terrace
Pembroke Pines, FL 33025, USA
Phone: 954-435-5971

Copyright © 2004 by A. Shakoor Manraj

All rights reserved under International and Pan-American Copyright Conventions including the right of reproduction in whole or in part in any form without express written permission from A. Shakoor Manraj and NDueCzon Publishing Group.

Cover design and graphic arts by Essex James of EJ Graphics

Edited by A. Shakoor Manraj and Bonita Manraj. Text edited according to standards and practices of formal English (U.K.) grammatical rules and usage.

Layout & formatting by Angela Judge for NDueCzon Publishing Group

Library of Congress Catalog Number available from the publisher upon request.

Printed in the United States of America

First Edition
10 9 8 7 6 5 4 3 2 1

ISBN: 0-9755679-1-8

In Pursuit of Justice

Dedication

This Book is lovingly dedicated to my Dear, Devoted and Caring Parents:

My Understanding, Helpful and Devoted Mother,

JANE MAKBULAN MANRAJ (Deceased),

and

My Kind, Knowledgeable and Caring Dad,

AZEEZ RAHAMAT MANRAJ (Deceased),

who, by their love, wisdom, kindness and sound principles, have enriched my life and given beneficial guidance to my efforts.

Acknowledgements

I am grateful to all of the following, for their permission to cite and reproduce extracts from their publications. If I have failed or inadvertently overlooked to obtain the requisite permission for any quotations or passages from any publication from which I have cited, I hasten to add that I am in error and apologize. I can only enter to such an oversight my plea of guilty and seek your understandable forgiveness.

I thank my esteemed and learned friend, Mr. Roy Black, for his gracious permission to cite two passages from his scholarly-written Introduction to his engrossing book, "Black's Law." Those passages relate to the attainment of Justice, the protection of one's client and the duty of defence counsel. I must also thank Butterworths Canada Ltd. 1991, for permission to cite from the 2nd Edition of my book: "The Law on Speeding and Radar" by A. Shakoor Manraj, Q.C. and Dr. Paul D. Haines, Ph.D., the passages relating to speeding as an absolute liability offence.

I thank Sweet & Maxwell Ltd. for their kind permission to cite from "Archbold Criminal Pleading, Evidence & Practice" the passages relating to "Right of Jury to stop case," "the onus of proof," the direction of Lord Sankey in Woolmington-vs-D.P.P. (1935) and the observations of Lord Goddard, C.J. regarding the Jury being "satisfied" and "sure" of the guilt of the accused, "the reverse onus" and dicta of Humphreys, J and the "Elements of the Offence of Theft," (the old Larceny under the Larceny Act) all of the above cited by me in Chapters 5, 8 and elsewhere in of my memoirs.

Further, I want to say how grateful I am to Sweet & Maxwell Ltd. for permission to cite from the 1955 Criminal Law Review, p.746, the famous words of Mr. Justice Humphreys and from the 1956 Criminal Law Review, pages

289-290, thc weighty words of Mr. Justice Devlin on "suspicion," all appearing in Chapter 2 of this book.

My thanks to the publishers of the All England Reports, (AER), [1961] 3 All E. R. p. 996 for my citation of the Privy Council judgment in the SHOUKATALLIE –v- R. Murder Appeal and the judgment delivered by the late Lord Denning, who presided at the Privy Council hearing of the Appeal. Further, I wish to express my sincere thanks to Professor Alan M. Dershowitz, Professor of Law at Harvard Law School, for giving me his kind permission to cite in my memoirs, "IN PURSUIT OF JUSTICE," in Chapters 12 and 15, page 60 of his revealing and superbly written book: "Reasonable Doubts," on the O. J. Simpson Murder trial. I feel that Professor Dershowitz must be loudly congratulated for exposing to the large and extensive readership of his book, the word *"testilying."* Professor Dershowitz is also a very competent lawyer who has defended many high-profile cases. I just could not only say thanks, but I also want to add how much I admire his contribution to the law.

A. Shakoor Manraj, Q. C.

Preface

Although this book deals for the greater part with my practice and relations with the Courts of Law, it is not a textbook on the Law. I have given myself more latitude in writing this book. If this were a textbook on the law, the footnotes and references would have taken up valuable space on almost every page and the legal arguments would have been very extensively covered.

This book is primarily intended to place before my readers in a less formal manner, the experiences and involvement of a Barrister at Law/Attorney at Law, who has spent over fifty years of his life as Criminal Defence Counsel, searching and wrestling for Justice, not only in the Courts of Law, but in all the related areas and departments of the law, whether judicial, quasi-judicial, social, religious, commercial, civil rights enforcement agencies and organizations, where Justice is the fountain-head of their goals and achievements.

I really set my mind on writing my memoirs when, as a Junior Barrister, I was invited to give talks to all different types of organizations covering a wide spectrum of activities. The activities and participation in public life continued and when I became a Senior Member of the Bar and was appointed a Queen's Counsel (Q.C.) in 1969, the invitations to deliver lectures and take part in forums, debates and discussions became more frequent. This was good, as I was able to keep in touch with the mainstream thinking and views of the time and of the people. I kept copies of my various speeches and lectures I delivered to the many organizations. These lectures and speeches, although based on the general law relating to different topics, did not have the potential to be called or labelled law lectures. Many of them were based on actual experiences I encountered in my practice – some of them very humorous.

These activities generated a motivating force in me to put my experiences in the form of my memoirs bringing to the surface, the cases in which I appeared and the clients with whom I had to deal.

When one sets out to write a book of this type, it must of necessity appear to the writer that he has something to pass on to his readers, which he feels will interest them. There is so much of one's daily life that is inextricably mixed with what is just, good and morally right, that I thought a book, recording my memoirs would be the proper and appropriate vehicle to achieve my goal.

In the course of my long practice, I have had exposure to those many caring and interested people who love reading about Court cases, the legal arguments involved, the art of cross-examining witnesses and most important of all, the verdict of the Jury. Those two beautiful and powerful words, *"NOT GUILTY"* never fail to bring joy, hope and pleasure to so many others, besides the freed defendant and his immediate relatives and close friends.

An old family friend once said to me, "Lawyers have the best stories to tell. They are all based on human behaviour, frailties, weaknesses and victories." My encounters and discussions with many people regarding my intention of recording my memoirs so that the many interested individuals could read about the life and practice of a criminal defence counsel, have left me convinced that what I have achieved and completed in my fifty years at the Bar, would find a ready audience via this book. At least, this is my sincere hope. This is my goal. This would be the ultimate compensation for my efforts.

I hope that I will have succeeded in giving my readers what they expect from a book of this category and satisfied their ever-growing interest in Justice and its attainment, which so often erroneously appears to be only a philosophical concept without pragmatic application. To help me to achieve what I stated earlier as the primary purpose of this book, I have, where I feel it is relevant and necessary to bring into prominence some of the very important features of the case under review, included parts of my cross-examination of witnesses who gave evidence in Court. To have attempted to summarise the impact of the cross-examination, would have been to obfuscate the significance of the point and the manner in which the evidence in support of it was elicited. I have tried to curtail complex legal arguments in the book.

It is not unusual for writers of books to seek the advice and help of friends, well-wishers and professional colleagues and all those who are so supremely qualified to give guidance. This book is about me, my fifty years at the Bar in the pursuit of Justice. I take sole responsibility for the opinions and views expressed in the Chapters of this book. But if my views, thoughts and opinions find acquiescence and concurrence with you, dear readers, then my views become our views, resulting in that feeling of satisfaction that a writer strives to attain.

I have to say thanks and express my appreciation to so many persons. First of all, I must express my deep appreciation to my Dear Wife, Bonita Manraj, who had to be highly inspired and superhumanly guided, to transform my almost illegible manuscripts into fair and respectable typescripts worthy of submission to my Publishers. Her patience is unmistakable evidence that she is a descendant of the Patriarch Job, as despite the daunting task that my manuscripts presented, she never wavered.

I am also happy to express my thanks to my eldest child, my elder son, Michael Manraj, who trained as an air-line Captain, is very methodical and assisted me in the sequence of the chapters. My eldest daughter, Anne Edun was very helpful in the selection of the human-interest cases covered in the text. To my son-in-law, Azam (Andrew) Edun, M.Sc., I owe a debt of gratitude. I am the beneficiary of his superb computer skills and his resourcefulness as my researcher.

I am so happy to express my thanks to my Granddaughter, Anya Edun, first year student at the University of Miami, Florida, for her industry and tenacity in researching the legal authorities entrusted to her. Her younger sister, Alana Edun, High School Junior, was always ready and willing to get the initial printing of the text material completed. She earns my sincere thanks. My younger son, Andrew Manraj of Toronto, Canada, may not fully realize how very helpful he has been. At the time of our departure from Guyana, Andrew was the Managing Clerk and Supervisor of my Chambers in Georgetown. He preserved and kept in safe custody, many of the files, minute books and records on which I had to rely to write this book. When I started to prepare to write this book, I asked him if he had my minute books and files. I was overwhelmed when he went into his garage and brought out two boxes containing the important minute books and files I used in the course of the trials in which I appeared. Thanks Andrew for your perspicacity and constructive suggestions.

I must also thank my daughter Elizabeth Sorayah of Victoria Island, British Columbia. Her sense of humour is so refreshing. When I was discussing the proposed title of my book with her, I told her that I was thinking of the simple title: "My fifty years at the Bar." Elizabeth's ready response was "Daddy, be careful. You will be inundated with enquiries for the name and address of the Bar where you spent so many years of your life!" I thank her for her constructive suggestions resulting in the elimination process of titles. My youngest daughter, Marcina, gave up some of her valuable time and helped in the proofreading of the typescripts. I thank her for her sagacity. I thank all the members of my family for their unfailing support and constructive suggestions and textual criticisms.

I also wish to record here my thanks to Dr. Paul D. Haines, Ph.D., my devoted friend and co-author of "The Law on Speeding and Radar," for his useful suggestions and advice given to me before and during completion of this book. Dr. Haines' encyclopaedic knowledge was always accessible to me. My close and dependable family friend, Mr. George Mangar, of London, England, earns my sincere thanks for forwarding to me, at my request, all the information on the late Lord Denning. I would also like to record my thanks to my trusted friend, Mr. David A. Clark, CEP, of Fort Lauderdale, Florida, a competent and respectable Certified Estate Planner and Financial Consultant, for the useful suggestions and advice he gave to me on the selection of reader-favourable materials.

I must also here express my thanks to my sincere and kind friend, Mr. Nassim Baksh and his Dear wife, Fazey, who spent many hours with me well into the night going through typescripts with me for publication. Angela Judge of Tampa, Florida, a very fine and efficient consultant made available to me her skills and deep knowledge of printing and publishing problems. For her remarkable efficiency, I am deeply grateful.

To my Printers, Father & Son Associates, Inc. of Tallahassee, Florida, I express my appreciation for their patience, understanding, ready help and dedication. To my Publishers, NDueCzon Publishing Group of Tampa, Florida, I offer my sincere thanks for the efficiency and sound advice resulting in the publication of this lovely and beautifully bound book. To my youngest sister, Mrs. Zaleena Misir of Toronto, Canada, I wish to say thanks for the photographs of our parents appearing on the Dedication page of my book.

Finally, to all those well-wishers and many individuals who helped in so many ways and insisted on anonymity, (you know who you are), I here acknowledge with gratitude their useful observations and timely suggestions so readily and unselfishly given.

A. Shakoor Manraj, Q.C.
Pembroke Pines, Florida.

Table of Contents

Introduction

My Father, Azeez Rahamat Manraj, wanted me to become a surgeon but I knew I was not endowed with that kind of aptitude. Just at the time when I was finishing College, My Dear Father asked me if I had really made up my mind to become a lawyer. I told my Dad that I could not think of myself as anything else but a lawyer. He then very adroitly and pensively said, "My Dear Son, I think you are making a great mistake. I would like you to be a doctor."

My Dad looking very forlorn said, "I did not achieve my ambition to become a doctor because of your grandfather's negative attitude towards my leaving home to go to England to become a doctor, when there was his already successful and expanding real estate and general merchandising business to be looked after. You see my Dear Son, I was the eldest son and child." Before I could say anything, my Father continued, "I want you to ponder over this my son. Lawyers are not as honourable as doctors. Lawyers thrive on the misfortunes, transgressions and weaknesses of human beings. Doctors on the other hand, are lifesavers. They are honourable men and they help suffering humanity. I would really be very pleased if you study to become a surgeon, rather than study to become a Barrister-at-Law."

I was very concerned about what my Dad said to me. He hinted on many occasions that he would like me to become a doctor but I never realized how deeply he was committed to this idea. All sorts of things started to pass through my mind and flood my thoughts.

At all times, I was fully cognizant of the differences in the two professions. I said to my Dear Father, "Doctors have to be very deeply knowledgeable in their professional skills and at times they have to fight to save their patients' life." As a lawyer, I saw myself as a gladiator, fighting sometimes against overwhelming odds, to get "JUSTICE" for my clients who had put their trust and confidence in me.

I told my concerned father that I understood his position and that I respect his feelings and views but I felt, since my very early days in primary school, that the Law was my calling. Add to this the fact that my maternal Uncle, the late P. M. Benson, was an East Indian Guyanese, who studied law in England, became a Barrister-at-Law and was called to the Bar of the Honourable Society of the Middle Temple Law School in England in 1925, the same year in which I was born. Before studying law, he was in the teaching profession. My Uncle Benson died in 1939 and I felt that I could carry on the family tradition albeit that he practised at the Civil Bar and did only Civil Cases and Real Estate Law.

My Dear Mother, Jane Makbulan Manraj, was elated from the very first time I ever mentioned that I had made up my mind to become a Barrister-at-Law and what is more, I intend to attend the same Law School that my late Uncle had attended – the Middle Temple Law School in London, England. After my pre-law years at three Universities, I was successful in securing my Law Degrees and I applied for and gained admission to the Middle Temple in 1948 to study for the Bar. I was called to the Bar in England (remember British Guiana as it then was, was a British Colony and the English Law and practice were entrenched in Guiana) at the Middle Temple on February 9, 1954.

The years I spent studying law and related subjects – logic, political science, philosophy, psychology and legal ethics and advocacy – were the most important and rewarding years of my academic life. I just did not want to pass the Bar Final Examination. I wanted to be well-rounded and fully prepared professionally and academically to embark upon my career as a Barrister-at-Law and an able and competent Lawyer. The Law has been, is and will always be my love, my heart and my everything. I am not surprised at the recognition and status I have achieved as a lawyer. I thank God for His Help, Guidance and Blessings of Good Health He gave to me to achieve my goals as a practising lawyer. One does not have to be a mathematical genius to do the simple arithmetic.

On February 9, 2004, I was at the Bar for fifty long and exciting years. I still do legal work. I was involved in an attempted murder case in New York in May, 2001. Many law firms seek my services as a consultant, but, I am happiest when I am at the Bar table in any Court, in any Jurisdiction, appearing for a defendant in a Criminal Jury Trial or any other legal matter.

When I appear in Jurisdictions where I do not normally practise, I am usually called *pro hac vice* on the Petition of the local lawyer who has retained me, for admission to the Bar of that Jurisdiction. This facilitates me to practise in many of the foreign jurisdictions where I do practise. But to revert to my Dear Dad, when I told him after our discussion mentioned earlier how I saw it and felt, he concluded with resignation by saying to me, "My Dear Son, JUSTICE is an illusory thing. You will have to fight all the time to achieve it."

I accepted this judgment from my father, as it was coming from a man who had spent years in the British Guiana Police Force and had earned a good reputation as a Detective. My Dad eventually retired from the British Guiana Police Force as a Sergeant. After his resignation, he went into business and when I went back to Guyana in 1954 to practice law, both he and my Mom were still very much alive.

At my suggestion, my father gave up business and joined me as Office Manager of my Chambers in Georgetown. He was a reservoir of legal skills. I profited immensely from his knowledge and experience. He gained many medals in recognition of his ability and devotion to the Force. The paradox here is this: here is a man who wanted to be a surgeon. He did not achieve his goal. He wanted me, his son, to be a surgeon. I did not become one.

A. Shakoor Manraj, 9:00 a.m. on February 9, 1954, the day he was admitted to the English Bar.

A. Shakoor Manraj, 9:00 p.m. on February 9, 1954, robed as a Junior Barrister for appearance in the High Courts in England; this marks my admission to the Bar 1954.

My father then saw service in the British Guiana Police Force. He was a good investigator and a good statistician – he compiled all the relevant statistics for the Police Gazette for many years. He did well in life and raised a family of eight children with the faithful, devoted and dedicated help and loyalty of my Dear Mother. At present, we are only four. I am the only brother with three sisters in Canada – Mrs. Jameela Mohamed, Mrs. Zaleena Misir and Mrs. Walima Mohammed.

Now that I have set about writing my experiences, encounters and practice at the Bar, the title that comes to mind, as I give to this effort to chronicle those experiences and my career so far is: "IN PURSUIT OF JUSTICE – Fifty years as Criminal Defence Attorney." That is exactly what I have been doing for the past fifty years – a total of some twenty-four years in England and Wales, in Guyana, where I was also admitted to practise in 1954 and in the Caribbean Territories and the following years after 1978 to the present time, in Canada, Turks & Caicos Islands, many islands in the Caribbean, the U.S.A., Australia, New Zealand, Venezuela, Jamaica, Cayman Islands, Bermuda, Bahamas, Trinidad & Tobago, Barbados, St. Vincent, St. Lucia, Grenada, Antigua and an appearance in Surinam (Dutch Guiana).

After fifty years at the Bar as Defence Counsel in several countries mentioned supra and then as Crown Prosecutor in the Ministry of the Attorney-General in Toronto, Canada, from 1979– 1988 and having been exposed to both sides as Defence Counsel and Prosecutor, I can only conclude that Justice is a nebulous, relative and illusory concept that is best understood in its philosophical assessment, rather than in its pragmatic application. Justice and many legal rights appear, at the first blush, to be abstract rights. Mr. Roy Black in his scholarly-written Introduction of his Book, "BLACK'S LAW," states, "Lawyers are the ones who transform abstract rights into reality." This is so true. Perhaps, it is this truism, that that doyen of the Florida Bar, my learned friend, Mr. Roy Black, had in mind when he also stated in his powerful, riveting Book, "BLACK'S LAW," that a "defense attorney must do everything in his power to protect his client." I fully endorse that comment.

I went to Bermuda on two occasions to advise on two very important cases on speeding and the method of dealing with the essential features of this offence as set out in my first book – "The Law on Speeding and Radar" by A. Shakoor Manraj, Q.C. and Dr. Paul D. Haines, Ph.D., published by Butterworths & Co. (Canada) Ltd. Legal, Professional and Academic Publishers. Businessmen, Salesmen, Drivers of Commercial Vehicles and Professionals like Medical Practitioners, are very mindful of protecting their driving records especially when the demerit point system kicks in after certain speeding convictions, with consequential suspension.

To set aside the suspension, the conviction for the speeding offence resulting in the suspension must be quashed. The assignment of demerit points varies in accordance with the excess of the speeding, which is an absolute liability offence. Many people do not quite understand the true nature of speeding as an absolute liability offence. My book explains it all. See: "The Law on Speeding and Radar" 2nd Edition by Manraj and Haines; p.8 (Butterworths).

I worked long and difficult hours when I started my practice in Georgetown, British Guiana (later, the Republic of Guyana). After a very full and hectic practice in the Magistrate's Courts throughout Guyana appearing in every conceivable type of case, criminal and civil, I decided to concentrate on a Supreme Court practice. I was retained to appear in the first of the very many murder cases in which I had the honour, the responsibility and the privilege of appearing for the accused. The trial lasted five days, the Jury retired for a short while and then returned to Court and delivered the verdict of *"NOT GUILTY"* – the sweetest and the most mellifluous sound of music to the ears of any defendant. Many friends, well-wishers and the relatives of the defendant were congratulating me.

My Mom and Dad had come to the Court to hear the verdict of this, my first murder trial in Guyana. They were so pleased. Then I was somewhat puzzled when my Dad said to me, "Son, I owe you an apology." My consternation must have been most obvious. My father hugged me and said, "I was so wrong when I thought of you as a doctor. You are on the correct course. You have achieved your goal. I pray that you have a long and successful career." Those words of endorsement from my father filled me with great exhilaration. I always had a deep love and respect for my Dad. He was not too big to admit his error in his assessment of my professional choice.

My very devoted mother passed away on July 27, 1969 – just two days after my birthday. She was barely audible but gave me her Blessings before she passed away. She told me that I would receive a great honour before the year is ended. She did not spell it out. However, on December 31, 1969, I realized to what she was referring. On that day, I received my "Letters Patent Constituting and Appointing" me a Queen's Counsel (Q.C.). His Excellency, the late Sir Edward Victor Luckhoo, himself a Queen's Counsel signed it. Sir Edward Victor Luckhoo was at the time, the Acting Governor-General and Commander-in-Chief of Guyana.

The appointment as one of Her Majesty's Counsel, (Q.C.) is a rare honour reserved only for very successful and experienced leaders of the Bar. I achieved this status and honour and the right of adding Q.C. after my name just only after fifteen years at the Bar. It normally takes a longer period. At this time, I was forty-four years old. I was born on July 25, 1925 in Georgetown, British Guiana, as it then was. In 1970, Guyana became the "Co-operative Republic of Guyana." After my mother's demise, my father and I became very close. He passed away in 1975.

My parents were descended from East Indian Immigrants, from India, who immigrated to British Guiana in the late 1890's. My Mom and Dad were very upright-living people and were very loving and caring. They were well-respected. The dedication of this book had to include my very Loving and Understanding Mother, JANE MAKBULAN MANRAJ and my Dear and Helpful Dad, AZEEZ RAHAMAT MANRAJ. With their Help, Love, Devotion and Encouragement, my Life and Achievements became more meaningful and relevant to my ideals.

During my student days in London, I met a very lovely and adorable young lady – GLADYS MAY GOODWAY. She was the younger of only two daughters of the late Mr. Walter and Mrs. Ada Goodway of Wimbledon Park, England. We became very much devoted to each other. Gladys and I got married on January 23, 1954. She came out to British Guiana six months after I returned there to set up my law practice. She bore me four children – two boys and two girls – the first, a boy – Michael, the second, a girl – Anne, the third, a boy – Andrew and the fourth, a girl – Elizabeth.

Gladys, who was a very dear, devoted wife and a source of great inspiration, passed away on December 14, 1976 after a short illness. My four older children are married and they have given me nine grandchildren. My two sons and their families live in Ontario, Canada and my daughter, Elizabeth and her family live in Victoria, British Columbia, Canada. My daughter, Anne and her family, as well as my daughter Marcina, live in Florida. None of my children studied Law although I would have loved so much to have one of my boys or girls qualify at the Bar and come to assist me in my busy practice. The nearest I got to inducing one of my sons to become a lawyer, was when my second son Andrew decided to come and take over the Management of my Chambers in Georgetown. I thought he had the makings of a good and witty lawyer.

After their mother died in 1976, we all left Guyana in 1978 and went to Canada to live. We all subsequently became Canadian Citizens. My eldest child, Michael, is now an Air-line Captain in Canada. When my second son, Andrew, came up to Canada, he became very much a computer person and that became his passion. He is in the computer-related field. My daughter, Anne, used to broadcast at one of the Guyana Radio Stations. She now lives in Florida, U.S.A. and is a Federal Government employee in Florida. Elizabeth went into child psychology and now teaches in Victoria, British Columbia, Canada. I saw all my children safely settled in their matrimonial life and eventually on October 26, 1990, I married my present wife – Bonita Mangal. Her father, the late Dr. Krishna Mangal, was a medical doctor in Georgetown, Guyana and Bonita, the fifth child of the late Dr. Mangal and the late Mrs. Muriel Mangal, brought into my life her young daughter, Marcina, from her previous marriage. I adopted Marcina and so I have a fifth child, Marcina Manraj, who is now a Registered Nurse in Florida, U.S.A. She lives not far from us in Florida, U.S.A.

We all live very happily together and I would be remiss if I did not mention all the members of my large and happy family. Michael married Esther Alvarez and they have two of their own children, Christopher and Natalie, both still in High School. Esther has a son from a previous marriage, Frank, who is now Frank Manraj. My son, Michael, adopted him. He is in business and lives in Barrie, Ontario, Canada. Anne married Andrew Edun, the son of the late Mr. Justice Edun and the late Mrs. Gladys Edun. They have two daughters – Anya, now at the University of Miami in Florida and Alana, who is still in High School in Florida. Andrew married Anabela Santos and they have two sons – Ryan and Kyle who are in Elementary School. Elizabeth married Ken Johnson of Cochrane, Ontario, Canada and they have two girls, Samara and Elyssa, who are in Elementary School. I am called Grandpa, Grand-dad, Pappy, Grandpy and many other affectionate names but one Christmas my youngest Grandson, Kyle said, "I know your name. You are Grandpa Shakoor." This was good enough for me. They are all a wonderful lot of grandchildren. Behind my back, I know they call me affectionately "Shaks."

I was called to the Ontario Bar in Canada on April 15, 1988, and on the same day, I was admitted as a Solicitor of the Ontario Supreme Court on the Fiat of the Honourable W. D. Parker, Chief Justice of Ontario. I had joined the Ministry of the Attorney- General of Ontario, Canada, in 1979. I resigned my position with the Ministry of the Attorney-General in July 1988 to return to private practice. On my resignation from the Ministry of the Attorney-General, my colleagues presented me with a very lovely and expensive plaque and this beautiful stanza. It says everything. The book referred to is my text on "The Law on Speeding and Radar." For more on the text see end of this Introduction. I miss all of my colleagues. All the members of the prosecuting team were kind and most understanding people. It was a real pleasure to have worked alongside with them.

This is the stanza to which I referred:

"SHAKOOR"

A lawyer named Shakoor had many degrees
He made prosecuting seem like such a breeze
The courtroom was his favourite place to be
Arguing and Sentencing were his cup of tea
In his spare time a book he did write
On speeding, he knew he could shed some light
Now on his own, off he will go
But back to the courtroom for a different kind of SHOW

I had a wide and varied practice in Canada and outside of Canada as well. My practice in the Caribbean Islands and other Islands developed rapidly again and on May 20, 1993, I was called to the Bar of the Turks & Caicos

Islands. I had a very successful Criminal Law practice there appearing before five Chief Justices of those Islands.

Except for the nine years of service with the Ministry of the Attorney-General of Ontario, Canada, as a Prosecutor, I was always engaged in private practice and for the better part of my years at the Bar; I practised as Defence Counsel in Criminal Cases. However, I also practised in other areas – civil cases, traffic cases and matters involving Family Law, Arbitration, International Law, appearances in Military and Police Tribunals, appearing for lawyers before the Disciplinary Committees, appearances before the Full Court to have delinquent disbarred lawyers re-instated. A real and distinct honour was my appearance before the Privy Council in 1961 presided over by that very famous and learned Judge, the Hon. Lord Denning, now deceased. Another high-powered retainer took me before the International Commission of Jurists when that Commission came to Guyana in 1965 to investigate and report on the inter-relationship, economic, educational, social and political conditions of the six races of the then British Guiana.

Over my years of practice as a Junior member of the Bar and after I took "Silk" and became a Queen's Counsel in 1969, I had, in the course of my practice, the privilege and distinct pleasure of presenting the Petition of thirty-two freshly qualified Barristers for admission to practise their profession in the Courts of Guyana. This was a real honour, as new incoming Barristers had to select the lawyer who will present their Petition for Call to the Guyana Bar. It was also my pleasure to present the petition for admission to practice, of two female Barristers. At that time, female members of the Bar were rare gems that adorned the Legal profession. They were a refreshing and stabilizing infusion to the hitherto predominantly male Bar. They brought a new spirit to the Guyana Bar and a welcome competence reminiscent of the Shakespearean Portia as portrayed in "The Merchant of Venice."

One important point I would like to make before proceeding further. In this book, the cases referred to are real, but for the greater part, I deliberately refrained from mentioning the names of the defendants, the Prosecutors or other parties involved. I feel it is the right thing to do. Perhaps I should clarify and explain that the terms "Barrister," "Barrister-at-Law" and "Barrister for the Defence" are used in England and Wales. They were also used in the former British Colonial Territories in the Caribbean and Africa to refer to the advocate (the Barrister) who was in practise in those territories and who had to be called to the Bar in England.

The references to "Counsel," "Defence Counsel" and "Criminal Defence Counsel" are also used in the Caribbean, African and other British Territories to refer to the Barrister who is a practising advocate in those territories. Finally, we have the same individual or legally trained and qualified lawyer, practising as an advocate in the U.S.A., Canada and some European Countries, being referred to and called "Attorney," "Criminal Defence Attorney" and "Attorney-at-Law." They are all the same person – the advocate pleading the cause or matter for the client in Court. To put it succinctly, it is just a case of different titles for the same person, performing the same function.

A final reference to the book, "The Law on Speeding and Radar," which I co-authored with Dr. Paul Haines, Ph.D. In the text, I wrote the chapters relating to the law on speeding and Dr. Haines, wrote the scientific and technical chapters regarding radar as a speed detection device and how it operates. The text was published in 1985 in Toronto, Ontario, Canada by Butterworths & Co. (Canada) Ltd., Professional & Academic Publishers. R. Roy McMurtry, Esq. Q.C., then the Attorney General of Ontario wrote the Foreword to the First Edition of this text. Mr. McMurtry was later appointed Canadian High Commissioner to the United Kingdom in 1985. He is presently the Chief Justice of Ontario, Canada.

In 1991, the text – "The Law on Speeding and Radar" was fully updated and revised by Dr. Paul Haines and myself and appeared for circulation it its 2nd Edition, by Butterworths Canada Ltd. 1991. A paperback Edition of the First Edition was produced and marketed by Macmillan of Canada, A division of Canada Corporation, Ontario, Canada. Macmillan had completed all the required negotiations with and permission from Butterworths before publishing the Paper Back Edition of "The Law on Speeding and Radar" by A. Shakoor Manraj, Q.C. of the Middle Temple, London, England, Barrister-at-Law, quondam Crown Prosecutor in the Provincial Offences Appeal Court at Old City Hall, Toronto, Ontario, of the Ontario Bar and Paul Douglas Haines, Ph.D. formerly Consultant to both Canadian and United States Remote Sensing and Defense Research Establishments and Research Analyst in Satellite and Airborne Image and Information Processing Systems. That paper-back edition was easily within the means of non-lawyers including taxi drivers, bus drivers and generally, the ordinary motorist in Canada, the U.S.A. and many other countries, where speeding is a moving offence as opposed to a non-moving violation, for example, illegal parking.

Chapter 1

What Is Justice?

If you were to ask any number of people the question, "What is Justice?" you will get many different answers. Some would say Justice is Fair Play; others would say that Justice is what is reasonable. Still, others would say it is an expression that connotes what is right: "Let right be done." Justice may be theoretically discussed fully in the pages of a book, but Justice is to be found in the consciousness of man. It is really a philosophical concept. *"Don't stifle your conscience" really is perhaps another appeal for* Justice, reasonableness and fairness.

Ever so often, we hear from politicians, demagogues, lawyers, academics, sceptics and read "Liberty and Justice for all." "Liberty" is a purely comparative term like "Democracy" and "Freedom." "Justice" is sometimes considered to be what is morally right and acceptable. Justice is an illusory goal. The expression *"Justice has been done"* reflects the sentiment that the outcome or decision arrived at, has been so realized by the proper application and use of the machinery of the Law. The expression, *"The wheels of Justice turn slowly,"* clearly indicates that whatever procedural practice is initiated, it will, no matter how long it takes, once it is based on the existing law, result in achieving fairness.

The aim of all legal systems and practice is to apply the law, whether statutory or common law, through the Judicial process in any given particular set of circumstances, so as to achieve fairness and balance, which together result in *Justice*. It is this aspect of Justice that we, as lawyers, are most concerned about. This concept of Justice which is symbolized by the traditional female figure with sword in one hand scales in the other and a *BLINDFOLD* to ensure that Justice is impersonal and impartial and does not allow any personal or other considerations to enter into the determination and assessment of Justice. Standing majestically on top of London's famous Central Criminal Court, the Old Bailey, is the Statue of Justice, in Greek mythology, *Themis*, the perfection of Justice, who presided over the assemblies of gods and men. Below this famous statue, these simple words are carved: *"Defend the Children of the Poor and Punish the Wrongdoer."*

The question "What is Justice?" is very often asked. The answer is not easy, but is based fundamentally upon two concepts. They are: (i) every man has a right to a fair hearing and (ii) no man should be a judge in his own cause or matter. This second concept embraces that whole area of morality and law dealing with the duties and functions of Judges, the most important duty being that Judges must be free from bias. Justice and clear conscience, in analysis, seem to be synonymous terms.

There is a higher, a more enlightened moral system that is in existence to supplement the established procedures of Law and adjudication. It is based on the fundamental principle that right must be done, justice must prevail and the conscience of the Court to see that Justice has prevailed and has been dispensed. I am referring to the doctrines and *Maxims of Equity*. The term Equity is used in various senses. In its popular and purest sense, it is equivalent to "natural Justice."

There are many matters of natural justice wholly unprovided for, from the extreme difficulty of framing any general rules to meet them and from the doubtful wisdom of policy of attempting to give a legal sanction, to duties of imperfect obligation, such as charity, gratitude and kindness. Perhaps the best way to put it is to say that Justice is the product of the conscience of each individual. That is why it is a fundamental rule in the application of these principles that where LAW and EQUITY conflict, then *Equity* must prevail - "Equity looks to the intent rather than to the form." The intention may be inelegantly or erroneously pleaded in the particular pleadings filed. Equity can go behind the document or pleading to see what is the real intention of the parties. There are other *Maxims of Equity*, which can assist in the full understanding of the equitable jurisdiction of the Court.

To the layman, the basic concept of *EQUITY* is essentially fair dealing. Equity is a concept, which the Judge may employ to temper the rigidity of the law, whenever the strict rule of law might result in a grave injustice. Equity is a collection of rules applied by a Judge to temper the rigidity of the Common Law Rules, which can at times be harsh and without the application of the *Maxims of Equity*, can prove to be unconscionable and unjust. Let me just set out some of the most important of the many *Maxims of Equity* so as to give you an idea what Equity is all about:

1) Equity will not suffer (allow) a wrong to be without a remedy.
2) Equity follows the Law.
3) Where there is equal equity, the law shall prevail.
4) Where the equities are equal, the first in time shall prevail.
5) He who seeks equity must do equity.
6) He, who comes into equity, must come with clean hands.
7) Delay defeats equity.
8) Equality is Equity.
9) Equity looks to the intent rather than to the form.
10) Equity looks on that as done which ought to be done.
11) Equity imputes an intention to fulfil an obligation.
12) Equity acts in personam – equity exercises a jurisdiction over the defendant personally.

The concept of "Freedom" is like the concept of "Democracy." The expression "Freedom" is a comparative term. "Justice" has been described as fairness, equality, that which is right, correctness, morally right and that which does not offend against good conscience. But, even when all those qualities are taken together, there is still an indefinable quality embracing the nebulous, all-inclusive concept of fair play. Does "Justice" mean the outcome, the result or the end-product arrived at by the proper marriage of the substantive law and procedural law?

In this book, I am dealing with the "Justice" that one expects under any Criminal Justice System. When we apply our minds to this aspect of "Justice," we immediately think of the Metropolitan Countries like England and the whole of the United Kingdom, the U.S.A., Canada, Holland, France, Germany and many former British, French and Dutch Colonies. But Criminal Courts are not Courts of Equity. Cases involving equitable principles are usually heard and determined in the Chancery Courts in England and generally in the Civil Courts. Equitable principles are applicable only in Civil Cases and Courts, which exercise a Civil Jurisdiction. In the most popular application of the word, "Justice" (fairness, that which is right) arises in the Criminal Judicial processes and reasoning.

If a verdict of the Jury is bad, it can be appealed on the ground that it is perverse, against the weight of evidence and unreasonable on the findings of fact. The verdict can be bad in law because of procedural problems, misdirection of the presiding Judge to the jury, legal problems and serious misconduct of any person taking part in the trial. These are just examples I am giving. I cannot in a book of this type, which is not a law book, discuss all the relevant principles of the attainment of Justice. But, this *is* the memoirs of a practising lawyer who has clocked up over fifty years of all types of practice – criminal, civil, divorce, traffic, immigration and cases involving International Law – just to mention some of the areas of practice in which I was engaged.

Whatever qualities or standards Justice has, it is something we all strive to attain. Sometimes it is illusory. At times, it defies concrete definition. At other times, it is just a by-word for anyone who feels that he or she has been wronged. Whatever is the realty of Justice, something metaphysical, abstract general reasoning, visionary or realistic, whatever it is, it is what the Courts, the Judges and the legal practitioners – Defence Counsel and Prosecuting Counsel – and the Public at large all aim for. Here is the interesting part of this complete conceptual approach to Justice. *It works*. We find it. We know when it has been achieved. Even in the young undeveloped minds and thinking processes of our children, we find that they know what is just when they exclaim, "But Daddy (or Mommy) that isn't fair."

We all know what is fair, just and morally correct – just don't let us try to dissect and destroy the existence of this integral part of our daily life. "Justice" like "Love" is a "Many-splendoured thing." It is a lofty but understandable concept. Let us always fight to attain it and preserve it even if we as lawyers and all members of the populace have to preserve it at great personal inconvenience and risk. "Justice must not only be done but must be seen to be done" is an old guiding principle. This is still a powerful guide-line protecting the preservation of Justice.

When a jury returns a verdict that is so inconsistent with the facts of the case, then something must have gone wrong and this type of verdict, known as a perverse verdict, tarnishes the whole institution of Justice and Fairness. In such an unhappy state of affairs, Justice was not done. The fair name of Justice was left tarnished. Judges have tried to express the true quality and appreciation of Justice. One particular Judge, Lord Atkin, in 1936, made use of these memorable and important pronouncements on the concept of justice. He said, "Justice is not a cloistered virtue: she must be allowed to suffer the scrutiny and respectful, even though outspoken, comments of ordinary men."

Today, we are fortunate, as the advances in social legislation and legal reform clearly secure and protect the access to the Courts of Justice of all, regardless of financial status, race, religion, sex, political persuasion or nationality. The study of the evolution of Justice is to a lawyer very exciting. As Counsellor Playdell in "Guy Mannering" stated, "A lawyer without history or literature is a mechanic, a mere working mason; if he possesses some knowledge of these, he may venture to call himself an architect." I see it this way: Defence Lawyers particularly and generally all Lawyers, Judges and Prosecutors and all law enforcement Officers, if properly guided, are the architects of Justice.

We have travelled a far way since the early beginnings of trying to attain Justice. "Wager of law," "Ordeal by Fire," "Ordeal by Water," were procedures that existed in the Anglo-Saxon Period. The law has developed, jury trials by twelve men "good and true" came into prominence, the rule that the prosecution must discharge the onus of proving the guilt of an accused person who remains innocent until proven guilty, are all slow and deliberate advances made in the search for Justice. Justice has evolved today as the quality that embellishes any Judicial System that seeks to see that "right is done" between man and man and between the "citizen and the state."

The enforcement of the law aims at achieving Justice, which in its final application is the delicate balance of the rights of the State vis-à-vis, the rights and privileges of the citizen. Justice blossoms when the administration of Justice is immune from the influence of politics. Judges in England are practically irremovable; consequently, they are more free and detached and enjoy an independence that is an essential ingredient in the administration of Justice. We will discuss more on this in ensuing chapters.

Chapter 2

Wrestling For Justice

The Onerous Duties and Responsibilities of Defence Counsel

The duties of Defence Counsel in a Criminal Trial are very onerous, time-consuming and demanding. It is literally true to state that we, at the Defence Criminal Bar, have to wrestle and fight every inch of the way to achieve Justice in a hotly contested criminal trial. There are reasons why this is so. But whatever the reasons, we must not forget our onus and conduct at the Bar.

In the British and American legal systems, we have the established adversarial system. The champion, the wrestler, the fighter who stands between an accused person (defendant) and imprisonment or penalty of death on conviction of the alleged offence, is the Criminal Defence Barrister-at-Law or Attorney. A present day criminal trial is open warfare. This is where the highest traditions of the Bar become relevant if the attainment of Justice and Fair Play is to be achieved. Whereas it is the duty and task of Defence Counsel to wrestle for an acquittal, it is never the duty (and should never be the function) of the Prosecuting Counsel or Attorney (State or Federal) to wrestle for a conviction. In 1955, Mr. Justice Humphreys, a famous English jurist and judge, succinctly stated, "His (the Prosecutor) duty is Justice first, Justice second and conviction a very bad third!" (See 1955, Criminal Law Review. P. 746)

Rights may be enshrined in written Constitutions and other documents. It is the duty of *all* members of the Bar, Prosecutors and Defence Counsel alike, to so conduct their professional duties in order to make sure that at all times those enshrined constitutional rights and all other rights are interpreted and transformed into reality. Put very simply, whereas defence counsel can skilfully fight, nay, wrestle, for an acquittal of his client, prosecuting counsel is duty bound to present the facts of the case he is prosecuting carefully, truthfully and in a fair manner. There is no room for semantics and at all times prosecuting counsel must be truthful about disclosures to defence counsel. Perhaps, it is this guide-line that motivated the highest courts and the most learned Judges to expound repeatedly the test of "equal reason" flowing from inferences.

After many years of careful consideration and deliberation, our Judges have ruled that, where from any given set of facts there are inferences that can be drawn and the inferences can with, "equal reason," be beneficial to the prosecution and the defence, then the inferences in favour of the defence must be accepted. This seems only *"fair"* and *"just"* as it clearly indicates that in such an event, the prosecution has failed to prove its case "beyond a reasonable doubt." The prosecution simply cannot take one interpretation of the inferential facts favourable to their case and tell the jury that that is the only interpretation they must accept. Of course, the trial Judge will have to direct the Jury fully and properly. In the topic under review, the Judge must tell the Jury that they must give consideration to the inferences drawn from the facts, which enure to the benefit of the accused.

During my fifty-odd years at the Bar, I have had the opportunity to see first hand the many sides of the conceptual thinking of what is interpreted as *"Justice."* As I mentioned earlier, I was a Prosecutor in the Ministry of the Attorney-General, Toronto, Ontario, Canada. I had the opportunity to study the attitude, the thinking processes and trial philosophy of most Prosecutors. Most of them see that their sole role is to secure a conviction. They regard securing convictions as the only function of their position and Justice is incidental to that purpose. This specious reasoning of many prosecutors follows the fallacious and illogical reasoning (mainly adopted by the laymen) that Police only charge people who are guilty of crime.

The syllogistic reasoning here is so unsound. I have heard many prosecutors (mind you, they were young and not fully matured prosecutors) say, "Why would the Police charge the defendant, if he is not guilty?" These prosecutors feel that they have discharged their "duty" once a conviction had been recorded. All the prosecutors want is a conviction "by hook or crook," but this is far from the standards required by a fair and competent prosecutor. The Prosecuting Counsel is, at all times, under a duty to be utterly frank with the Court and the defence. There is no exception to the application of and obedience to this rule.

Perhaps I should mention that I was attached to Canada Law Book, Agincourt, Ontario for six months in 1979. Then I joined the Ministry of the Attorney-General in 1979. The then Attorney-General was Mr. R. Roy McMurtry, Q.C. (now, the Hon. R. Roy McMurtry, Chief Justice of Ontario). I served in the Provincial Offences Appeal Court for a substantial period of my years with the Ministry of the Attorney-General and I have to admit that together with the late Judge Robert Dnieper, we gave this new Appellate Court much-needed status. The late Judge Robert Dnieper was a keen student of the law, quick at grasping facts, impatient with lawyers who were ill-prepared to present and conduct their cases properly and at heart a very kind and considerate man. He was a scholar. He loved the law. He was an asset in putting the newly created Provincial Offences Appeal Court of Ontario in its true perspective, importance and function. It was a rare pleasure and honour to have been the "Crown" in the Provincial Offences Appeal Court presided over by His Honour, the late Robert Dnieper. His premature death was a severe loss to the Provincial Courts of Ontario. I feel he was destined to go

A. Shakoor Manraj was appointed Queen's Counsel on December 31, 1969. Here he poses in full Queen's Counsel Robes.

This is the Court of Appeal Building in Georgetown, Guyana, where Shakoor Manraj argued many of his Appeal cases.

higher, but death stepped in and robbed the Law and Justice of a brilliant mind and jurist.

The role of Defence Counsel/Attorney is not an easy one. Once he accepts the responsibility of representing a defendant, he must do everything in his power and competence to protect his client. He is there to see that nothing irregular or unfair takes place. He must be vigilant and he is there as the Guardian of his client's rights. He has to be attentive to what is going on. Much of Defence Counsel's role is actually determined by the Judge's attitude and learning. With respect to the learning and competence of the Judge, it is like a breath of fresh air when one appears in any case before a Judge who is competent, unbiased and willing to clamp down on attempts to introduce inadmissible evidence that is sought to be adduced by either the Prosecutor or Defence Counsel in a criminal trial, or by either the Plaintiff or Defendant in a civil action.

Many Judges, who preside over the Criminal Courts, were once prosecutors and when they ascend the Judicial Bench, they forget (sometimes very conveniently) that they are no longer prosecutors. Judges sometimes do not hide their shameless efforts to aid and advance the prosecution. The Judges lean in favour of what the Prosecutor says and requests. Defence Counsel/Attorney appearing before Judges like these, have a rather rough time and believe me when I tell you, that he must be prepared at times for an outright war. What is distressing is when a Judge from the Bench tries to give Prosecutors advice as to how to deal with certain difficulties relating to evidential and procedural problems. On one occasion when I stood up before a certain Judge in order to protect my client, I was threatened in the presence of the Jury with imprisonment for "Contempt of Court." Defence Counsel/Attorney must never succumb under threats from the Bench. I will deal with this experience at a more relevant time.

For Defence Counsel to give of his best in defending his client he must know his case, know the legal principles applicable to the case, must be articulate and must not be afraid to do everything in his power to protect his client from a dual battering from the Prosecutor first and then from the Judge, who, sometimes, to redeem an incompetent prosecutor, asks more questions than the prosecutor asked. The Judge does this under the guise of "questions by the Court to clarify certain facts." All of this is done in the presence of the Jury.

It takes courage, dedication and rhetoric to stop a Judge from pursuing this path. A criminal trial becomes sometimes an all-out battle between the Prosecutor and Defence Counsel who, must of necessity, object and keep on objecting whenever the Prosecutor seeks to do what he is not permitted to do, hoping that the former Prosecutor, now the presiding Judge, will not allow him (the Prosecutor) to continue the travesty. It is a battle of wits. If you do not have the ability to think fast on your feet and fight for your client, then the Criminal Defence practice is not for you. It is not a calling for the faint of heart. Add to this these facts: the government (State or Federal) has all the advantages and resources. They have everything at their command – police officers, money, government pathologists, crime-labs and all the resources to secure information readily, not to mention the availability of all kinds of experts they feel they need. Sometimes the unfortunate defendant can hardly put together the retainer and fees for experienced defence counsel.

Just as there are inexperienced and dull Prosecutors, there are also inexperienced, ill-prepared and lazy Defence Counsel. Fluency of speech, ornate, mundane, colloquial language and their niceties and the ability to think quickly and constructively while on your legs, a thorough grasp of the facts and law relating to the case in which you are appearing, full understanding of your client and his background, the patience of the PATRIARCH Job and an inexhaustible reserve of mental and physical energy, are the tools of trade of Defence Counsel. Sometimes, a Defence Counsel's worst enemy is his own client, especially if the client has been exposed to the “senior and seasoned prison practitioners” while he is in prison awaiting bail. Those “practitioners” in prison claim to know the Law and they do tremendous harm to the novice inmate awaiting bail. Let me give an example.

On one occasion, in Georgetown, Guyana, I was retained by the parents of a young man charged with the murder of a man in a Hotel Bar to appear for him. The parents told me a long story but, as is my custom, I told them I would have to see the young man and hear from him. The defendant was in prison. In Guyana, as in many other countries, accused persons charged with the offence of murder are not admitted to Bail, but every facility is made for Defence Counsel to see his client in prison. From what the parents told me, I concluded that the young man (he was only 23) had a good case to defend.

There used to be a little café on Camp Street opposite the prison. The parents said they would accompany me to the prison and wait in the café until I had finished interviewing their son. I raised no objection. They paid me the retainer fee and on the appointed day when I was to see their son, they came with me to the prison. I was let in and the parents remained in the café. The prison officers all knew me well because I frequently visited clients who were held in prison pending Bail. I was escorted to the room to which they had brought my client from his cell. A prison officer always remains a discreet distance away. I went into the room and after an exchange of some pleasantries, I told the young man to let me know truthfully, what happened. I told him, as I always tell all my clients, “Tell me the truth and let me be the lawyer. Do not tell me what you have concocted thinking that that will be your defence and you will be set free.”

The young man started to tell me a story with all sorts of legal implications and misstatements of the law. I allowed him to talk. (I always do this with my clients). I did not interrupt him for about forty-five minutes. He then concluded, "There you have it, Sir, a perfect case of self defence."

He was not very educated and his flow of garbage amused me. I then said, "No, my friend, a perfect case for the gallows." He became visibly deflated. In Guyana, the penalty for murder is death by hanging. I asked him from where he acquire all the legal phrases and expressions he used. He hesitated and then eventually confessed to me that some of the prisoners serving long sentences, had spoken to him and told him that he must tell the lawyer the concocted story as if you tell him the truth, you will be convicted. I said to the young man, "All you have told me is untrue, your parents are waiting for me across the road, I will go to them and refund the retainer fee and you can retain another lawyer who may act on all the nonsense you told me."

He quickly apologized. He said he thought he was helping me. He undertook to tell me the truth, (the parents had told me what they understood were the allegations). I listened to him. He told me what actually took place. I decided then to accept his case. He seemed pleased. I told him not to discuss his matter with anyone in the prison or elsewhere. As and when I need more information, I will see him in prison.

I rejoined his parents. We went to my law offices ("Chambers" as the Barrister's office is called in England and some Commonwealth Countries) and there I was properly retained. It was a case based on facts and I thought I would have to convince the Jury by relying on that famous doctrine of "reasonable doubt." He had told me that although he was in the Hotel Bar, he did not commit the offence and he did not wound the deceased.

At the conclusion of the Preliminary Investigation, I submitted to the Magistrate that there was not enough conclusive and reliable evidence to found a *prime facie* case on which to commit my client for trial for murder. There were too many discrepancies and flagrant contradictions. This resulted from the prosecution calling too many witnesses who claimed they saw what happened. The Magistrate over-ruled my submissions and committed my client to stand trial at the next Criminal Sessions of the Supreme Court of Guyana. At the time of the trial, some of the witnesses could not be found, the Police Officer had left the Force and the Pathologist had left the Country: this was the beginning of the end.

The Judge was an experienced Judge. The Prosecutor was reliable and was known for his fairness. (He eventually ended up on the Judicial Bench and was a good and fair Judge.) I made submissions at the close of the case for the prosecution, but the learned Judge over-ruled my submissions and said it was a matter for the Jury, at that time, an all-male Jury selected from a wide cross-section of the country. (The Jury list verified this). This was murder trial number 101 for me, but many more were to follow.

I addressed the Jury for about two hours and I hammered home the weakness of the prosecution's case and the "flagrant and fatal" discrepancies in the evidence of the prosecution witnesses. Their evidence could not be reconciled. That drove me to ask the Jury to find that the witnesses, who were present, were merely witnesses of convenience. That was my sincere feeling and I canvassed it vigorously to the Jury. In Guyana, the Prosecutor always replies last. He did his job. The Judge summed up fairly and explained fully the meaning of "reasonable doubt" as is understood in the Criminal Law.

The Jury took one hour and thirty minutes to deliberate. This is the most agonizing time not only for the accused, but for Defence Counsel, as well. The Jury returned a verdict of *"Not Guilty."* Those are the two most delightful and eloquent words from the foreman of the Jury an accused person can ever wish to hear. It is the most mellifluous sound of sweet music to his ears.

While on this topic of guilt or innocence, I would like to add this aspect of practice, which sometimes confronts the Criminal Defence Attorney. Ever so often, I have been asked laymen and non-legally trained individuals whether I can defend a man who tells me he is guilty. The answer is very straightforward. First of all, lawyers follow instructions from clients. We are not at the scene. If a client were to confess to me that he is Guilty of the Offence for which he is charged, then it is my duty as Defence Counsel to advise him to enter a Plea of Guilty. If he does not accept my advice, then I am, in duty bound, as a member of the English Bar, to withdraw from the case. But one problem remains. If a defendant is charged with an Offence by way of summons or indictment, which is defective to such an extent that the prosecution cannot proceed with it in its present form, then what does Defence Counsel do?

I take the view, having regard to the oath I took to give of my legal skill to those who consult me, that I must inform the client of the defective summons or indictment, which cannot be cured by amendment and then, before the plea is taken, I must make legal submissions on the unamendable defects or errors and ask that the summons be dismissed or the indictment be quashed. It is wrong professionally, to advise a client to plead not guilty and "see what happens" when the client tells you that he is guilty of the offence. Many legal practitioners hold the view that the defendant must always plead *NOT GUILTY* and put the prosecution to prove its case. In the course of so doing, if the prosecutor fails to prove some essential ingredient of the offence, then defence counsel can take advantage of this lapse and make a no-case submission. It is the duty of defence counsel to fight, wrestle and stand up bravely in the defence of his client and his rights.

We are the protectors of our clients' rights. We are the ones who have to give all we have to transform abstract Constitutional rights into meaningful reality especially where you have a Judge who is a "prosecuting" Judge. To him, the Prosecutor is always right and one has to use every skill and professional dexterity to obtain a proper and correct ruling when objection is taken to the manner in which prosecuting counsel adduces evidence, sometimes not only leading the witness but literally "dragging" him to get what he wants from the witness, who does not want to be dragged into "gilding the lily." Judges have gone so far at times saying to Defence Counsel, "Why don't you be quiet and let prosecuting counsel get on with the job."

The only reply is this,: "That perhaps, My Lord (or Your Honour), is what you would like me to do, but, Sir, I will not be brow-beaten into abandoning my responsibilities as Defence Counsel to see that the rules of law are observed especially with respect to the admissibility of evidence."

Several times I have been asked if I do not feel somewhat afraid to answer a Judge in a forthright manner. Not really, once it is done respectfully. We were trained to stand up for our clients' rights and to see that the law is properly applied and followed and say what we have to say clearly and respectfully. But, Criminal Defence Barrister (Attorney) is a human being and there are occasions when tempers become frayed and things are said which ought not to be said. A very hotly contested criminal trial can be a very tense affair for all the participants. But, hope springs eternal in the human breast and throughout the whole trial, everyone concerned is hoping that "Justice" will be done and "Right" will prevail. Perhaps, I always felt that Justice will be done even if it means that Cicero's Latin peroration and exhortation, "FIAT JUSTITIA, RUAT COELUM," ("Let Justice be done, though the Heavens should fall") must be invoked to achieve this "many splendoured thing" called "Justice."

Justice is not as illusory and unattainable as many people would like the public to believe. A lot depends upon the Judge who is sitting on the Bench. Some Judges are reluctant to take initiatives to see that Justice is done. A good example of a Judge who took the initiative to attain Justice can be seen from a murder trial in 1956. A prostitute was found dead in her flat. She was killed by eight wounds in the head, which had been inflicted by an axe or similar weapon.

The man charged with her murder, admitted that he was with the prostitute until 2.15 a.m. on the morning in question but he maintained that he left her alive in her flat as she had told him she had another visitor coming to see her at 3.00 a.m.

What were the allegations of the Crown Prosecutor? Let us examine them. The principal scientific officer at the Metropolitan Police Laboratory carried out certain tests on the various articles of clothing belonging to the defendant. Apart from a handkerchief there were no bloodstains but certain garments give a positive reaction to the presence of what looked like blood but the scientific officer was not prepared to state in evidence that it was human blood. Further, a copy of the magazine TRUE DETECTIVE was found in the defendant's room outlining a case of motiveless killing, which the Crown Prosecutor alleged was similar to the murder of the prostitute. The Prosecutor said that the case for the Crown was the accumulation of small items of circumstantial evidence, such as these.

Mr. A. P. Marshall, Q.C., a distinguished Barrister and Queen's Counsel appeared for the defendant and he submitted that in this case there was nothing more than mere suspicion pointing to the accused and there was not a single piece of evidence which had the quality or weight of implicating the defendant. Not often Defence Counsel succeeds in this type of submission. Most Judges often take umbrage under the general rule of "Let the Jury decide." However, in this case under review, Mr. Justice Devlin, a learned Judge, accepted the submission made by Defence Counsel and directed the Jury to return a verdict of *NOT GUILTY*. His Lordship gave his reason and explained that an accused person had every right to demand and expect that the prosecutor's case against him should be proved before he went into the witness box and say anything in answer to the allegations against him. Mr. Justice Devlin continued:

"Where one has a case where the evidence is purely circumstantial, then I must satisfy myself, in my judgment, that there is some piece of evidence that is more than mere suspicion, that there is some piece of evidence which would justify me in saying that points to the accused. You cannot put a multitude of suspicions together and make proof out of it.

It may be that if you were asked now whether on the evidence you would convict the accused in a case of this sort, you would not think it safe to do so, but it is not for me to put that responsibility upon you until after I have discharged mine and my responsibility is the one I have stated. Having formed the view that I have, I tell you now that as a matter of law, there is no evidence on which you can convict, even if you wished to do so."

This judgement produced the foundation of the guiding principle used by Criminal Defence Counsel that '*suspicion upon suspicion*' could never amount to criminal liability. The learned Judge then directed the Jury to return a formal verdict of "*Not Guilty*" and the defendant was discharged. Justice was done. Where there is a complete compliance and merger of the substantive law and the procedural law, then there is an achievement of Justice in the sense that right has been done and fairness has triumphed. The defendant is protected once the rules of law and the evaluation of evidence are observed.

Many Judges shirk the responsibility they first have to discharge, before allowing a case to go to the Jury. The criminal defence attorney must always be vigilant to protect his client and see that his rights are not compromised. I was happy to be able to use the forceful words of Mr. Justice Devlin just after his outstanding ruling. I was appearing in an Arson trial before Mr. Justice Kenneth Stoby (Later Sir Kenneth Stoby) in January, 1957. The Crown Attorney, who later became a Judge in Jamaica, was a very experienced lawyer. The defendant was charged with committing the offence of Arson at a place called Enmore in the County of Demerara, British Guiana (later the Republic of Guyana). Enmore is about sixteen miles outside the capital of British Guiana, Georgetown.

Before the Magistrate at the Preliminary Investigation, the only eye witness testified that he was returning from the cinema around mid-night and he saw the defendant running away from the house, which was already on fire. He was running away from him so he caught a back and side-view glance of the defendant. On this very unsatisfactory evidence the Magistrate committed the defendant to stand trial. It was this Jury trial that I am referring to.

At the Jury trial before Sir Kenneth Stoby, later Chancellor of the Judiciary in Guyana, the Crown Prosecutor led all the formal evidence. I did not cross-examine any of these witnesses. An experienced Defence Counsel knows when not to cross-examine. It is just that simple. The simple and golden rule is that if the witness says nothing to incriminate your client, don't cross-examine him. I have seen many young and inexperienced lawyers stand up and embark upon a senseless cross-examination sometimes to their detriment as some witnesses, if cross-examined long enough by Counsel who wants to indulge in gallery-grandstanding, can become very resentful and give some very damaging and incriminating evidence against the defendant.

As a Queen's Counsel a Senior Member of the Bar, I have guided many lawyers on the art of cross-examination and I have lectured at University Level on the General Law of Evidence and the art of cross-examination. My silence in not cross-examining the Prosecution witness in this Arson trial prompted Sir Kenneth Stoby to remark that I was uncharacteristically silent in Court. I explained to His Lordship that I was waiting for the eyewitness. He and the members of the Jury had a chuckle. At this time, I was about three years at the Bar, but I had already earned the reputation of being a skilful cross-examiner. As I proceed, I will discuss other cases that will clearly support my proposition.

Eventually the Crown's main witness came on the stand. I became visibly aware of his presence in the witness box. He was not a very articulate person. I knew this from the Preliminary Investigation before the Magistrate. My learned friend, the Prosecutor in the Jury trial was having serious difficulties adducing the evidence without leading the witness. That is not permitted in examination in chief. I saw my friend struggling to get from the witness how he identified the defendant. I was becoming very much amused. The witness specifically told the Jury that it was dark and he could not identify the defendant. Apparently, the witness may have told the Police that he had a flashlight, but even with the flash light he could not properly identify the defendant. I could see the frustration on the face of the Prosecutor. Eventually this took place:

Prosecutor:	"Did you have anything with you that helped you to see the Defendant?"
Mr. Manraj:	"My Lord, I object to that question. My learned friend is leading the witness."
Judge:	"Objection sustained."
Prosecutor:	"Did you have a torch light?"

I could not keep my composure anymore; I rose to my feet and forcefully objected.

Mr. Manraj:	"My Lord, I ask that the question be noted as that was strenuous dragging, not leading, the witness to give evidence to the effect that he could have identified the defendant, whereas, he clearly stated in examination-in-chief, that it was dark and he could not have identified the defendant. My learned friend, the Prosecutor, is trying to put words in the witness' mouth. He must know he cannot do this."

Judge: “Objection sustained. Mr. Prosecutor, you know the rules. I can understand your frustration with the witness. He is not giving you what you want. You cannot lead him, however, to give you the answer you want. You know that. The objection is sustained.”

I declined to cross-examine the witness. It could have been grossly dangerous even to ask him to repeat what he said in examination-in-chief about it being dark and that he could not identify the defendant. Identification of the defendant was the whole case. The witness in examination-in-chief gave me what I wanted. I just saw no need to cross-examine him and I did not.

At this stage, the Prosecution closed its case. The words of Justice Devlin came to my mind plus the fact that there was no evidence before the Jury that the defendant was the person who started the fire. Even in the Preliminary Investigation, the evidence was open to so many explanations. I submitted what Justice Devlin said in the murder case which I mentioned ante and relied on the dicta of Lord Sankey, Lord Chancellor, in the Woolmington Case in 1935, regarding “reasonable doubt.” The learned trial Judge upheld my submissions and stated briefly that he accepted the law as stated by Mr. Justice Devlin a year earlier and directed the Jury to return a formal verdict of *“NOT GUILTY.”*

There is one thing I must make clear. Although it may appear to the general public that, the Prosecutor and Defence Counsel were having a “go” at each other that is common occurrence in the course of the case. There are sometimes deep differences and conflicts of opinions between defence and prosecuting counsel as to the Law and the admissibility of evidence. That is quite in order. It is an adversarial system. Heated debates and repartees are part and parcel of the adversarial system. The important thing is that we do not normally become abusive towards each other, there are no fistic encounters and when the case is finished, we normally are quite civil and polite to each other. Of course, some Prosecutors take it as a personal defeat if you get a favourable verdict from the Jury or the Judge (as in the case I cited supra) but those Prosecutors are usually the younger and inexperienced ones who are just having their baptism as Prosecutors.

The legal profession has been described as a gentleman's profession. In England, there are two branches of the profession: Barristers and Solicitors. However, there is agitation to have the two branches merged. It is canvassed that such a move would be expedient and economically beneficial for litigants. In the two-branch system in England, the client sees the Solicitor first. The Solicitor does all the preparatory work and then he retains Counsel (a Barrister) and forwards the "brief" (the paper work he has prepared) to the Barrister he selects.

The Solicitors usually know the Barristers who excel and specialize in the various areas of the Law. The interposition of the Barrister between the litigant and the Judges produces a cooler, calm and more harmonious climate in Court.

There has been a merger of the two branches of the profession in many of the former British Colonies and in many of the Commonwealth Countries. In Canada, for example and more particularly, the Province of Ontario, a lawyer practises as a Barrister and Solicitor. Lawyers belong to a brotherhood. The traditions of the Bar are still very much alive, but in the areas of conduct and honesty, there has been a precipitous deterioration. Even in language, dress and behaviour, lawyers are remiss. Integrity is important. It is the backbone of the reputation of being a reliable and responsible lawyer.

I have witnessed with chagrin, how the quality and standard of language have deteriorated very badly. It is always a delight to hear the flow of good, acceptable, correct and polite English. I am happy to report, that despite the lowering of standards and ethics, especially among the newcomers to the Bar, there is still, in many quarters, deep respect for the honest, capable, competent and industrious Barrister-at-Law and Attorney-at-Law. Lawyers themselves have to take a lot of the blame for the widespread deterioration of the high respect and esteem that they enjoyed in the recent past. The "get-rich-quick" mentality so prevalent in the mind-set of many practitioners has resulted in unhappy disbarments and the disciplining of quite a number of practitioners.

It is one thing to be nice and friendly with clients and the public at large, but quite another thing to stoop to uncomely, uncouth and coarse behaviour. The inelegant and inappropriate language that one hears today, not only from some senior members of the Bar, but from Judges as well (when they are off the Bench) leave the responsible members of the Bar somewhat deflated.

It is a different world today. I have had many experiences where opposing counsel and I have had heated and sometimes profoundly divergent views on some weighty principles of the law and the salient factual issues applicable to the cases engaging our attention. But when the day is finished, we could both walk back to the robing room and exchange some pleasantries and part courteously, but looking forward to the next day's encounter in Court when the matter in question continues.

That is the camaraderie that makes the legal profession what it is: a legal fraternity. To put it in a paradox, it is a practice where we can agree to disagree agreeably. This was and still is part of the training of lawyers at any reputable Law School. Debate and discussion can be animated and intense but must never descend to the low level of abuse, derision and open resentment.

This reminds me of a humorous story told to me in my early days at the Bar, by the late Sir Eustace Woolford, Q.C., a very senior member of the Bar in Guyana, formerly

British Guiana. He was soft spoken, but he had a tremendous good sense of humour and a ready wit. He was one of the best raconteurs I ever encountered. Sir Eustace was a kind and very much a senior member of the Bar. I was at the time Junior Counsel to Sir Eustace Woolford in a Land dispute action before Mr. Justice Boland, then acting Chief Justice, who had admitted me to practice my profession at the Bar of British Guiana (now Guyana).

Sir Eustace and I were in the Court Gallery, both of us fully robed, waiting for the Court to get started. Justice Boland was a very punctual Judge and it was always wise and convenient to be on time in his Court. This is how the story goes: Two lawyers appeared before the trial Judge in a Civil Action. Without formally entering appearance and informing the Judge who was appearing for which party, they embarked upon their opening speeches. In the course of their opening speeches, they abused each other violently, one calling his adversary a rogue, a scamp and a charlatan, while his opponent retorted that his so-called friend was deceitful, dishonest and a masquerade who has a smattering knowledge of the law.

The learned Judge, very much amazed at this exhibition of unprofessional behaviour, then intervened and, addressing the two lawyers said, "Now that you two so-called gentlemen have been fully and properly identified by each other, let us get on with the case. Which one of you two misfits is appearing for the Plaintiff and which one is appearing for the Defendant?" The effect was devastating.

Chapter 3

The Battle Royal For Justice

After Discovering Evidence of Tampering While Court Exhibits Were In Police Custody

This is an experience I will never forget. It remains indelibly impressed in my memory, as I could not believe that what took place actually happened in a Court of Law administering Justice, fair-play and good conscience. The facts of the case are not very remarkable, but it is what took place behind the scenes and in open Court that leaves a blot on the achievement of Justice, Honesty and Fair- Play in an independent, unbiased Judiciary.

Three men were charged indictably and it was alleged that they broke open a stall in a market place and stole articles worth more than $2,000.00. There was a Preliminary Investigation held before the Magistrate and at the close of all the evidence, he committed the three men to stand trial at the Supreme Court of Guyana Criminal Sessions. Let me examine what happened in the Magistrate's Court, as this is vital to appreciate what transpired at the subsequent hearing before a Jury. Let me also hasten to add that in the Preliminary Investigation, the prosecution witnesses gave evidence on oath and I cross-examined them.

Before the Magistrate were about two hundred odd Exhibits including panties, brassieres, skirts, dress-materials, umbrellas, flasks, cosmetics, radio, roll-ons (pantie girdles), bucktas, beach pants, vests, socks, kerchiefs, towels and handbags. Quite an array of merchandise!! The well of the Court looked like a lingerie shop and a general store, offering all sorts of personal garments, hardware and other merchandise. My main concern was to hear the evidence of the market stall-holder with respect to her reason for claiming these many articles as her merchandise. Suffice it to say, that when she was finished giving her evidence-in-chief, I started my cross-examination.

There is much debate over the role of Criminal Defence Counsel in a Preliminary Investigation. It is felt by some of the pundits of the profession that Defence Counsel, in a Preliminary Investigation, ought *not* to cross-examine the witnesses thereby "showing his hands" to the Prosecution and further, the defendant under no circumstances should go into the witness box and *give* evidence. I think that all these arguments are more academic than pragmatic. As Counsel for the Defence, I evaluate each case as I see it and apply my experience and knowledge to the case I am defending.

There are times when I *do not* cross-examine the prosecution witnesses. I hear what the prosecution's case is and to what extent it is supported by the evidence adduced. The client is not a lawyer. He retains me to secure the necessary, relevant advice and guidance to help him get Justice. In the case under review in this chapter, I cross-examined the virtual complainant as to her ability to identify the Exhibits she was claiming as her merchandise. My cross-examination before the Magistrate, set out below, produced the following important admissions:

Mr. Manraj:	"Are there other stalls in the market that stock and sell the same items that you carry and sell in your stalls?"
Witness:	"Yes."
Mr. Manraj:	"If you were to be shown unmarked items you sold in your stalls along with similar items with no marks or identification on them taken from another stall, would you be able to tell which items are from your stalls and which items are from the other stall?"
Witness:	"No, they would all look alike. I could only say that they look like mine."

Mr. Manraj: "These Exhibits tendered here in Court do not have any marks on them? For example, price tags or initials?"

Witness: "That is correct. They are unmarked."

Mr. Manraj: "You did not put any price tags on the various pieces of garments you are claiming as yours, did you?"

Witness: "No. I did not have the time to mark the prices on the various garments and items, but I know the price of each."

Mr. Manraj: "Look carefully at all the Exhibits tendered in this case and tell me why you are claiming that they are yours?"

Witness: "I know that the items I purchased and the Exhibits look like the ones in Court. I would say they are mine from 'general appearance.' They look like the items I had stocked in my stall."

Mr. Manraj: "What marks do you usually put on your items?"

Witness: "I put price tags on them attached to the various garments and other items with scotch tape."

Mr. Manraj: "Do you see in Court here today any items tendered as Exhibits in this case with a price tag on them or any other identification marks on them?"

Witness: "No."

Mr. Manraj: "Do you see any marks or initials on any of the items in Court?"

Witness: "No."

By this time, I had all the admissions I wanted from this witness. The gist of the cross examination is that she claimed ownership of the items from their *'general appearance.'* They *looked* like the items she stocked in her market stalls. In cross-examining a witness, one must know when to stop. I have seen many young Counsel keep on and on in order to put on a gallery show. As I've stated previously, a Counsel asks a witness many questions of no relevance and the witness can become very hostile and say things that you *do not* want. When Defence Counsel then tries to get those answers struck from the record, the Prosecutor will ask the Court to have the answer recorded as it was in answer to a question put by Defence Counsel. Fortunately, in this case, I saw all the Exhibits as each one was tendered in Court and none of them had any marks, price tags or initials on them.

At the close of the evidence adduced by the Prosecutor, I submitted to the learned Magistrate that there was no *"sufficient"* (and I stress the word "sufficient") evidence that the items were the property of the virtual complainant. The Magistrate was somewhat hesitant to commit the accused but *ex abundante cautela*, he overruled my submission and very courteously stated that he was of the view that the matter should be sent to the Jury for them to decide whether or not they were satisfied "beyond a reasonable doubt" that the items being claimed by the stall-holder were really her merchandise. That was the ruling of the Court.

I could understand the reluctance of the learned Magistrate (Some years later, he was appointed a Judge of the Supreme Court. He was always courteous and a gentleman.) to throw out the case. I specifically requested the Order of the Court that all the Exhibits in the case be securely kept by the Police to be produced at the Jury trial. From my experience at the Bar, I know that Exhibits have been known to disappear and evaporate into thin air, while in others there was clumsy tampering with some important Exhibits.

In this case, as it turned out, this was the most brazen, clumsy tampering I ever witnessed. My clients were not in any way disappointed. They were in Court and they heard all that transpired in the Magistrate's Court before the learned Magistrate. They told me that, in view of what transpired in Court, they hoped for an early trial at the Supreme Court Criminal Sessions. Since the day when my clients were committed to stand trial in the Supreme Court, I never saw the Exhibits again until they were in the well of the Supreme Court on the day of the Jury trial.

The trial started before a Judge and Jury on Monday, May 7th, 1973. Prior to his appointment to the Judicial Bench, the Judge in this case was a very popular Crown Prosecutor, the State Prosecutor as they were called after British Guiana became a Republic. The State Prosecutor assigned to the case, was a young member of the Bar. He was pleasant and genial young man with whom I never had any encounters while he was practising at the Bar. Everything seemed to be quite normal and I was happy to get this matter heard as I had a lengthy murder trial coming up later at the same Session.

The accused men were put in the dock. They were properly arraigned and pleas were taken. They all pleaded not guilty. Jurors were empanelled. Everything was following the normal and regular procedure. The State Prosecutor asked that the matter be adjourned to 1.00 p.m. I noticed then there were no Exhibits before the Court. No reason was given for the request for the adjournment. Normally, Counsel would inform the Court why the adjournment was being sought. I did not resist the application.

The learned Judge asked me (as Defence Counsel) about how long the case should take to be completed. I told the Judge that I thought that the case should be completed by Thursday of the same week as there were not many witnesses to be called for the Prosecution. Names of witnesses to be called by the State are listed on the back of the Indictment. Everything was going just right.

At 1:00 p.m. the matter started. Never in my wildest dreams could I have ever thought that this simple case would turn out to be the cause *célèbre* it became. This was one of the most important cases in my professional life.

When the Prosecutor opened his case, he told the Jury that the owner, the virtual complainant, locked up her stalls in the market place on the night before the incident but upon return to her stalls the next morning, she observed that her stalls were broken into and articles were missing. She reported the matter to the Police Station nearby. The Prosecutor mentioned that some goods were taken away from the accused. Here, I noticed how things were beginning to take on new dimensions.

The Prosecutor told the Jury in the boldest of language that the virtual complainant identified the goods. He steered away from specifics. He neither told the Jury that she would identify the goods by *"general appearance"* nor by specific markings she had placed on the various pieces of goods. The nature of the identification is normally told to the Jury at an early stage. I immediately concluded that something "fishy" is developing. Then the Prosecutor told the Court and the Jury that in due course, the State would produce the Exhibits and the virtual complainant would identify said Exhibits as hers by marks, initials and price tags. I knew there and then that this was going to be a battle as at the Preliminary Investigation, the Exhibits had no marks, no initials and no price tags. My cross-examination of the owner of the stalls during the Preliminary Investigation made this pellucidly clear.

At this stage, there was nothing I could have done. I simply had to wait for the correct and appropriate moment. I previously appeared in several criminal trials before this same Judge and I was well acquainted with his attitude when things were not going very well for the Prosecution. The Judge knew full well that I was *always* very careful and thorough in my cross-examinations. He knew that I would not waste time by cross-examining witnesses when there was no need for me to cross-examine them. I kept my peace.

My whole case rested on the cross-examination of the virtual complainant and her evidence from the witness box. Two formal witnesses (as they are called) gave evidence of the location of the market place, the stalls, how they were made and secured. They further testified as to the results of their inspection of the complainant's stalls when they inspected them after her report at the Police Station. I asked each of the two witnesses about the location of the stalls in question and established that both stalls were clearly visible by anyone walking on the roads running along the front and right sides, which is the eastern and northern sides, of the market. My reticence must have been noticeable as after I was finished with the first and second witnesses, the Judge said to me, "Is that all, Mr. Manraj?"

I courteously replied, "Yes, Your Honour, that is all from me for now." I stressed *"for now."* You see, I was waiting for the main witness, the virtual complainant who was the owner of the stalls; she was the person who claimed ownership of the Exhibits. To my delight, following the order of the names listed on the back of the Indictment, the Prosecutor called the third witness, the woman who owned the stalls. After the usual preliminary questions, she bravely and stoutly started to identify the Exhibits by her initials on some, her price tags on others and yet on others, by pieces of scotch tape with prices marked on the scotch tape. On one exhibit, a flask, the witness told the Jury that she claimed the flask because it had the sale price on it in her handwriting when she saw it at the Police Station. The mark was made with red crayon but the mark was now rubbed off. I found this very interesting. I immediately jumped on my feet and objected to this evidence being led. I told the Court very slowly and deliberately:

"This witness is now saying that when she saw it at the Police Station it had a mark but yet here she is telling the Jury that the flask has no mark. We have four stages to go through the Exhibits in her market stalls, the Exhibits at the Police Station, the Exhibits at the Preliminary Investigation before the Magistrate and now, a new version of identification of the Exhibits before the Jury. These are the facts that made me apprehensive of fraud and tampering of the Exhibits and I am now fully confirmed of that. I had cross-examined her very carefully and fully tied her down at the Preliminary Investigation."

I further submitted to the Judge: "Your Honour, you can see the difficulty involved and patience one has to possess to cross-examine this witness who is taking us through a labyrinth of identification of the Exhibits."

The Court ruled that when the Prosecutor connected the evidence, the witness can be recalled and the Court further ruled that the witness could continue with her evidence in chief. So, the "circus" continued until the witness had identified all the Exhibits with price tags and initials as her merchandise and that she had them in her stalls before the alleged breaking-in by the accused.

I waited my turn. The evidence in chief was completed and I started a very careful cross-examination of the stall-owner. Already, very early in my cross-examination I saw how 'the breeze was blowing.' You, the reader, will recall from earlier pages that on oath, before the Magistrate, at the Preliminary Investigation, the witness conceded to me that she had no marks, no price tags, no initials on the Exhibits. After further agreeing with me at the Preliminary Investigation that she had no marks on any of the Exhibits, she concluded by telling me, "I would say the Exhibits are mine from *'general appearance.'*" She further stated under cross-examination that the Exhibits shown to her in the Jury trial are the same Exhibits shown to her at the Preliminary Investigation before the Magistrate.

Well, one does not have to be a Sherlock Holmes to conclude that somewhere, some interference, meddling and tampering took place with respect to the Exhibits before the Jury, as here the witness was identifying each item by price tags, marks and her initials. As I continued my cross-examination, the Judge constantly interrupted me to find out what I had in mind and where all this was leading. I told His Honour that there is no mystery in my cross-examination. The witness gave evidence under oath before the Magistrate and me at the Preliminary Investigation that she did not have "any marks" (price tags or initials or scotch tape) on the Exhibits shown to her. All she could swear to is that the Exhibits appeared to be hers only from *"general appearance."*

The Judge told me that he was not interested in what she said in the Magistrate's Court at the Preliminary Investigation – that is not before the Court. He said he was only concerned with what she told the Jury. Here, I saw some real problems coming into focus. I explained to His Honour, in the most polite manner, that where a person gives evidence on oath in a previous proceeding involving the same matter and then subsequently changes the evidence that was given on oath, then as Defence Counsel, I am entitled to bring her previously sworn statement to the attention of the Court and Jury. Furthermore, Defence Counsel should be able to cross-examine the witness on the previously sworn statement.

The Judge told me he did not agree with me. I was amazed and I urged again that my cross-examination would go to the credibility of the witness in the case, who was making statements that were in direct conflict and at variance with the sworn statements she made in the Magistrate's Court. Both statements could not be correct. Before the Magistrate, on oath and under cross-examination by me, she told me in the clearest of language that she had no marks on the Exhibits shown to her in the Magistrate's Court. She only relied on "general appearance."

When legal arguments of this nature are being made, the Judge usually orders the Jury to retire until the legal arguments are concluded. I could not help observing the expressions on the faces of the Jurors and the nodding acquiescence coming from them as I advanced my arguments to the Judge. It is not my duty to direct the Judge on matters that he ought to know, but the Judge did not order the Jury to retire, as he ought to have done during my legal arguments regarding the admissibility of evidence concerning the credibility of the witness. It is established practice and procedure, that during legal arguments, the members of the Jury are directed by the Judge to retire to the Jury room for obvious reasons. Instead, His Honour told me to carry on with my cross-examination.

I asked the Court Orderly to pass to me all the Exhibits bearing the witness' initials. The Jury watched intently as this took a few minutes. Armed with these initialled Exhibits now in Court, I took them one by one and showed them to the witness. I then asked her if these were the Exhibits she had seen in the Magistrate's Court. She said, "Yes." This was the break-through I sought. I then reminded the witness that the Exhibits she identified in the Magistrate's Court did not have any initials or marks on them. I reminded her that she only relied on *"general appearance"* to identify them during those previous proceedings.

Before the witness could answer me, His Honour said, "Mr. Manraj, what are you asking the witness? This is a trial in the Supreme Court."

I do not get easily riled. I told His Honour that he was interfering with my cross-examination of the witness. I made it clear to him that as Defence Counsel, I had taken an oath to defend my clients to the best of my ability. I had to make sure that I did everything for them that would help them to get justice in this Court of Law. It is my duty to show the Jury the witness' lack of credibility.

This is what I meant when I said earlier that we do not only have to fight for the protection of our clients' rights, we also have to "wrestle at times to get justice done." His Honour did not make any comments on the reply I gave to him. I continued with my cross-examination and at the end of the day, the matter was adjourned to the following morning at 9.00 a.m. for continuation. I was fighting with the

Judge to get my questions answered and he interrupted me every time I got the answers I wanted.

The proceedings were just reaching the stage when I was going to deal with the witness's initials, which were all made on each item in black ink. They stood out to me as it appeared that the ink was very fresh on the items. Between the Preliminary Investigation before the Magistrate and the trial now, the Exhibits were in Police Custody (I hope) for almost three years. The ink marks were fresh. Here I profited from my previous cases involving the evidence of handwriting experts. So I started simply to ask where she was when she put these initials on the Exhibits which she admitted did not have any initials on them when she saw them in the Magistrate's Court.

I clearly saw that the Judge was getting very jittery over my cross-examination of the witness. It appeared to me that the Judge understood clearly what I was doing and there was no way the State Prosecutor could successfully re-examine the witness to restore her credibility. The physical facts were established. All the unmarked and un-initialled Exhibits that were tendered before the Magistrate were now marked, priced and initialled with the witness' initials. Two principles occupied my thoughts: my duty toward my clients and the pursuit of Justice.

First of all, as Defence Counsel for the three men in the dock, I owed them the right to a fair trial and was in duty bound, to use all my skill, learning and experience to see that they obtained Justice. I kept my calm and did everything according to the rules. The Judge, I observed, did not feel very happy about that, as he saw where I was going. This was the fight. I was wrestling for Justice. It appeared to me that the Judge believed that the three men were guilty and did not want me to pursue the cross-examination. I did not budge. I could see the Judge thinking of what a tight spot he would have been in if he were the Prosecutor, as the answers elicited from the State witness under my cross-examination were so adverse to the prosecution's case.

Secondly, I felt that if these were the thoughts and feelings in the Judge's mind, he ought to decline hearing the matter further and not continue with the trial of the three men. He ought to recuse himself. These three men are innocent until they are proven guilty. That is the burden on the prosecution. That is the fullest attainment of Justice. That is what I was pursuing at all times.

On every occasion that I was able to impair the credibility of the witness with respect to the identification of the Exhibits that were being shown to her by the Prosecutor, the Judge would interrupt. It soon reached the point of explosion, which I was trying very much to avoid. I had a few more questions before concluding my cross-examination.

To my chagrin, the Judge started again to interfere by way of interruptions of my cross-examination. He again said to me, "Mr. Manraj, let us get on with it."

My reply was, "Your Honour as soon as I have concluded this aspect I would be finished with the witness. I am not quite finished with her."

I then asked the witness if she has the pen, which she used to put her initials, as she is claiming she did, on the Exhibits. Before the witness could answer me (a legitimate question by me), all Hell broke lose and His Honour blurted out, "Mr. Manraj, what are you doing, why don't you shut up and sit down!"

That was the limit!! Clearly, the Judge saw the end coming and that the accused men would have to be set free. A million replies flooded my thoughts. Here I am, a Senior Member of the Bar and one of Her Majesty's Counsel (the greatest Honour a practising English qualified Barrister can achieve) conducting my case on behalf of my clients, being told by the Judge to 'shut up and sit down.' What inelegant coarse and abrasive language coming from a Judge on the Bench in open Court! It was clear that he wanted the three men before him convicted of the offence.

I stood there and replied,

"Your Honour, you are not a Queen's Counsel, but you ought to know you cannot speak to Senior Counsel like that. I would like to respect your knowledge regarding the law on cross-examination and what cross-examination lets in. I strongly resent and object to the manner in which you have spoken to me just now, but it is all the more ridiculous, when you use coarse language telling me to 'shut up and sit down' in open Court, before my clients and the Jury. That is unforgivable and shows a lack of decorum on your part."

Then I told him,

"You cannot today speak to your servants like that. If this is your way of behaving at home, please keep that kind of behaviour at home and not bring it into your Court. Please don't speak to me like that. It is not only rude. It is unprofessional and is not becoming of a Judge to use such unrefined language."

When I was finished, I felt very relieved but I knew what was coming. Defence Counsel's work in Criminal trials is no bed of roses. Let me hasten to add that immediately after, I felt hurt for being involved in this ridiculous and uncalled for encounter between Bench and Bar. I was practising my profession in the highest traditions of the English Bar. The Judge had no right to behave in the manner he did behave. It brings the High Honour of being a Supreme Court Judge into ridicule and unfavourable respect.

Immediately, again in the presence of the Jury, His Lordship told me that the matter is adjourned to 1.15 p.m. for me to *"show cause"* why I should not be committed to prison for Contempt of Court. That was adding insult to injury. His Honour left the Bench and without giving the

Jury the usual admonition when adjournments are taken, went to his Chambers, stating that the Court is adjourned. I do not know where the people came from. The Courtroom was filled and there was some confusion as Jurors were trying to get out, people were trying to get in and Police Officers were hustling to the Court-room to restore order. My clients were very disturbed and concerned. I can understand that, as everything happened in the presence of the Jury.

The mid-day newscast was all about the incident and gave it unusual full coverage. I did not fully realize the full impact of the Judge's ruling and how to assess the situation. So many people came up to me and congratulated me for standing up to a "Prosecuting Judge." Yet others told me I might go to prison. Most of the working people were delighted that I stood up to the Judge. At that time, my eldest daughter, Anne, was attending Bishops High School – the leading Girls School in Georgetown, Guyana. The Radio discussed the possibility of my going to prison for Contempt of Court. There is the human side of all this drama.

My late wife, Gladys, phoned me. She was very perturbed over the whole incident and wanted to come to me at my Chambers immediately. She said that our daughter, Anne, did not want to go back to school that afternoon as everybody is going to tell her that her Daddy is going to prison. I told my late wife, Gladys, to put Anne on the phone. I told her not to be worried and I assured her everything would be put right. I assured her that by the time she gets back home from school everything will be back to normal.

I then consulted the late J. O. F. Haynes, Q.C. and the late Ayube McDoom, Solicitor. "JOF" Haynes as he was affectionately known was the most senior practising Queen's Counsel (Q.C.) at the time. He and I had a very good professional relationship and I was Junior to him in many important cases before I became a Q.C. When I took "silk" and became a Q.C. our good professional relationship continued although, on many occasions, we were opposing Counsel in many high-profile cases. I told "JOF" Haynes exactly what happened and he was very upset over the incident but told me that perhaps I went too far in rebuking the Judge for his utterances. I told him I will accept his criticism but I was shocked at the Judge's outburst.

In a short while, many members of the Bar made contact with me and offered their assistance. I was overwhelmed by the show of support and understanding from my fellow members of the Bar – young ones and older ones. They all offered to come on board and give me all the help I needed. During this very short period, many members of the Bar also contacted His Honour, the trial Judge. He told them that he would accept an apology for the remarks I made to him and put the matter behind us. I was moved by this show of solidarity from the practising members of the Bar. After several interventions by practitioners, including Mr. Frederick Ramprashad, Q.C., the Judge disclosed a willingness to accept an apology and forget the incident.

At 1.15 p.m., the Court Gallery was crowded and the Court itself was packed. Mr. Haynes entered appearance for me, Mr. Frederick Ramprashad accompanied him and both had the late Ayube McDoom as Instructing Solicitor. Mr. Haynes informed the Court that I would like to make a statement. I apologized for what I said, "Perhaps," I said, "my remarks went too far. Although I was not the originator of the unfortunate incident, which occurred in the Court the day before, I sincerely regret what took place."

"JOF" Haynes was really the true representative of the Senior Bar. He told the Court that it was regrettable that the incident ever happened. He continued, "Speaking for my learned friend, Mr. Manraj, we will ask that the outspoken apology be accepted as true and complete. One must bear in mind that there are two considerations, which might have contributed to this unhappy event. You will understand that in the course of battle in criminal trials, counsel on both sides might be indiscreet and remarks are made in the course of heated arguments which ought not to have been made."

The Judge remarked that he knew that behind it all there was no malice. His Lordship accepted the apology and did not make an Order of Contempt. The Judge requested that I meet him in Chambers and adjourned the Court for a few minutes. He told me he would not continue the trial and would adjourn the matter until the next Criminal Sessions. When the Judge returned into open Court, he addressed me and said, "Mr. Manraj, I am feeling that in view of the incident in Court in the presence of the Jury, your clients might very well feel that they would not have a fair trial."

I stated that my clients informed me that they would like you to continue with the hearing of the case and conclude the trial. The Judge stated that in the interest of Justice, he would halt the trial and adjourn it until the next Criminal Sessions. The Judge then discharged the Jury.

Justice and the achievement of Justice are the concerns of all the parties involved in the administration of the substantive law and procedural law that are in place to marshal and facilitate the attainment and realization of Justice. It is as much the concern of the Judge and the State Prosecutor as it is the vital concern of Counsel for the defendant in a Criminal trial. Justice must be done even if there are conditions and circumstances that may detract from its attainment.

Respect, courtesy and good breeding are not three lanes in a one-way street. You have to show respect, courtesy and behave in a manner that inspires mutuality and reciprocity of these values. Not because one is placed in high authority, that that gives that person the passport to ride roughshod over others. Except for the nine years I served in the Ministry of the Attorney General of Ontario, Canada, I have always been an employer. What you give out, is what you get back. Being civil and polite can move people and things over the roughest spots. My Staff was always appreciative of the kind and understanding manner in my dealing with them.

Now my clients, who were committed to stand trial at the next Criminal Sessions of the Supreme Court, were very upset because, as they told me, they could not raise any more legal fees to pay to me for the continuation of their trial. I hastened to assure them that I wanted no more fees from them. I also promised them that I would take steps to have a *nolle prosequi* entered in view of the obvious tampering of the Exhibits.

I took a copy of the depositions of the Preliminary Investigation in the Magistrate's Court and a record of what transpired before the trial Judge and went to the then Director of Public Prosecutions, the late Mr. E. A. Romao. He was a fair man and when I pointed out to him the evidence given by the virtual complainant in the Magistrate's Court and the evidence she gave in the Supreme Court culminating in the interchanges and exchanges between the Judge and myself, he told me there and then that he, as the Director of Public Prosecutions (DPP), will not prosecute the case any further and a *nolle prosequi* will be entered. This was properly executed.

This brought me great relief. I went back to my Chambers where I had left my clients with strict instructions not to leave until I returned from the DPP. I gave my clients the good news. That was another big event. They left my Chambers and within half-an-hour, they were back with a large following. They came into my Chambers and they were very loud in their praises of the manner I conducted the case and the resolution of the upheaval that arose. Practice at the Criminal Bar is not for the faint-hearted practitioner. One must have stamina and courage.

It is extremely important that the case for the accused persons be made clear to the Jury at the earliest moment in cross-examination. Once Counsel conducts his case properly, with propriety and integrity, no Judge whose role is to see that Justice is done, has the right to interfere with Defence

Counsel's cross-examination or to tell him to "shut up and sit down" when things are not going well for the prosecution. That militates against the dignity and esteem of the entire Bar. One good thing emerged from all of this.

An avid Press lavishly covered every step in the proceedings of this unplanned incident. I would be less than honest if I were to state that I was not pleased with the outcome. It all resulted in a terrific upsurge of my already established practice at the Bar and my reputation for being a lawyer who goes all out to protect his clients and see that Justice is done. With humility, I must state that I earned, through my practice, this reputation.

I wrote the Commissioner of Police, the Chief Justice and the Director of Public Prosecutions about the dishonest, unlawful and clumsy tampering of the Court Exhibits that were put in the care of the Police for safekeeping until the Exhibits were to be produced in Court for the Jury trial. There was fraud, tampering and dishonesty when the initials and other marks were put on the Exhibits during the time they were in Police custody. The markings and initials were not on the Exhibits at the close of the case for the prosecution at the Preliminary Inquiry. The virtual complainant herself told me this under my cross-examination.

When were those initials and marks put on the Exhibits? Only the Police Department can answer this question as all the Exhibits were in their custody. It is clear that the virtual complainant had access to them as she said the initials, which appeared on the Exhibits in the Supreme Court, were her initials. The Police must have facilitated this dishonest and unlawful interference and tampering of the Exhibits while they were in their custody. They probably realized that their case was very weak and they tried to embellish the evidence of identification via a clumsy tampering. I would like to think that no State Prosecutor or any legal functionary of the Attorney-General's Chambers or the Office of the Director of Public Prosecutions had anything to do with the interference of the Exhibits.

What is shameful is this: Here I am fighting with all my professional skill to expose the fraud and tampering and the Judge turns on me for exploring and exposing the fraud and tampering. I would have thought that when the State Prosecutor saw what was happening, he would have there and then entered a *nolle prosequi*.

But the Judge, being a former Prosecutor, thought he would turn me off and subdue my zeal and intent in exposing the tampering, the dishonesty and the fraud. I had to fight and battle every inch of the way to secure Justice for my three clients. That is what Criminal Defence Counsel has to do ever so often to see that the limpid stream of Justice does not become adulterated or polluted by those who only feel that a conviction is a synonym of "Justice," – which has to be fought for, resulting at times in defence counsel having literally and figuratively to wrestle with Judge and Prosecutor to see that Justice is done.

Up to the time I left Guyana in 1978 for Canada, there was no report published or circulated by the Police Department, the Chambers of the Chief Justice or the Chambers of the Director of Public Prosecutions regarding the enquiry over the tampering. The battle for Justice does not only take place in the Courtroom. Much of the pursuit of Justice is done outside the Courtroom. If I were still in Guyana, you can rest assured that a report on the investigation would have been forthcoming, resulting in the proper sanctions being taken against the perpetrators of the tampering of the Exhibits in order to defeat Justice. The fair name and concept of *JUSTICE* must never be compromised.

Chapter 4

The Guilty Plea

Its Importance and Ramifications

The important applicable maxim is as old as the hills, *"A plea of Guilty is a solemn confession."* Ever so often one hears from the Court: "I take into account that you have pleaded guilty and by so doing, you have saved the Court, the Administration and the Tax Payer a lot of money. You will be fined the minimum for the Offence." Or continues the Court as an alternative, "You will be given a warning on this occasion, but please don't come back before the Court, as you will then be fined the maximum or sent to prison." Of course, the nature of the offences plays an important part in helping the Court to determine to what extent leniency can be invoked. There are so many variations of the considerations that are taken into account when deciding what penalty will be imposed.

Before discussing a few matters, which I would like to bring to the readers' attention, I would like to deal with some important aspects of the plea of guilty. First of all, it is not sufficient for counsel to tell the Court that the defendant wishes to plead guilty. The defendant himself must plead guilty. Ever so often, defendants have told the Court, on an application for change of plea, that they never authorized their counsel to enter a plea of guilty. The procedure on such an application to change the plea is for the charge to be read again to the defendant and the new plea should be made by the defendant himself and not someone on his behalf. Experience has guided counsel to be very careful and cautious and therefore he should always let the defendant tell the Court himself that he is guilty.

This is how the procedure unfolds. Let us take a case where the defendant is charged with the Summary Offence of making an unsafe lane change. The defendant retains me and tells me that in an unguarded moment, he did make an unsafe lane change but there was no accident and no one was injured. The only harm that resulted from his action was that the driver behind him had to brake suddenly and very hard to avoid an impact. He tells me he wants to plead guilty and put an end to this *"Sword of Damocles"* that is hanging over his head. Most people are motivated to travel this route and get the matter out of the way. Normally, the fee charged for a plea of guilty is far less than that charged for a *"Not Guilty"* plea, when the matter has to be contested fully.

On the appointed day, the parties go to the Summary Court. When the matter is called up, the defendant appears (not always necessary). The charge is read to him by the Magistrate, the Judge or by whoever is the presiding officer of the Court. The presiding Magistrate then asks the defendant: "How do you plead?" Or words to that effect.

The defendant says "Guilty." It is always safe for the defendant to be present in Court and himself inform the Court of his plea.

The Prosecutor (whoever he may be – Police Officer, State Attorney, Provincial Prosecutor or whoever is discharging the functions of the Prosecutor in that Court) then states the facts to the Court. Defence Counsel (or the defendant himself) then addresses the Court and urges on behalf of his client, all the mitigating facts and circumstances that are in the defendant's favour, for example, no previous convictions, his charitable services to the community and the like, all intending to show that the defendant is a reliable and decent citizen.

The Court then pronounces its judgment – the defendant can either be fined or reprimanded or ordered to do some community service. Sometimes the Court would say to the defendant: "You have done the right thing. You have pleaded guilty thereby saving a lot of the Court's time, administration expenses and tax-payer's money. There was no injury or impact. Please be careful. Don't come back to this Court. I will give you a reprimand today. You are free to leave." Usually if there is a fine imposed and the defendant requests time to pay the fine, reasonable time is granted. In my early days at the Bar, I did quite a lot of these types of cases. It was a good way of building up a clientele and getting established.

A good lawyer never turns his back on the clients who came to him in his early days. As one lawyer puts it, "I will appear in any case in any Court once my fee has been paid." This is the practical approach. In my own practice, after I became a Senior member of the Bar and my practice developed into a very substantial High Court practice, I had under my wings several Junior members of the Bar. I helped them, guided them and many of them became my Juniors in the serious Supreme Court cases. To these Junior Barristers, I handed over the Magistrate's Court practice.

I have had the pleasure and privilege of presenting the petitions of many young lawyers for admission to practise their profession. I feel very happy to state that I have trained and presented the Petitions for Call to the Bar of many young lawyers and then took them into my Chambers and trained them. Three of them in time became Judges, quite a few became Magistrates, one became Attorney-General of Guyana and very many became "Crown Prosecutors" later on, designated "State Prosecutor or Counsel" after British Guiana became the "Republic of Guyana" within the Commonwealth in 1971. On many occasions, some of those same "Crown Prosecutors" or "State Prosecutors" prosecuted many of the important criminal jury trials where I was counsel for the accused person.

A simple plea of guilty is very straightforward procedurally. But a rather interesting situation arises where a defendant tells his counsel that he did not commit the offence with which he is charged, but insists on pleading guilty to it, for reasons of his own. Counsel must continue to represent him, but only after he has advised his client what the consequences will be and that which can be submitted in mitigation can only be on the basis that his client is guilty. The client cannot have the best of both worlds. The obvious setback to the instant situation is that counsel is very circumscribed as to what he can urge by way of mitigation.

There is one case I would like to deal with to show how a plea of guilt can be useful, economically beneficial and timesaving. My client came in to see me. He told me what happened. He was upfront with me and I admired his honesty. In an unguarded moment he had made an unsafe lane change. He did not execute the established caution of looking in his mirrors before changing lanes. There was no accident, no impact and no one was injured. The only thing that caused an officer to be aware of what happened was the screeching of brakes from the vehicle behind. My client was pulled over despite the fact that the driver in the vehicle behind had made no complaint to the officer. He did not stop. After applying his brakes very firmly, he continued driving. My client was eventually served with a citation for "unsafe lane change." He had no previous convictions, had a good and respectable driving record and assisted in the local school basketball team. This was his first encounter with the law.

On the appointed day we went to Court. The Magistrate was an experienced Magistrate and ran his Court in a very systematic manner. I had appeared before him in my early days on several occasions in various matters. He usually saved time and accommodated members of the public, by calling on all those who wished to plead guilty to step forward. The Prosecutor would soon produce their dockets and the cases are called. This makes good sense as those cases, which are to be tried, can take up the rest of the day.

Eventually my client's matter was called and he pleaded guilty. I rose to address the Court and I stressed that

This is Victoria Law Courts building in Georgetown, Guyana, where Mr. Manraj had many of his famous trials.

After more than 50 years as a Barrister-At-Law, A. Shakoor Manraj still practices his profession.

This is a picture of the Manraj Family Home in Georgetown, which now houses the Ministry of Foreign Affairs.

No break for the busy; even at breakfast, Mr. Manraj is hard at work on behalf of his clients.

the change of lane was an unconscious act by my client. There was no accident. This is his first encounter with the law and the Prosecutor will confirm (Counsel usually checks with him first) that the defendant has no record of any serious or minor traffic violations. To be more precise, he never appeared before a Court on any charge whatsoever. The Court seemed impressed as in many of the other cases before mine; the defendants had some shocking records. This was psychologically an advantage for my client. I then rounded off what I had to say by telling the Court about his community work at the school and eventually stated what I wanted to say by stating to the Court:

> "Your Worship, Counsel can never dictate to the Court what it should do or what penalty it can impose but, Your Worship, in this matter before you, you have a young man who is frank with the Court, honest with his lawyer and has an enviable good driving record which is confirmed by the prosecution. Your Worship, I most respectfully ask that you apply the section of the Magistrate's Court Ordinance which gives you the power, in proper cases, to warn the defendant and not fine him or do anything that would result in a conviction being recorded. Bearing in mind the standard of driving in today's crowded streets, I respectfully submit that my client has a good and enviable driving record."

I was so happy. The Court thanked me for putting it so forcefully and the part about his community service at the school weighed heavily with the Magistrate. He dismissed my client under the relevant section. My client thanked him and I also thanked him and asked "permission to take my leave." He was so pleased at this gesture of politeness. He commented on it. I joined my client outside. He could not have been happier and he thanked me profusely. So much for the plea in mitigation in that type of offence.

The Teacher vs. The Student

Talking about Juniors, who did their "pupilage" with me, brings to my mind one incident, which really touched me. One of my Juniors had just been appointed a "Crown Attorney" (or Crown Counsel, whichever you choose to call them). He had spent one year in my Chambers as a Junior Barrister. He was bright and matured into a fine lawyer. He came to me one afternoon and told me he was the "Crown Attorney" assigned to do the murder trial in which I was appearing for the accused man.

The case was due to start that same month before a Judge and Jury. He told me how diffident he felt doing the case in which I was appearing. I put him at ease. I told him that I would like to think that I trained him to strive for Justice at all times and to be like the blindfolded Statue of Justice and hold the scales evenly. "Get on with the case." I said "Forget the role I filled as your Principal and Tutor in your very green days at the Bar. Just do your job and don't worry about personalities."

Of course, there are instances where he cannot prosecute in a case e.g. if a relative or close friend or previous client was charged. In that case, he would ask to be relieved, as there was either a real or apparent clash of interest. That situation did not arise in the instant case that he was to prosecute. He thanked me for putting his mind at ease. When he was leaving, I said to him, "Know your Law, apply it properly and above all see that Justice is done." He thanked me and left.

At the trial, we had a very noble and decent Judge – he was very good on the Bench and was very highly respected. My young and learned friend, the Prosecutor, did very well. It was a hotly contested trial. It took the Jury a long time to arrive at their verdict. I had urged them in a long and passionate and detailed address, to return a verdict of *"Not Guilty"* based on their findings that there was reasonable doubt in which case they are bound by law, to give the benefit of that reasonable doubt to the accused. They did that. No sweeter sounds could have reached the ears of my client. I felt he was innocent from the beginning. I was fully satisfied and there was an inner glow in me as “Justice was done.” It was fought for and it was attained.

Guilty or Not

There is one other case I would like to deal with to show the full effect of entering a plea of guilty at the propitious time. That case is one in which the defendant was charged with the Offence of Speeding. I will deal with this later on in the chapter, but suffice it to state here that speeding is an absolute liability offence in the Province of Ontario, Canada, where you will recall that I practised after I resigned my position with the Ontario Ministry of the Attorney-General. A powerful plea in mitigation is like a healing remedy and properly orchestrated can, at times, despite the plea of guilty, achieve a fair and just determination of a matter. That is what I was pursuing in the case I am about to discuss.

My client was a young member of the Bar. I knew him very well. I had attended his wedding two years before. He came to me at my Office, which at that time was on Carlton Street, Toronto, Ontario. He showed me a speeding ticket. It charged him with doing 80-kph in a 50-kph zone, an excess of 30-kph. That offence even at that time (1990) on conviction carried a stiff fine and an assignment of three demerit points to his driver’s licence. Speeding up to 15-kph in excess does not carry any assignment of demerit points, but any conviction for speeding can result in a steep increase in insurance rates. He had read my book, “The Law on Speeding and Radar” by A. Shakoor Manraj, Q.C. and Paul Haines, Ph.D., 2nd Edition at pages 7-9. The police and the Courts regarded my book as an authoritative source on “The Law on Speeding and Radar” and for some time, I was very active in the Provincial Offences Courts defending speeding tickets where the speeding was detected by Radar.

My client's elderly father had a serious heart problem and for a while, was staying at the home of his only son (my lawyer friend and client) pending admittance to the famous Sunnybrook Hospital for surgery. My client had received a telephone call from his home informing him that his Dad was in a bad way and that he should get home immediately. He tells me that he cannot remember all the details of what happened.

All he could think of is getting to his Dad as quickly as he possibly could and see what could be done. Bear in mind he is the only son and he wanted to get to his Dad. With that mind set, he was speeding towards his home. He has no recollection of seeing any Speed Limit signs. He was most truthful to me. He really could not remember how fast he was travelling but he admitted to me that he was speeding. He wanted to get to his Dad before anything more serious developed. He felt once he got to his Dad, he would be able to get him to the hospital.

As he was approaching near to his home, he saw the flashing blue lights of the Police car. He was overtaken and told to pull over. He told me he spoke to the young officer but cannot remember what he told him. All he can remember is that the Officer told him, "Come on you can do better than that. I hear that all the time." My client was anxious to get home. He told the Officer please hurry with the ticket. The Officer gave him the ticket charging him with doing 80-kph in a 50-kph zone. He could not remember whether the police caught him on the radar or was just "pacing" him. At any rate, he got home and saw his Dad's condition and he immediately called the ambulance heart unit service. His Dad was taken to hospital the same afternoon. The doctors told him that his father had a serious heart attack.

After he spoke to me, I told him I wanted him to get from the admission doctor at the hospital a certificate showing when his father was admitted and how serious was his condition. I had previously explained to him that the excessive speeding carried a stiff fine and demerit points. He was not worried about the stiff fine. He was really concerned about the demerit points as he was clearly in the category of excessive speeding that carried a suspension of his driving privileges.

Driving in a sense was the key to his "bread and butter." He had time to reflect and my client told me that he did not mind what fine he had to pay but he could not carry on without his driver's license. I told him I quite understood his concern. He put a heavy burden on my shoulder when he told me: "Apart from being a close friend and a Senior Member of the Bar, I have great respect for you. You have written the accepted text on the Law on Speeding and Radar. You have to find something in there to come to my rescue." I had to chuckle.

The speeding ticket indicated the date, time and Court where he will have to appear. The Court was to be one of the Courts at Old City Hall, Toronto. That was my "Stomping Ground" during my service as a Prosecutor with the Ontario Ministry of the Attorney-General. I knew the disposition and mentality of many of the Justices of the Peace presiding over the various traffic Courts. I knew the Provincial Court Prosecutors. Some of the Justices of Peace were like stone walls. You plead guilty. You are fined and on to the next case. They really administered the law without any human feelings. Those were just human machines. There were some others who were more Jurists and not merely Justices of the Peace. They understood the whole philosophy behind summary infractions and punishment. I told my client that I cannot select my Court or the J.P. but whoever we get on the Bench, I will have to get through to his better side.

We appeared in Court. It was a cold day and in the early morning, some of the Justices of the Peace, (J. P.) are still a bit grumpy. Nevertheless, I am happy to say that my reputation at the Bar always came to my rescue when I was "in a jam." To my great delight (and one must know one's

Court. That is one of the secrets to success) the J. P. was really a fine gentleman. He had a good sense of humour and his English was very refined and correct. He knew me well during my days at Old City Hall.

The matter was called and after the guilty plea was entered, the Prosecutor just got up and said in the usual summary manner, "Your Worship, he was doing 80 in a 50-kph zone." The learned Justice of the Peace said to me, "Mr. Manraj was his house on fire?"

That opened the door for me. I said, "No, Your Worship, it was something far more serious than that."

J. P.:	"And what, pray tell, is that?"
Mr. Manraj:	"Your Worship, it was his Dad. I will explain."
J. P.:	"You have got to make it a good one, Mr. Manraj, as this is doing an 80-kph in a 50-kph zone."
Mr. Manraj:	"I do not know, Your Worship, whether you will call it a good one but it is the truth and since I was a boy I was always told, "Tell the truth and shame the devil."

I was succeeding. Things were going my way. I continued: "Your Worship, one can come before you with some concoction or some sad story which cannot be supported, but in this case, I will respectfully ask the Court to let the milk of human kindness and understanding flow freely. This unhappy reason for speeding could befall any one of us."

I mentioned to the Court the very close relationship between the old man and his son and the depth of the filial affection of a son for his elderly Dad. In this day, that is something to admire - the deep veneration an only son has for his elderly and loving father. I went on to tell the Court what actually happened and told the Court about the unfeeling remark of the police Officer when my client told him the truth. I went on with my submissions, the main one being that speeding is an absolute liability offence. Be that as it is, my client had only thing in mind – getting to his father before anything more serious took place.

At this stage, I produced the Medical Report. My client is not deceiving the Court or trying to find some excuse. His Dad was really in a very bad way. It is the normal human reaction to a situation that my client was facing. In a situation like this, certain faculties do not function within the strict application of rules and sanctions and stress can be a very upsetting factor. I am sure that perhaps many of us might have had the same reaction to the news involving a much loved member of the family.

I told the Court that my client was an understanding practitioner. He was not asking to be set free and unaccountable for his wrong-doing. He pleaded guilty. That is in his favour. He has saved the Court and the administration and the tax payer a lot of money and I did not have to cross-examine the young doubting Police Officer. I am respectfully asking the Court to reduce the excess of the 30 kph having regard to the extenuating circumstances and deal with it as if it were a 15 kph in excess. There was no accident or any incident resulting from the fact that my client was hurrying to get to his very ill Dad.

The Court was very patient with me and heard me through my plea in mitigation without interruption. The Court asked the Prosecutor if he had anything to say. He seemed very understanding of the stressful situation that confronted my client and simply said to the Court: "No Your Worship. I certainly would not like ever to be in the defendant's shoes," I thought that was decent of the Prosecutor. The Court granted my application regarding the excess; fined the defendant the fine based on the reduced speeding and finally moved everyone when he addressed the defendant and said, "And how is your father today." The defendant replied, "My Dad is recuperating very comfortably and I thank you, Sir, for your kind enquiry." I thanked the Court and took my exit.

That did it. I think everyone was satisfied with the outcome. I know I was and my client was overwhelmed and came and hugged me and said: "I knew you could do it." This was a plea of guilty. Pleas in mitigation must be dextrously handled. Some lawyers call themselves "Mitigation experts." Even though this was a plea of guilty, it had its complexities. One must be able to navigate in troubled waters without running into difficulties. That is really coming to grips with the facts and the system that promote Justice.

I feel that my client got Justice. Justice is not unattainable. We must know how to travel along the sometimes rough road that leads to Justice. If we strive to obtain Justice, we will find a warm welcome in her open arms, with sword in her outstretched right hand and scales in her outstretched left hand and blindfold around her eyes.

Chapter 5

Never Plead Guilty Rule:

What Is The Rationale To Support This Rule?

Many lawyers believe that a defendant should never plead guilty. He should always plead "Not Guilty." He is before the Court not as a spectator. The Prosecution takes him there. It was not an invitation to a picnic. Let the Prosecution or the person who caused him to be before the Court prove their case. They have selected their weapon. Let them use it and "get their victim." This in short is how the thinking works. "I did not ask to be here," says the defendant, "you brought me here and you prove that I did or caused or was responsible for what you are alleging."

Many have argued that this is the correct approach. Even in Civil Actions, it is felt by the advocates of the "Never Plead Guilty" Rule, that the Plaintiff sued the Defendant and it is the Plaintiff's duty to prove his case against the Defendant. However, there are distinct differences, procedural and legal, between the Criminal Trial and the Civil Trial. In this chapter, I am only dealing with the Criminal trial. A person is charged or is summoned or indicted to appear before the Court to be tried for certain offences or violations.

We have heard ever so often the expression that the "Prosecution must prove its case." This is the onus placed on the Prosecution. However, there are certain instances where that burden shifts and the Defendant has to discharge the onus. Let me begin by citing a passage from a celebrated English case, delivered by that famous Judge, Lord Sankey, Lord Chancellor of England, in 1935 in the celebrated case of Woolmington-v-Director of Public Prosecutions. This deals with the standard of proof if the legal burden lies on the prosecution. While the prosecution do not have to make the jury feel certain of the defendant's guilt, they must, however, satisfy the jury upon the whole of the evidence called by the parties, of the accused's guilt beyond all reasonable doubt or "a" reasonable doubt or "any" reasonable doubt.

This is what Lord Sankey said:

> *"Throughout the web of the English Criminal Law, one golden thread is always to be seen, that it is the duty of the prosecution to prove the prisoner's guilt, subject to the qualification involving the defence of insanity and to any statutory exception. If at the end of and on the whole of the case, there is a reasonable doubt, created by the evidence given either by the prosecution or the prisoner (defendant), as to whether the offence was committed by him, the prosecution has not made out the case and the prisoner is entitled to an acquittal. No matter what the charge or where the trial, the principle that the prosecution must prove the guilt of the prisoner is part of the common law of England and no attempt to whittle it down can be entertained."*

Lord Goddard, Chief Justice of England, expressed the view in 1952, that it was better to tell the jury that before they can convict, they must be "satisfied so that they are sure" of the guilt of the accused. This form of direction on the standard of proof has frequently been used by Judges since then and has been approved by the Privy Council (the Highest Court of Appeal in England) in 1960.

However, the standard of proof changes where the standard of proof lies upon the defendant (for example alibi). As I said earlier, this book is not a legal textbook. I would not delve too deeply in the many legal principles applicable to the cases I am reviewing. I will deal with them if those legal decisions or principles were the ones that were the foundations on which my defence rested. However, before proceeding, let me state the principle.

Dealing with the standard of proof if the legal burden lies upon the defence, Humphreys, J., said, in 1944:

> *"In any case where, either by statute or at common law, some matter is presumed against an accused person 'unless the contrary is proved', the jury should be directed that it is for them to decide whether the contrary is proved, that the burden of proof required is less than that required at the hands of the prosecution in proving the case beyond a reasonable doubt; and that the burden may be discharged by evidence satisfying the jury of the probability of that which the accused is called upon to establish."*

Another aspect I would like to deal with is this: sometimes a case against a defendant may look good on paper, but the evidence called in support of the case and the cross-examination of the witnesses may cause the case to crumble and fall to pieces. Therefore, when a person pleads "Not Guilty" all he is saying in layman's language is this: "I do not have to admit or deny anything. I do not even have to answer any questions. If you feel I have committed an offence and you further feel that you have a case against me, then proceed."

If the evidence against him is strong, the prosecution discharges its burden and the jury convicts him then he is deprived of some important pleas in mitigation. Judges have been heard to say after the jury returned a verdict of guilty: "Instead of coming before the Court and invoke the mercy of the Court, you chose to defend the matter and wasted so much of the Court's time, not to mention the expense involved." Some Judges hold it against a defendant when this happens and can be very robust in the penalty imposed upon the defendant. I personally feel that this is wrong and improper. The defendant exercised his right provided for him in law to say that the prosecution "must prove its case against the defendant beyond a 'reasonable doubt.'" The defendant is innocent until proven guilty. Another important feature is that a jury must not convict on the weakness of the Defence, but rather on the strength of the prosecution's case. That is the onus cast upon the prosecution. The prosecution must establish through reliable, relevant and cogent evidence, the guilt of the defendant.

In jury trials, it is always the best course to follow by pleading "Not Guilty." It happens sometimes that the Prosecutor may be willing to accept a plea of guilty to the lesser offence e.g. in a charge for murder, the Prosecutor, after reviewing the evidence, may say to Defence Counsel, that he is prepared to accept a plea of manslaughter and then discussions usually take place over the penalty phase of the trial. These negotiations and acceptance of the plea to a lesser charge can be very useful especially where the client has a bad record.

I have always held the view that the "Never plead Guilty," rule is relevant to serious matters and to all jury trials. Where one is charged with minor traffic offences or offences like parking in prohibited areas, defective vehicles, disorderly behaviour, indecent language or summary offences of this class, then the defendant, if he is guilty and did commit the offence, should plead guilty and save himself some time and a harsh fine usually imposed because the defendant showed no contrition and wasted the Court's time. Some argue that the Court is there to hear cases so what is the problem of a person pleading "not guilty" and put the police or other summary prosecuting functionary to the proof of the case. This is not really the jurisprudence behind simple summary matters. Traffic tickets for simple matters should not take up the valuable time of the Court when matters that are far more important await trial.

Let me give you some examples of cases that I actually defended after the defendant pleaded “Not Guilty.” In the first place, defence counsel must be fully acquainted with the essential ingredients of the offence and must know what the Prosecutor has to prove to secure a conviction. If the Prosecutor fails to discharge this onus, then a submission can be successfully made that the prosecution has failed to prove its case and the defendant will have to be dismissed. Here is an experience I had with the Jury, which was not repeated often. Sometimes in the whole of a career at the Criminal Bar, it may happen just once. My records show that on three occasions I had the privilege and surprise of living through this experience.

Two men, one a custom’s clerk and the other a motor-cart driver were charged with stealing fifty bags of flour from the bond (warehouse) of the large company. The Prosecutor, a very energetic junior who was steadily rising to be a very successful Prosecutor, told the Court that the custom’s clerk, employed at a city Firm went to the bond clerk of the large company’s warehouse and received a tally slip for one hundred bags of flour. It was later discovered that fifty bags of flour were missing from the bond and after investigations, it was alleged by the State Prosecutor that delivery was taken by the custom’s clerk and the flour was laden on a motor-cart driven by the second defendant who used a false name when he signed for the flour.

On these facts, both men were charged with the Offence of Larceny of the bags of flour. There was a Preliminary Hearing before a Magistrate and he committed both men to stand trial after he found that there was sufficient evidence to commit the men to stand trial before a jury. I remember that at the close of the prosecution’s case at the Preliminary Investigation, I had submitted to the Magistrate that there was not “sufficient” evidence on which to commit the two defendants.

Here, the process became reversed. The Magistrate has to find that there was “sufficient evidence” not a mere "suspicion," before he could commit for trial. I do not think there was even a mere "suspicion" in this case that warranted a committal. However, the Magistrate was far from being enterprising and courageous. He felt that in all matters that came before him by way of Preliminary Investigation, even where there is not a scintilla of evidence, he must commit for trial and let the Jury shoulder the responsibility. This is not the function of the Magistrate in Preliminary Investigations. If there is no evidence or if there is a mere suspicion, he should have the courage to say that he does not find that "sufficiency" of evidence as would warrant a committal for trial before a jury. You will see the full merit of my no-case submissions before the Magistrate, as the outcome of this case unfolds.

The matter came up before a jury and a Supreme Court Judge. The Prosecutor opened his case to the Jury and for the first time I saw my young friend in difficulty trying to show that the defendants were guilty of any offence or wrongdoing. Under cross-examination by me, none of the witnesses could testify what really happened to the fifty bags of flour missing from the bond. Apart from the many discrepancies in their testimony, there was no evidence of the number of bags of flour in the bond. There was no evidence of the distribution of the flour from the bond. All that was established was that the custom's clerk received a tally slip for one hundred bags of flour. One prosecution witness actually said under my cross-examination that one hundred bags of flour were actually taken by the custom's clerk and removed from the bond by the other defendant. There was no evidence of larceny.

The Prosecutor closed its case and then for the first time in my career at the Bar, I decided not to address the Jury and waste precious time. The State Attorney, to my surprise and delight said that he too would not address the Jury. Then the Foreman of the Jury told the trial Judge that because of the many discrepancies and inconsistencies that were brought to the surface via my cross-examination, they were unanimous in their decision and did not want to hear the summing up.

They found there was no case established by the State against the two accused men and that the two men were not guilty. The learned Judge was quite unprepared for this and asked for my comments regarding the legality of the Jury's request not to have a summing up. I told the learned Judge that there is provision for that in the law and cited to him the authorities from that *vade mecum* of the Criminal Defence Counsel: "*Archbold Criminal Pleading, Evidence and Practice.*" There was nothing that the Judge could do but to accept the Jury's finding and verdict of *"Not Guilty."*

My clients were so excited and happy over the results. They told me they did not commit any crime and that they were not guilty. I followed their statements that they gave to me and under cross-examination, the prosecution witnesses could do nothing to destroy the suggestions I had put to them. The plea of "Not Guilty" was the only plea that could have been entered when the trial started and they were asked how they pleaded to the indictment. The plea was *"Not Guilty."* The Jury entered this as the correct plea as soon as the Prosecutor closed the case. Justice was not only done; it was a clear demonstration how Justice stands out if any attempt is made to meddle with its pristine nature. "Justice must not only be done but must be seen to be done."

Justice simply did not fall in the laps of the defendants. It had to be fought for every step as the prosecution unfolded its case, which was completely destroyed by cross-examination. What a sweet reward to fight for and how satisfying the tranquillity that emanated from the fact that the prosecution failed hopelessly in its attempt to get two honest men convicted. It is the role and function of Counsel for the Defence at all times, to assist the Court, presided over by a Judge who is there to see that Justice is done, even if this assistance means a vigorous and assiduous application of all the rules that are in place to protect the interests of both the State and the accused person.

Chapter 6

Judges

How They Influence the Administration of Justice

There is a tremendous difference between writing a biographical sketch about a certain Judge or Judges of the High Court generally and writing one's experience as Counsel appearing before Judges at all levels of Jurisdiction. A biographical sketch is objective. It gives the personal facts about the Judge – his place of birth, date of birth, his background, his education lower and higher, his Law School, when he was called to the Bar and a survey of his professional life – when he or she became a Crown or State Attorney, a Magistrate, a Judge and his or her promotion up the Judicial ladder. One also examines some of the well-known and important cases (if any) over which he presided.

A lawyer writing about his years of practice and experience before Judges is of necessity a subjective approach as he writes about the cases, which he conducted before certain Judges. Here, he examines the character of the Judge, his attitude, his learning, his shortcomings, his sense of humour and generally his ability to administer Justice and see that "Justice is done." The lawyer ever so often encounters the aversion of the Judge to certain types of cases, his idiosyncrasies and his reputation as a "convicting" Judge or a Judge before whom a rape defendant or an indecent assault defendant hasn't got a "ghost of chance."

Yes, Judges do have pet aversions and antipathies to certain types of offences. Sometimes one learns the hard way through actual appearances. You cannot select your Judge who is to adjudicate in your case and try your client. However, after a few harsh experiences, Counsel becomes skilled and is in a position to ensure that his client is not put up for trial before that type of Judge. In Canada, I had an experience which educated me as to the steps to be taken not to have your client put up before a single Judge who is hell-bent on convicting for certain offences. Your client can always opt for trial by Jury. No one must ever under-rate the ability of counsel to exercise court-craft and manoeuvrability in deciding the best course for his client. We owe it to our client.

My client was charged with living off the earnings of prostitution and rape. He retained me. I insisted on knowing the whole truth and nothing less. He admitted that he knew his girlfriend "walked the beat" in the evenings. By day, she was a different individual working as a most efficient salesperson for home products. That is how they met. My client was a successful night cleaner and had many contracts under his belt. He told me he found out after they met, that this young lady had this salacious occupation, but he loved her and they decided to live together. His girlfriend agreed to give up the prostitution as he earned very good money. She decided to give up this "Jekyll and Hyde" life style. In the meantime, they both had expensive cars and a very up-beat standard of living. Eventually, the milk went sour and realizing that she did not intend to give up her prostitution, he decided to call it quits. This was where she took over. Hell hath no fury than a woman's scorn unleashed!

She alleged that she gave him money to buy the car and maintain a high life-style and then further alleged that he raped her after they separated. It was not an easy case to defend and I had to go into details of my client's earnings. I had to get his Bank Accounts to show deposits but above all, I had to get documentation regarding his earnings to justify his deposits. The rape allegation was that he went to her house one night and after an altercation, he raped her; this despite the fact that the door locks were changed. It was a lot of preparation and a mass of investigation to be explored. My client denied the rape allegation. I got evidence to show that on the night of the alleged rape, he was working from the 6 p.m. to the 2 a.m. shift. The rape was alleged to have taken place at "about midnight."

This is what I had to work with after careful investigation. There was an indictment and it was at this stage my client consulted me. I did not know that a person indicted with these charges had no chance at all before this particular Judge. He was hostile from the beginning. The case was listed before him and my client elected to be tried by this Judge rather than by a Judge and Jury. The Judge muzzled my cross-examination and treated my witnesses in a most degrading manner. The State Attorney was happy when the Judge took over the prosecution of the case.

> *"A judge who observes the demeanour of the witnesses while they are being cross-examined by counsel has from his detached position, a much more favourable opportunity of forming a just appreciation than a judge who himself conducts the examination. If he takes the latter course he, so to speak, descends into the arena and is liable to have his vision clouded by the dust of the conflict" – per Lord Greene, Master of the Rolls, in 1945.*

At the practising Bar, we have a formula to fit this type of behaviour and conduct – "A much- talking and interfering Judge is a non-thinking Judge." It is clear. He loses concentration on the developing issues and unfolding facts of the case. I saw the writing on the wall and began there and then to lay the foundations for an Appeal based on suppression of evidence, admission of inadmissible evidence, hostility of the judge, who had at one stage refused to make notes of my submissions regarding admissibility of evidence adduced by the State. My client was, needless to say, convicted by the Judge and given a stiff sentence. I immediately appealed. My client was denied Bail pending Appeal even though I agreed to surrender his Passport and have him report on any day or days that the Police requested.

I had to appeal this too. Eventually, my client was granted bail.

I had my day in Court. Justice was done. The Appeal Judges were appalled at the behaviour of the Judge and the mass of inadmissible evidence he admitted. I had no difficulty in convincing their Lordships that the conviction was against the weight of the evidence and was glaringly perverse. My Appeal was successful. My client was happy and grateful for the work I put in. The sequel to that is that the Judge retired shortly after. I learnt a great lesson – never agree to a trial by a single Judge unless you have had some previous exposure before that Judge.

There are still on the Bench, Judges who are learned, unbiased and fair – one must know one's Court before proceeding with a case. This is a cardinal rule that Defence Counsel at the Criminal Bar must observe at all times. However, Judges are human beings. *Humanum est errare*. They are not always right in the way they feel, think and decide. They are not machines. You just don't put them on the Bench, wave a magic wand and convert them from human beings into a mere functionary governed by rules and regulations controlling the manner how they must discharge their onerous duties.

Some Judges are kind, some are stubborn, haughty and arrogant and some are just mere bullies who are carried away by the power they can wield. Others are great actors. They exude a sense of caring, understanding and human kindness when deep down, it is just a gallery show. Some are far from being erudite or "learned in the law" and sometimes it surpasses the intellect and understanding to fathom out why they were appointed in the first place and how they can continue to function when their decisions are repeatedly over-turned.

The story goes that when Counsel for the Appellant got up in the Court of Appeal to argue his Appeal and started off by saying, "My Lords, this is an Appeal from the

Judgment of Judge X." (I would not mention his name even though he is no longer with us).

The President of the Court of Appeal said very crisply, "Counsel, are there any other grounds of Appeal?" That Judge whose decision was under Appeal was on the Bench for many years. His Judgments were always taken to the Appellate Court. Only once was his Judgment upheld. Yet he kept on toiling on the Bench, dedicated to a complete misunderstanding of the Law and the analysis and assessment of evidence adduced before him at the trial. It seems he could not separate facts from law.

That is only one side of the coin. There have been and there are still on the Judicial Bench some very learned men. It is a pleasure to practise before this calibre of Judges. They listen. They cogitate. They are quick to see the legal point that is being canvassed. Discussions between Bench and Bar are courteous and reach a high standard of legal debate. Sometimes, a learned Judge poses a question, which really calls for sound legal reasoning and the ability to appreciate the difference between the facts upon which that decision was arrived at and the inapplicability of the legal principles advanced in support of the problem, which the learned Judge had formulated.

In many of the former British Colonies, a Judicial Service Commission appointed Judges. Today, the whole English legal system depends on the judges in London, for it is these judges who try cases in the High Court and at certain fixed intervals travel around the country administering justice at Assize Towns in a system which is substantially the same now as when it was fixed in the reign of Henry II in the twelfth century. It was essentially this centralization of the Judges in London, which has led the English Law being forensic and strictly professional in origin, whereas Roman Law, (which is a compulsory subject at the Bar Examination) and many systems deriving from it are scholastic.

These Judges always have been and still are, selected from the ranks of the experienced and successful practising barristers. There is no question of the State examining and selecting a candidate. The men who have come to the top of their profession, who are held in high esteem by their colleagues and by existing judges are appointed, regardless of political considerations, on the advice of the Lord Chancellor of England, who is head of the Judiciary. Once approved, they are entirely free of State control, for a judge cannot be dismissed except on an express resolution of both Houses of Parliament (House of Commons and the House of Lords) a thing that has not happened in over one hundred years.

A Barrister-at-Law in England appointed as a Judge, has usually to give up a very lucrative practice and settle for a salary – far less than that which he is earning. But, it is part of the tradition of the Bar that when one is asked to ascend the Judicial Bench, one accepts. It is high honour to be a Judge. In the U.S.A., Judges are elected. They advertise the fact that they are running for a particular Judicial Office and they ask the people to vote for them. In many instances, lawyers and others contribute to their election fund. This is peculiar to the U.S.A. A Judge must have no obligations to people who elected him – but it does not always work that way.

In the days of the British Colonial Empire, Judges used to be sent out from England to the Colonies but as those Colonies became more and more progressive and independent, Judges were appointed from the members of the local Bar or from the existing Magistrates or Crown Counsel in the said territory.

When the Justice system is so established as to facilitate an adversarial system as in the U.S.A. and the U.K. and most common law Jurisdictions, then the two opposing litigants have an ongoing battle in Court to find out which one of the two is correct and on whose side are the facts and the law applicable to the established facts. The Judge sits there to see that the law is correctly interpreted and applied and to ensure the practise complies with the established rules of procedure. However, there are times when the presiding Judge "descends from the Judicial Bench and enters into the arena" and allows his vision to become clouded by the "dust of the conflict."

This conduct clearly indicates where he is leaning or which side he favours. This is when the Judge opens himself to ridicule as he besmirches the fair name of Justice. Justice is not tarnished by the lawyers but by the very person, the Judge, who is there to preserve and protect the fair name of Justice. When this happens, the fairness of the system is grossly eroded and abused. Justice is not a flower on the wall just waiting to be plucked. You have to win her acquiescence before she surrenders her virtues to your cause. These thoughts come to my mind as I write. I will give some examples later. Remember there is a *blindfold* over the eyes of the Lady of Justice.

There are times when the law on a certain issue is rather complex and there are areas of such law that need to be fully settled and established by a competent Court of Appeal. If a trial Judge errs by accepting one aspect of the unsettled law, he cannot be criticized for that. The losing side in such a case usually takes the matter further, to the Court of Appeal to have the Appellate Judges give a ruling in the matter and settle the law. Depending upon the system, that may be the end of the matter but if there is still a further appeal available, then the matter should be taken further to have the law settled once and for all times. This is easier said than done. Costs for Appeal Court are high and it depends upon the interest of the client and the means. Let me give an example.

Take the simple case of a violation of parking. A retired Army Colonel once retained me to fight his parking ticket. He had loaned his car to an old acquaintance who was visiting him and who parked the car in a prohibited area. Eventually a parking ticket was issued and put on the windscreen of the Colonel's car. This seems to make sense as no parking officer could tell who the driver of the car was.

My Colonel-client was furious. The fine was only at the time *$7.50*. He said he would not pay it as a matter of principle. He did not park the car. Why should he pay? I explained to him in detail that the parking officers just issue the parking ticket and put it on the windscreen. The owner gets the ticket and must pay the fine. This seems the only way that parking violations can be enforced. If this were not so, then parking violations would become a mockery.

Despite my explanation to my client, he insisted that he wanted to test the practice. He did not pay the fine. Eventually, he was served with a notice of the fine owing. He went to Court and raised the point that he did not park the car and therefore was not liable. Of course, he was fined. He told me he wanted to test the matter no matter how much it cost him. We went through every step of the appeal processes available until the matter reached the highest Court of Appeal.

The Judges listened to the arguments that the Appellant, my client, could not be guilty for acts committed by another. The doctrine of "intention" was canvassed. Tickets for "moving violations" have a place for you to sign, but parking tickets have no place for you to sign. This makes sense, if not a parking officer will have to stand up by the vehicle until the driver/owner comes up and then get him/her to sign. Parking violations don't go on your driving record. The parking relates to the owner of the vehicle and not the person who parked the car.

My client had his "day in Court" and left the Court quite satisfied that his point of view was heard and that the Court explained to him the almost useless exercise of trying to find out who was the driver who parked the vehicle in the prohibited area. Most Courts usually allow you to plead "guilty with an explanation." You can then tell your story to the Judge who might reduce the fine or suspend the fine, if your explanation and excuse were good and reasonable. If the trial Judge makes an error where the law is unsettled this can be understood. However, if the Judge gives a decision based on bad law or out-of-date law, this is unforgivable. It just shows that he took no time to check the relevant legal principles and so assure himself that he was giving a decision based on current law.

That brings me to the role of counsel appearing in Court. Counsel is there to assist the Court and if a Judge is citing out-of-date law or incorrect law, then counsel appearing has a duty to tactfully inform the Court that that is no longer the law. Most Judges express their appreciation to counsel who has put the Court on the right track, in a very subtle and polite manner. I have had many experiences where Judges were relying on over-ruled decisions, to rule in my favour. The ethical and correct thing to do is to inform the Judge that those cases he is relying on are no longer the law. One then tactfully gives the Judge, the relevant current cases and then proceeds to show the differences to put him back on track, by showing that the current decisions are still in my favour. This is a difficult procedure. It depends upon how it is done and who is the Judge.

On one occasion, I was actually rebuffed by a Judge and told me that I had my remedy if I did not agree with his decision. I thanked him, as a Q.C. (Senior member of the Bar) should do. He ruled against me. I appealed. I won my Appeal and the Court of Appeal Judges (three in all) made some very caustic comments about the behaviour and attitude of the trial Judge. The Court reiterated the practise that it is the duty of counsel always to assist the Court and such duty must be tactfully and respectfully discharged. The Court very forcefully suggested that counsel who find themselves in similar situations should adopt the manner, in which I conducted the procedure.

Some Judges have a way of living out their fantasies on the Bench. It takes patience, dedication and a sharp wit to deal with them. Judges soon recognize the lawyers who read and prepare their cases. They tell their brother Judges and soon the word gets around. You are now on your way. You are in orbit. Nothing is more rewarding than to be sitting at the Bar table waiting for your matter to be heard. A case is in progress. Legal arguments develop. Lawyers on both sides apparently did not do their homework and they were both groping, but the Judge remembers that quite recently there was an Appeal Court decision on the point. He turns to me and in open Court and says, "Mr. Manraj, we know you are up on the recent decisions. You have been hearing the arguments, what is the recent decision? Can you assist?"

With heart pounding with pride, I got up and stated, "My Lord, the case is the recent decision in *X v. Y*. It is reported in the Weekly Law Reports (WLR) and the All England Reports (AER)." Then I knew I could go further and give them the names of the Judges who presided in that case in the Court of Appeal. This has happened to me more than once. You sit down feeling and knowing that you have arrived.

Erudite and dedicated Judges study the lawyers who appear before them – their appearance, their punctuality, their potential and their manners. I have made it a rule during the whole of my fifty years at the Bar, (even when I was a Crown Prosecutor in Canada) to be robed and seated at the Bar table fully five minutes before the Court is scheduled to begin. The golden rule is: *be honest to yourself and to the Court*. It is so easy to deceive at times and many young lawyers try this ever so often and think that they are impressing the Judge. They cite cases with fictitious names like: (Jones –v- Moody) but no reference is given where the case can be found. This is what happens. The Judge, anxious to read of this bogus principle asks the young lawyer for the reference. He apologizes and asks for leave to lay over the reference. This he cannot do. He has just "cooked his goose." This is malpractice. It has a way of coming back to haunt you.

I have always advised my younger colleagues that any diligent and honest lawyer should go through all the authorities – those in favour of your proposition and submission and those against you. Do not be deceptive and exclude those against you from your submissions. Cite them and try to distinguish the cases against you (if any) and show that they are not applicable to the instant case before the Judge.

Not all judges are lazy. Many of them do their own research and would know what the cases decide – the *ratio decidendi* of the cases. Those learned Judges are looking to see how honest you are. Always cite all the cases – for and against your proposition. Read them and study them. Remember that a good and dedicated judge most likely has read them. Be frank. This frankness is rectitude of the highest order and pays off handsome dividends. Judges talk in the Judge's Common Room. They discuss the lawyers who are dependable and reliable. Soon, one finds that one's standing in Court is immensely enhanced. People talk. Remember that. Remember what Shakespeare said in *"Hamlet"* where Polonius is saying farewell to his son Laertes as he was leaving to go back to University in Paris and tells him:

"This above all: to thine own self be true,
And it must follow, as night the day,
Thou canst not then be false to any man."

The Appeal Court can be caustic in their comments, not only with respect to the failure of a presiding Judge to keep abreast of the Law, but also regarding the inefficiency and incapacity of Counsel, to cope with and keep abreast of the changing Law. Know your Court. Know your Judge. Each Judge has his or her own idiosyncrasy and pet aversion. It pays off to prepare your case well. Master the facts and law and never go to Court unprepared in a matter set down for trial. The results can be devastating to your client and most damaging to your reputation.

Younger Judges are now being appointed. I would like here to pass on this advice based on my long practice at the Bar. First, come to terms with yourself. Know what you want to do as a lawyer and go after it. If you decide on a career as a Judge, get into the system early (either as a Magistrate or Crown or State Attorney) and for goodness sake be a good Judge – honest, compassionate, stern when necessary, human and above all, a Judge who likes the law and reads law. So many Judges ascend to the Judicial Bench and view their appointments there as a pre-retirement leave. Nothing is more frustrating than to appear before a Judge who is on "nodding acquaintance" with the law – if that much.

On several occasions, I was invited to take an appointment as a High Court Judge. On one occasion in 1985, I was offered a position in Australia. I did not accept. The late Judge Robert Dnieper of the Provincial Court in Toronto, Ontario, Canada, was very intent on my accepting a position as Judge. He felt I would be an asset on the Judicial Bench, especially in the Appeal Court.

Apart from the nine years I spent with the Ministry of the Attorney-General of Ontario, Canada, I have always been in private practice. You will recall, I mentioned earlier, KNOW YOURSELF. Know what you want to do as a lawyer. The practising Bar was my choice and I am still a practising Barrister-at-Law and Attorney-at-Law. To the young practitioner, let me give a hackneyed, but true advice, "THERE IS ALWAYS ROOM AT THE TOP."

Nothing that I have stated so far is intended to convey the impression that a practising lawyer must not be firm, fearless and ready to stand his ground. Practising what I preach has landed me in some very dicey and contemptuous situations. I have dealt with those situations in separate chapters. Some Judges like to intimidate young practitioners and then they go to the Judges' Common Room and boast that they gave young so-and-so a good shaking up in Court and that they had given him the Baptism of fire in Court.

This happens all too frequently and I recall the numerous occasions when I had to stand up in defence of young colleagues and ask Judges to give my young friends an opportunity to conclude their arguments free from the frequent and distracting interruptions from the Bench. This is what is called the CAMARADERIE at the Bar. I prefer to call it SOLIDARITY FOREVER. Perhaps one is disposed to conclude that many Judges have a sadistic attitude in their treatment of young lawyers. At the right time, with the right words, one can become famous for being a lawyer who knows how to stand up for his rights. An incisive wit can be an asset. A sense of humour can disarm a most insolent adversary. Let me illustrate.

F. E. Smith, the great and legendary English Barrister, that notorious wit, who later became the First Earl of Birkenhead (Lord Birkenhead), was appearing before a County Court Judge who despised brilliant lawyers. The Judge was not what one would describe as a scholar or brilliant Judge. After a scholarly and meritorious submission by the then Mr. F. E. Smith, the Judge said, "Mr. Smith, you see, all that you have been telling me has just come in one ear and gone through the other."

To this statement, F. E. Smith (later Lord Birkenhead) replied, "That is understandable, Your Honour, there is nothing in the middle to stop it." The effect was shattering. However, be careful. We are not all Lord Birkenhead.

On one occasion, very early in my career in Guyana, I was addressing the Jury in a very difficult murder case. It was a case that was fraught with problems regarding admissibility of evidence and I had to fight it all the way. The pressure never eased up. The Judge, who had come to Guyana on promotion as a Judge, from Jamaica where he was a Magistrate, accentuated this pressure. He was never happy when the prosecution was not having an easy ride. Off the Bench, he was a pleasant man with a wonderful sense of humour. I enjoyed his company at many civic and professional functions, which we both attended. This Judge later returned to Jamaica, was appointed Chief Justice of

Jamaica and was Knighted by Her Majesty, the Queen and became Sir Roland Phillips.

This is what took place before Mr. Justice Phillips, as he then was. I was very young at the Bar and I was really making in-roads in the prosecution's case. I could observe from the Jury's reaction that I was getting my points across and I was really making headway ripping the prosecution's case to shreds. This was a strongly contested case and I wished very much to have a verdict in my favour.

The presiding Judge, very conscious of the fact that I was having sway with the Jury, blurted out much to my surprise and astonishment, "Mr. Manraj, I find it necessary to protect the Jury from you." Immediately my inner feelings surged forward and I told the Judge that I felt his remark was offensive and improper. He quickly adjourned the Court and ordered me to appear in his Chambers (office). He told me that his first reaction was to lock me up for the rest of the day for Contempt of Court. When you are practising at the Criminal Bar, you cannot be "chicken-hearted."

You must have a conviction and your resolution must be firm but always, one must be very moderate in one's speech. I told the Judge very sternly that he ought not to have said what he said in the presence of the Jury and that what he said is not acceptable judicial conduct. He told me to sit down. I did. He and I chatted seriously about "conduct at the Bar." I cautiously and skilfully shifted the conversation to "conduct on the Bench." I was skating on thin ice but I knew I was right and throughout my whole career, I have been fighting to protect my client's rights and ever so often, my own. Each of these encounters and there were quite a few, increased my stature at the Bar and my reputation for being a very blunt and outspoken practitioner, calling a "spade a spade" and not cringing before the abuse of authority.

I never conceded to the Judge that I was guilty of unprofessional conduct. My remark was a natural response to his improper remark. His did not have any exclusive right to be offensive. Eventually, he reprimanded me for being too rashly outspoken. I told him it was a spontaneous statement prompted by his offensive remark. He decided to adjourn the Court for the day and returned into open Court to do so. I thought that was the end of that incident. I was so wrong.

The next day, I concluded my address to the Jury. The Crown Prosecutor began his address and much to my amazement did not advert the Jury's attention to the many points I raised. If I were the Crown Prosecutor, I would have gone on a rampage and try to destroy the arguments that were raised by me. Perhaps he knew something I did not know. However, soon I was to find out. The Judge started his summing up to the Jury. He obviously felt my client was guilty and went far beyond expressing his views on the evidence adduced. He injected his inner feelings with relentless ponderous repetitions in his directions to the Jury. He sounded to me as if he was the Senior Crown Attorney in the matter.

After about one hour of this, I just could not sit there and tolerate what was going on, so I stood up and it just flowed mellifluously forward: "My Lord" I said, "I now find it necessary to protect the Jury from you." Holy Smoke! Goodness me! All hell broke loose. He again adjourned the Court and again ordered me to appear before him to show cause as to why I should not be committed for contempt of Court. I knew my Judge.

He gets very erratic in the afternoon hours. It was an ordeal for any dedicated and committed Counsel appearing before him when he is in that mood. I kept my cool. Suffice it to say, that after I expressed the view that he was going far beyond the latitude afforded him by law in expressing his views, I was never committed – not that I was afraid of that. I was of the view that if all came out in any investigation, the Judge would not have come out "smelling like a rose." I was never committed.

That Judge and I eventually became very firm friends. He even complimented me on my tenacity and resolute approach to the practice as a Criminal Defence

Counsel at the Bar. Years after, in one of my several appearances in Jamaica, he and I were able to sit back and laugh at the whole incident. He also, as Chief Justice, became the Head of the Judiciary of Jamaica. I felt righteous indignation triggered me to speak out and that added to my reputation. An avid Press fanned the whole incident and that can be useful in building your reputation as a good, outspoken and outstanding lawyer.

There was one particular Judge, a newcomer to the Bench, who had the reputation for looking askance at meritorious legal submissions. I had practised before this Judge when he was a Magistrate – a completely tolerant and understanding Magistrate. After I was honoured by the appointment as a Q.C. on December 31, 1969, I found that my retainers were becoming more and more complex, many of them bristling with legal arguments and intricate procedural problems. I was very happy with this new phase of my practice as I was very much at home doing legal research.

On one occasion, shortly after this Judge went on the Bench, I was arguing a matter before him, which involved the difficult concepts applicable to frustration of contract and rescission of agreement. In the middle of my arguments, this Judge asked if I had researched the point. I took time to couch the terms of my reply, as I felt that it was pellucidly clear that I had done so. I was somewhat annoyed at this useless and irresponsible comment. I said, "My Lord, unlike you, I know where the Law Library is. It should be a very tempting transition for you, having regard to the fact that the Law Library is just one door away from your Chambers. Perhaps your Lordship may be tempted one day to use its facilities."

This Judge never again trivialized submissions I made before him. Many Judges ascended the Judicial Bench after serving as Magistrates for several years. Some were bright and good students of the law and adorned the Judicial Bench. Many others left me wondering how they were able to confound the examiners at the Bar Final Examination! In the middle of my submissions in a Larceny case, the Magistrate said, "Mr. Manraj, I know the case you are referring to." I was pleasantly surprised. I kept quiet to hear his further pronouncements. He then started to outline the facts of the case. I respectfully adverted his attention to the fact that the case he is referring to has nothing to do with the case to which I was referring.

The case I was relying on was based on a completely different set of facts and the Judgment of the Court was based on the facts to which I was referring. He was obviously embarrassed. I told him that he interrupted my submissions at a crucial point to superimpose on my arguments, facts that had no relevance to my submissions. I told him that I am aware of the case to which he was referring and that that case dealt with the question of identification of the subject matter of the larceny only. My case was a completely different case. I had not yet completed my submissions when the Magistrate intervened. I was just about to resume my submissions when, to my horror, he blurted out, "Furthermore, I find your client guilty" – this is while I was still making my no-case submissions.

After years of practice, one soon learns how to handle interfering and pseudo–learned Magistrates and Judges who just enjoy a pretension to legal knowledge. The Magistrate sentenced my client to six weeks imprisonment. I bowed and took leave of the Court and went straight to my Chambers and had prepared two sets of documents, one, a Notice of Appeal stating the impropriety of the Magistrate and the invalidity of the decision which he handed down while I was addressing the Court and finally, the decision was erroneous and bad in law. The second set of documents was an application for Bail pending Appeal, just in case he decided not to let my client go, as an Appeal in these cases in the Magistrate Court "stays" all convictions and penalties. My client was allowed to go pending his Appeal.

The Appeal was filed and was heard about six weeks later. My client's conviction was set aside. The Appeal Court had no difficulty in allowing the Appeal and setting aside the conviction as bad in law. The Court did not even call on the Prosecuting Counsel to reply. He conceded that my Appeal had merit and that the Magistrate erred in law. The Appeal Court expressed alarm at the Magistrate's conduct and made some very uncomplimentary remarks about his behaviour and the citation by him of inapplicable case law.

Sometime after, through the effluxion of time, the Magistrate who had blossomed into a very good and reliable Magistrate was appointed a Judge. He had matured. I would like to think that the caustic comments from the Appeal Court Judges, awakened him and he kept moving upwards. As a Judge, he proved himself competent. My appearances before him were very pleasant and he handed down some good judgments. However, let me not leave you with any wrong impressions. Some High Court and Appeal Court Judges before whom I appeared in England, Canada, Guyana, Trinidad and Tobago and other Caribbean Territories including Jamaica, Barbados, Grenada, Antigua, Bahamas and the Turks and Caicos Islands, were capable and brilliant Judges.

It is a pleasure and source of great satisfaction to appear before capable and learned Judges. You are assured of a proper and professional consideration of your arguments. These men and women bring dignity, decorum and respect to the High Office of appointed High Court Judges. A practising Attorney must always be prepared to argue his cases fully and properly and he must make copies of the cases he is relying on for the Judge or Judges before whom he is appearing. That goes a far way in impressing the Judges of your consideration for an already over-worked Judiciary.

Some practitioners run away from the "cut and thrust" of private practise. It is not easy work. One must always be prepared to fight and wrestle intellectually and vigorously for the attainment of Justice. It is such an important cog in our social, economic and everyday life. The more incompetent the Judicial Officer, the more strenuous is the fight and struggle to achieve intellectualism leading to Justice and moral right. I have been doing this for the past fifty years of my professional life. To be very frank with you, my dear reader, it has become such an integral part of my life that I cannot see myself in any other capacity than as Senior Counsel at the practising Bar.

Chapter 7

Balancing The Scales Of Justice

Justice Must Not Only Be Done, But Must Be Seen To Be Done

British Guiana was the only British Possession (Colony) on the South American mainland. It is now the Republic of Guyana. It is on the North Eastern coast of South America. To be more exact, it is bounded on the North by the Atlantic Ocean, on the East by Surinam or Dutch Guiana, on the West by Venezuela and part of Brazil and on the South by Brazil. This once British Colony was the pride of the Caribbean and its Capital, Georgetown, was known as the "Garden City." As a British Colony, British Guiana was the Paradise of the British Caribbean Colonies. British Guiana eventually gained its Independence and in 1970 we saw the establishment of the Co-operative Republic of Guyana by Mr. L. F. S. Burnham, Q.C.

As a British Colony, the common law of England was the plinth on which our legal system and institutions were based. Guyana is still known as the "Magnificent Province" and Georgetown is still known as the "Garden City." These qualities ascribed to *"Our Dear Land of Guyana"* would never fade away. Before Independence, all the Barristers-at-Law practising in the then British Guiana, studied law in England at one of the four Inns of Court (Law Schools), The Honourable Society of the Middle Temple, Lincoln's Inn, Gray's Inn and Inner Temple. They are all governed by a Council of Legal Education which is responsible for conducting the Bar Examinations. One had to be called to the Bar at one of the four Law Schools before he or she would be allowed to practise in Guyana.

We also had the Solicitors Branch of the profession. Many of the Solicitors were "articled" to practitioners in Guyana and took the Law Society Examinations, which, if they succeeded, entitled them to practise as Solicitors in the Courts in Guyana. Guyana has always been known for its hospitality and its readiness to make friends with tourists and visitors. Even after British Guiana became an Independent Territory within the British Commonwealth of Nations, the English Law and practice remained the system adopted by Guyana. Before Guyana became the Republic of Guyana, the Privy Council of England was the final Court of Appeal.

This is important. I hope the reader now has a general appreciation and understanding of the background of Guyana. One last important fact I must mention about Guyana is that we have the highest water fall in the world: *THE KAIETEUR* Falls. Just imagine, billions of gallons of water tumbling over the brink with a vertical drop of 821 feet. It is magnificent. The Kaieteur Falls is about two hours flying time from the Capital, Georgetown. In Georgetown, the St. George's Cathedral is the world's largest wooden building.

Just twenty five miles East of Georgetown there is a place called Mahaica. The Mahaica River runs into the agricultural and pasture lands of the Mahaica area. There are several small tributaries or inlets of the Mahaica River. The front portion of Mahaica is the Town Square. There you have the Mahaica Magistrate's Court and the shopping area. One has to travel on launches or speed boats or corials (dug out canoes) to get to the rice lands and other agricultural lands along the banks of the creek. In this "back land" area a cow-farmer and agricultural farmer name Rampat had his holdings. He was more known as "Peeka."

Not far away lived Jehangeer Ali, his wife and family. They also had agricultural lands and raised cows. Over the years, the two families were not on friendly terms. There were allegations of cow-rustling and trespass on each other's land. Jehangeer had two sons – Showkat Ali (spelt

Shoukatallie) and Mohamed Ali (spelt Mahomed Ali) in the Privy Council Law Reports. There were over the years, some differences between the two families. I was always legal adviser to the Jehangeer family in many matters unrelated to the differences they had with the Rampat (Peeka) family. Mohamed Ali was a Land Surveyor's Assistant and Showkat helped his father, Jehangeer Ali and his mother, really gentle and cultured old couple with whom it was very easy to get along.

One February 10, 1960 Peeka was murdered. It was alleged that he had gone in the early morning to visit his cows at a creek on the Mahaica River. He was paddling a corial, which is a dug-out canoe. He never returned home alive. Five days later his body was recovered from the Mahaica River. It appeared from its condition that someone had shot him with a shot-gun, then his body (while he was still alive) had been tied to a log of wood by means of vine branches and it had been thrown into the river. Suspicion fastened on the two brothers named Shoukatallie (*No. 1* accused), the Appellant in this case and Mahomed Ali (*No.2* accused). They were both arrested and charged with murder.

Let me pause here for a moment. In my fifty years as a Barrister-at-Law, I successfully conducted and completed 329 murder trials, not to mention trials for other offences. I have never had an experience like the one I encountered in the present murder case. This case is bizarre. Travel with me along the road as I take you through this most interesting murder trial.

The Police suspected that these two Brothers were Peeka's murderers. Without any completion of the investigation or available statements, the police arrested and charged Shoukatallie and his brother Mahomed Ali (I am using the names as they appear in the Reasons for Decision of the Privy Council delivered by Lord Denning, one of the greatest and most learned Judges of this century).

Eventually four of the principal witnesses for the prosecution gave statements. Each one was closely related to the deceased Peeka and they were antagonistic towards the Jehangeer Family and particularly the two brothers charged. The fifth prosecution witness was bribed to give testimony. In the third world countries, like Guyana, accused persons and their family do not have the funds to conduct polls as to the opinions of members of the public who may serve as jurors and the possible challenges of such jurors.

Accused persons do not have the funds to have a Jury consultant to advise how the accused should dress at the trial and what should be his demeanour during the trial. All these sophisticated procedures are beyond the financial means of an accused person. Defence Counsel is the chief adviser and strategist. He has to do everything and direct everything once he undertakes the Defence of the accused. Defence Counsel's work in the Criminal Court is no picnic or bed of roses!!! It is hard work and painstaking preparation. Cross-examination did much to destroy the credibility of the prosecution witnesses.

Nevertheless, let me get back to the case proper. On May 16, 1960, both Shoukatallie and Mahomed Ali were in the Supreme Court of British Guiana for trial before Bollers, Ag. J (Acting Judge) and a Jury. I was retained by old Mr. Jehangeer to appear for Shoukatallie and Mahomed Ali. I felt that much of this case depended upon discreet, but piercing cross-examination and I was ready to tackle the problems. I succeeded.

Under cross-examination the prosecution witnesses proved to be unreliable and gave conflicting and irreconcilable evidence. My efforts paid off and proved very effective, as you will see from the Jury deliberation.

The case was heard between May 16 and June 3, 1960. This included a visit to the *locus in quo*. It was a picnic for the Jury. To my mind, no useful purpose was served, but the Jury requested it and the Judge accommodated them. In the early morning of June 3, 1960, at 1:35 a.m. to be precise, the Jury found both accused guilty of murder but in the case of Mahomed Ali, there was a very strong recommendation to mercy. Bollers, Ag. J sentenced both of them to death. Both appealed to the Federal Supreme Court of the Caribbean area. The Court was presided over by Sir Eric Hallinan, Chief Justice of the Court and sitting with him were Mr. Justice Rennie and Mr. Justice Marnan, Federal Judges. Hallinan and Marnan were white Judges and Rennie was a coloured West Indian Judge. On September 14, 1960, the Federal Supreme Court dismissed the Appeal of Shoukatallie but allowed the Appeal of Mahomed Ali and set aside his conviction and sentence.

Having secured the acquittal of the one brother, the parents Mr. and Mrs. Jehangeer then retained me to Appeal to the Judicial Committee of the Privy Council. I applied for special leave to appeal in *forma pauperis* to Her Majesty in Council and it was granted. My instructing Solicitor was Mr. Derek Wilkes, an able, competent and hard-working Solicitor with Offices in London, England. There was a lot of paper work to be done and I am grateful to Derek Wilkes for his ready support and guidance. I am told that Mr. Derek Wilkes voluntarily disbarred himself as a Solicitor and read for the Bar and qualified as a Barrister-at-Law. He is still a practising member of the English Bar.

In the Privy Council, presided over by Lord Denning, Lord Morris of Borth-y-Gest and Mr. L. M. DeSilva, I had as my leader, the late Mr. Phineas Quass, Q.C. while Mr. M. P. Solomon and I appeared with him. For the Crown, J. T. Molony, Q. C. and J. C. LeQuesne appeared. In 1961 I was not yet appointed a Q.C. I was at that time just seven years at the Bar but I had already established a tremendously successful practice at the Criminal Bar in the Caribbean area and elsewhere. Her Majesty the Queen appointed me a Queen's Counsel on the 31 December, 1969, eight years after this murder case I am writing about.

Just to complete the *dramatis personae*, let me give the reader a glimpse of the important persons in this unfolding drama. Bollers, Ag. J was a Magistrate in British Guiana and then Guyana for many years. He was promoted to an Acting Judge, then confirmed as a Judge and was finally knighted by Her Majesty the Queen to become Sir Harold Bollers, when be became the Chief Justice of British Guiana. He had fixed views on many topics, but was very pleasant off the Bench. The reservoirs of the Magistracy and the Attorney-General's Chambers (from where Crown Prosecutors practise) are usually the two sources from which Judges are appointed. Very rarely have there been appointments to the Judicial Bench from the experienced and competent members of the practising Bar.

A judgeship in the Supreme Court is usually the Mecca for Magistrates and Crown Prosecutors. There have been few occasions where Registrars of the Supreme Court were elevated to the Judicial Bench. Mr. Doodnauth Singh who joined me in the Appeals before the Caribbean Court of Appeal, known as Federal Supreme Court appeared for Shoukatallie. It was felt that it was good strategy as it gave us the opportunity of addressing the Federal Supreme Court of Appeal twice and re-enforce the arguments in the grounds of Appeal on misdirection of coercion of the trial Judge.

Mr. Singh was once a Crown Prosecutor and then he left the Attorney-General's Chambers to return to private practice. He became a Senior Counsel after Prime Minister Burnham discontinued the appointments of Queen's Counsel when Guyana became the Republic of Guyana. At the time of writing, my learned friend is the Attorney-General of Guyana. The Crown Prosecutor at the trial before Bollers, Ag. J was Mr. J. Gonsalves-Sabola. He left Guyana and went to the Commonwealth of the Bahamas. He is a brilliant lawyer and we had a "good and unforgettable legal and intellectual battle" in the Shoukatallie case before Bollers, J.

We remained good friends and we met several times when I went to the Bahamas on legal business. I actually did a long drawn-out land-dispute case before him when I appeared with the late David Bethell of the Bahamas Bar as my Junior Counsel. In 1992, my friend "Joe" Gonsalves-Sabola was the Chief Justice of the Supreme Court of the

Commonwealth of the Bahamas. A few years later, he was knighted by Her Majesty the Queen and became Sir J. C. Gonsalves-Sabola. When I telephoned him to congratulate him and addressed him as “Sir Joe” he remonstrated with me and said quite graciously that as far as he is concerned, he will always be “Joe” to me and to him, I will always be “Shakoor.” He said we have travelled a long road together and we both were honoured for our respective accomplishments at the Bar and services to the Law (in 1969 I was appointed a Queen’s Counsel for my service to the practising Bar and in 1992 Mr. Justice Sabola was knighted by Her Majesty the Queen).

Having set the stage and having given the personalities of the case their proper identification and their acquisitions of honour, I will now return to the Appeal before the Privy Council. I travelled up to London in 1961 to appear in the matter. The Appeal of Shoukatallie (remember that his brother was set free by the Federal Supreme Court when the Judges unanimously allowed my Appeal which I had filed on his behalf and set him free) was heard on July 4t and 5, 1961, when their Lordships said that they would humbly advise Her Majesty that his Appeal should be dismissed. Some weeks after, their Lordships gave their reasons.

Several grounds of Appeal were filed but the strongest and most potent ground for the Appeal was based on the conduct of the trial Judge. It was argued very forcefully that the Judge had exerted undue pressure on the Jury and coerced them into arriving at a verdict. For this reason, the verdict could not stand. There, the Privy Council was only dealing with the evidence and had no way of judging the quality of the evidence which came to the surface after careful and searching cross-examination by Defence Counsel. The point cannot properly be appreciated without some description of the nature of the case. The prosecution’s case was that Shoukatallie and Mahomed Ali were acting in concert in a common design to kill Peeka. The evidence from the prosecution witnesses, all related to the deceased Peeka and all fully aware of the bad blood between the two families, was as follows:

> Peeka was paddling along the Mahaica River in his corial. A gunshot was heard. It came from another corial in which, the two accused men, Shoukatallie and Mahomed Ali, were. The prosecution alleged that Shoukatallie was the man who had fired the shot. The prosecution alleges he had a gun in his hand. Mahomed Ali was steering the corial. Shoukatallie, continues the prosecution, fired the gun again at Peeka. Peeka fell on his face in his corial. Mahomed Ali then paddled their corial close to Peeka's corial. Shoukatallie got hold of Peeka's corial and pulled it across the creek. Mahomed Ali and Shoukatallie were seen near the two corials. The evidence from the family members goes on that Shoukatallie was seen chopping wood. Mahomed was twisting vine branches.

Let me comment. Mind you, all of this, with no sound of alarm, no call for help, no calling out to the two accused men assuming they were there. What happened to all these so-called eye witnesses bent on incriminating both accused? Why the silence? Not a word. No alarm.

Five days later a search was made in the river and a diver was employed. The body of Peeka was found tied to a log of wood by a vine. A post-mortem examination indicated that Peeka was shot, tied up and immersed in the river while still alive. Neither Shoukatallie nor Mahomed Ali gave evidence on oath. Both men made statements from the dock (which the law permits <u>them</u> to do) denying that they were in the vicinity or that they knew anything at all about the crime. Defence Counsel vigorously attacked the credibility of the witnesses for the prosecution, urging that the four principal witnesses were close members of a family who had a feud and an unhappy relationship with the family and the accused and that the fifth witness, had been bribed to give evidence. He was at sea under cross-examination. These are the facts that were made bare under cross-examination in Court.

Before the Privy Council, counsel for the appellant vigorously urged that, on the evidence, either both the Appellant and Mahomed Ali were guilty of murder or that neither was guilty. The Judge summed up to the Jury that it was a case of acting in concert to kill Peeka and that the act of one is the act of the other. Even if the evidence of the prosecution was accepted, was it altogether clear that the shooting was pre-arranged? Mere presence is not enough to constitute acting in concert. Might it not, perhaps, be that the Appellant Shoukatallie fired the shots on his own account (if the Prosecutor's case is to be believed) with Mahomed Ali merely a spectator?

True enough, the learned Judge told the Jury that if Mahomed Ali took no part in the crime and if his presence there was merely accidental, they should acquit him. But the Judge went on to say that "The cause of death was drowning.... If you feel that they were acting in concert.... Then they would be equally guilty of the offence of murder in the eyes of the law." The learned Judge failed to put the other principle of the law with respect to "accessory after the fact." Here there was not misdirection but a glaring non-direction, which is a serious flaw in the summing-up. Mahomed Ali may have been merely a spectator. The Federal Supreme Court acquitted Mahomed Ali. There was no direction by the trial Judge to the Jury about accessory after fact as it relates to Mahomed Ali.

Let me now turn my attention to *No.1* accused Shoukatallie. On June 2, 1960, Bollers J. could not have made his feelings of the case against Shoukatallie clearer. It looks from all that transpired that all he wanted was a verdict of guilty against Shoukatallie. During the conduct of the case, he showed his bias against the defendant *No.1*. His defence was an alibi. The prosecution witnesses were not independent non-partisan witnesses. They were all very closely related to the deceased and had no difficulty in saying what the Police wanted them to say. The witness who was bribed to give evidence was discredited under cross-examination. The Crown Prosecutor, had no difficulty, the Judge did a very fine job for the prosecution in his summing-up to the Jury.

Let me examine what happened on the final day of the trial. The Jury took their places at 8:40 a.m. The Judge came on the Bench at 9:00 a.m. Mr. Gonsalves-Sabola continued his final address until it was concluded at 10:00 a.m. The Court was then adjourned for a few minutes and at 10:14 a.m. the Judge began his summing-up to the Jury. There was a break from 11:20 a.m. to 12:30 p.m., one hour and 10 minutes. The summing up took nearly five and a half hours to deliver!!! The Jury retired at 4:50 p.m. In most civilized societies, the Judge should have ended his summing-up for the day and continue the next morning. Arrangements could have been made for the Jury to be put up at a Hotel under strict directions from the Judge, but the Judge saw it fit not to do this.

If the trial Judge was conducting this trial in a Court in England or any of the Metropolitan Countries of the world, he would have had to adjourn the matter to the next morning after ordering that the Jurors be given appropriate hotel accommodation for the night which would of course include dinner. But the Judge kept the Jury locked up and at 5:30 p.m., the Judge, a Guyanese, graciously condescended for the Jurors to be served with sandwiches, tea and ice cream. How noble!!!

They were treated like children at a party. But you see, my Dear Reader, the Jurors were ordinary Guyanese Citizens "good and true." That was the respect and treatment meted out to them by a Guyanese Judge sitting in Guyana. The whole Appeal before the Privy Council was based upon non-direction by the trial Judge and blatant coercion by the Judge. The evidence was complex and the Jury had to resolve the discrepancies and sometimes-irreconcilable bits of evidence from the various witnesses who had succumbed to the cross-examination of Defence Counsel.

Even the Privy Council found an excuse for the harsh and undue pressure via the exhortation by the trial Judge to the Jury when the Privy Council stated, "But, no doubt, he (the Judge) thought that the Jury would be able to reach their verdict in an hour or so." They were sent back at 8:49 p.m. and returned at 10:00 p.m. asking for further legal directions. At 10:15 p.m. the Judge concluded his further directions and the Jury retired again. They came out at 1:35 a.m. on June 3, 1960 with a "guilty verdict," this is after about eight and a half hours of being locked away in a small, hot and uncomfortable room. You have to see the jury rooms in the Supreme Court Building of Guyana to understand what discomfort and inconvenience really connote. There are no washrooms; just a large table in this very uninviting room with about a dozen chairs. If a Juror has to go to the washroom, he (at that time there were only male jurors) would have to bang on the door. The Marshal or the Keeper of the jury room would open up and if required, take the Juror or Jurors to the rest-room and wait there for him or them.

When females became part of the jury system in Guyana, then a female turnkey was put on duty to cater to the personal needs of female Jurors. This was the type of jury room that existed in 1960. From what I have heard, the situation has not changed to make accommodation in the jury room compatible with the jury rooms of the more advanced countries of the world. It seems that the Judge was hell-bent in getting a verdict that evening, no matter what was involved. You, the reader, will see the unswerving intent of the trial Judge to get a verdict no matter how. Let us see how things developed. At 5:30 p.m., the Jury was served with sandwiches, tea and ice cream. At 8:40 p.m. the Jury returned into Court after about nearly four hours of deliberation.

I have to take time off here to explain the verdicts that a Jury could return in Guyana. The verdict could be either guilty or not guilty or the Jury could disagree and cannot arrive at a verdict. In a murder case in Guyana, the verdict must be a unanimous verdict of the twelve empanelled Jurors in the case. I was in Court at all times throughout the whole trial right on down to the verdict which was returned at 1:35 a.m. on June 3, 1960. At about 8:40 p.m. my recollection is that they were ordered by the Judge to return to Court. They did and then this is what took place. It appears that the Judge had prepared his address when he ordered the Jury to return to Court for the Judge to enquire what was their verdict.

Marshal of the Court:	"Have the Jury arrived at a verdict?"
Foreman of the Jury:	"No, My Lord, we are disagreed on our verdict." (Note this was after about four hours of deliberation).

It was as plain as a pikestaff in a noon-day sun, that there was a disagreement. He must have had an idea that the Jury was not agreed on a verdict. The Judge had already prepared his further speech to the Jury. He wasn't going to have any such nonsense! The Judge then addressed the Jury and unleashed his broadside on the Jury with this salvo:

> *"Gentlemen of the Jury, I want to remind you of the oath that each and every one of you took at the commencement of this case. It reads as follows: 'You shall well and truly try and true deliverance make between Our Sovereign Lady the Queen and the prisoners at the Bar whom you shall have in charge and a true verdict give according to the evidence. So help you God.' I want to direct your attention to the last two sentences in that oath that you have taken –*

'And a true verdict, give according to the evidence. So help you God.'

Well, the evidence that has been led in this case by the Crown and by the accused persons is clear and I can see no difficulty at all why you should not arrive at a final conclusion in this matter. When you get into that jury room you must put all extraneous matter away from your deliberations. If you take extraneous matter and improper matter into your deliberations in deciding whether the case has been proved or not proved against the accused persons, then you will not be acting in accordance with the oath you have taken. It appears to me that this Colony is reaching a stage, or wants to reach a stage, when it can manage its own affairs. Well, this kind of thing that is going on amongst the Jury would not help.

In my very humble submission I cannot see how it will help one way or the other. Now, you must return to that jury room and consider the matter again and then make up your minds one way or the other. If you feel one way and another member of the Jury thinks another way, then you must examine the arguments of each other and accept reason. You must not be pig-headed. Not because you may feel one way or the other does it mean that you must never give way, even though sound common sense and good reason are placed before you.

The community is looking to you to return a verdict in accordance with your own conscience. If you fail to do that you will not only be bringing disgrace upon the community but you will be bringing disgrace upon yourselves, which is perhaps even worse. Gentlemen of the Jury, I am now going to order you to return to that jury room and consider the matter calmly and dispassionately and give you an opportunity of arriving at an honest verdict in the

> *case. Please see that you do not besmirch the fair name of your country. Please return to the jury room."*

So, if a Juror felt that he was not satisfied beyond a reasonable doubt that the accused men were guilty, he would be "pig-headed," if he did not go along with the others who felt that they were guilty. That Juror, according to the Judge, would be bringing disgrace upon the community and upon himself. He, according to Bollers, J. would be besmirching the fair name of Guyana. Never mind the wrong and the disgraceful treatment meted out to those men who swore to give a verdict according to the evidence. It is for the Jurors to assess the evidence, not the Judge to do so and word his exhortation to infer that if a man sticks up for what he feels in his opinion and inner feeling is right, that his conscience would not be affected if he ditches and abandons his real inner just feeling in order to give a verdict of the majority of the Jurors who have not considered the matter calmly and dispassionately. In other words, as Bollers J. saw it, the majority is right and must be followed even it means a man's life is involved.

At 8:49 p.m. the Jury retired to the jury room, hungry and tired now after a long and intense day of listening to complicated legal directions. At 10:00 p.m. the Jury returned to the Court and asked for further directions:

The Foreman: "We would like further legal directions as to accomplices after the fact."

This clearly indicated the difficulty of the legal aspects of the case and the confusion of the Jury. The Judge did not, in his summing-up, tell them anything about 'accomplices after the fact.'

The Judge: "I am not quite sure what that means. During the course of my summing-up, I did not mention the word 'accomplices.' What I did mention was 'acting in concert in pursuance of a common design to commit the offence for which the accused persons stand charged.' Do the Jury desire further directions on that aspect of the matter?"

The Foreman: "Yes."

Then Judge proceeded to direct the Jury about principals in the first degree and in the second degree, but, quite surprisingly did not give the Jury any directions on accessories after the fact. Presumably, he thought it did not arise. All the Judge was concerned with was his own view of the case, which he urged and canvassed *ad nauseam* in his summing-up to the Jury. The Judge only wanted and expected one verdict – a guilty verdict. In cold print, one cannot quite appreciate the devastating effect of intonations and over-emphasis of the Judge, of certain viewpoints, which he wanted the Jury to accept.

The Judge again went on to make his own view of the fact clear when he said:

> *"You may feel that in this case the (appellant – Shoukatallie) shot Peeka and having shot him, when he was in a helpless condition but still alive, he decided to drown Peeka and it was at that stage that the No. (2) accused (Mahomed Ali) proceeded to act in concert with the Appellant (Shoukatallie) and assisted him and was present at aiding and abetting Shoukatallie in the killing of Peeka. If you find that is so, then they would be equally guilty of Murder."*

Even at this late stage of further summing-up, as Their Lordships in the Privy Council observed, the Judge again missed one important point that he had earlier missed in his main summing-up and that is this: that Peeka may have been dead or to all appearances dead and that Mahomed Ali the No. (2) accused believed he was dead before he took any part in the matter.

This clearly shows the mind-set of the Judge. He had concluded, as the Crown alleged, that Shoukatallie and Mahomed Ali both took part in the killing of Peeka while he was still alive, they both had him immersed in the water and this caused him to die from drowning. That, put in simple terms, accounts for the many instances in the summing-up where the Judge kept on urging in strong tones, "I can see no difficulty at all (emphasized) why you should not arrive at a final conclusion in this matter."

The Judge stopped short in telling the Jury what was the final conclusion. I was in Court. I heard it all and it was clear from the views of the evidence expressed in the summing-up of the Judge, that the only verdict that would be a "final conclusion" is a verdict of guilty. He was so obsessed with his view-point that he forgot to address the Jury on accessory after the fact. However, Mahomed Ali's Appeal to the Federal Supreme Court was allowed and he was set free. This was due solely to the fact that the biased trial Judge could not see that aspect of the law that cried out for explanation to the Jury. Only one verdict was the proper verdict in so far as the Judge was concerned: *Guilty* of both accused.

At 10.15 p.m. (this late hour with no rest for the Jury and no dinner) the Judge concluded his further directions and the Jury retired again. At 1.35 a.m. on June 3rd, 1960, the Jury returned, looking haggard and very tired physically and mentally and gave the verdict as follows: "Unanimous verdict: No. (1) (Shoukatallie) accused guilty of murder. Unanimous verdict: No. (2) Mahomed Ali guilty of murder with a very strong recommendation to mercy."

What a convoluted and complex and irrational verdict. This was the hall-mark of this whole case. The penalty for murder in Guyana at the time (1960) and I think it still is death by hanging.

Their Lordships in the Federal Supreme Court of the Caribbean had no difficulty in pin-pointing the non-direction by the trial Judge on accessory after the fact. It was the failure of the Judge to assist the Jury on this important aspect of the case along with other reasons, which led the Federal Supreme Court to quash the conviction of the accused Mahomed Ali and set him free. So much for my client.

Obviously, I was not in the jury room during their deliberations. But, as one walked past the jury room in question, going from one Court to another, one could have heard the commotion. The next day, as I passed the then vacant jury room, I saw the results of the violence that took place in the jury room, on those Jurors who were pressurized and coerced to agree to a guilty verdict. This was really confirmed by Jurors after the trial was over and the verdict was delivered.

When the verdict was delivered, I was really stunned. At that early hour of the morning, the Judge got in his car and went home and the Crown Prosecutor did the same. I wanted space and fresh air. My mind was troubled, not because of the verdict as such, but by the procedure and means that were adopted to get such a verdict. I got in my very comfortable English Austin Westminster car and went to the "sea-wall" (a wall keeping the Atlantic Ocean out from the below sea-level coastal lands) and there took in some fresh air and went over in my mind the "rape on Justice," which I saw unfolding before my very eyes. I was determined to keep on fighting for Justice always.

The very next day, the parents of Shoukatallie came to my Chambers. They first said thanks for all the help and support I gave to them in their ordeal and wanted to know what was the next step. I explained to them that we would now have to appeal to the Federal Supreme Court of the

Caribbean. They gave me the authority to do so and the authority to do whatever I considered right and necessary and to take all necessary steps to pursue all the appeal procedures available. I explained to them the costs involved and they gave me the authority to proceed. My learned friend, Mr. Doodnauth Singh (now Attorney General of Guyana) and I decided to prepare the Appeal. To have greater leverage in the Federal Supreme Court, we agreed to have the Appeals argued by two Counsel, Mr. Doodnauth Singh for Shoukatallie and myself for Mahomed Ali.

It was clear that the Jury was swayed and affected by the strong opinions expressed by the trial Judge in his summing-up. Even while I was a student in London at Law School, I was always suspicious of the "shelter," the "haven" and the "last resort" that Judges took under the guise of expressing their opinions in summing-up to the Jury. Many times Jurors here have stated openly that the Judge in his summing-up expressed some very strong views on the evidence and this affected the outcome of their verdict of guilty.

One cannot really evaluate what weight juries under the British system attach to the "views" of the trial Judge. It is time for some research to be done on this aspect of the Criminal Justice System. If a thorough and extensive research is carried out and it resulted in establishing that the "views" or "opinions" of the trial Judge are too strongly worded or they carry much weight in the Jury's deliberation, then remedial steps can be taken and Judges should not be allowed to comment or offer their own opinions upon the evidence.

In my fifty years as a Criminal Defence Counsel, I am of the very strong opinion, based on my experiences and the declarations of jurors who do not think that it is right for a Judge to inject his own personal feelings or views on the evidence. I think the time is ripe to stop this anachronistic practice. Jurors today are far more educated, well informed and capable of deciding facts for themselves, than the jurors of many past years. Leave the Jury to do its work. Stop the Judges from interfering with the right juries have, to make their own assessment and evaluation of the evidence without trial Judges embarking in their summing-up on long, ponderous and over-excessive expressions of their views. Bollers, Ag. J. went far beyond what is judicially permissible in the expressions of his own views.

Steps must be speedily taken to stop this anachronistic practise. The Judge directs the Jury on the Law, but for Heaven's sake, let the Jury make their own findings of fact. One old Judge many years ago adopted this odd formula of sheltering under his very authoritative view to and personal affliction of his opinions upon the Jury. This is what he always told the Jury after almost telling them how they should decide the case and the verdict they should return: "Gentlemen of the Jury those are my views and they remain my views, but if you accept them they become your views. In such an event they become our views."

If proper research is done and this can be effectively done only by interviewing jurors who sat in cases, then we will know exactly the extent of the mischief done by Judges expressing their own views and then the necessary steps can be taken to stop Judges from expressing their views and comments upon the evidence.

In England and the previous British Colonies, it appears as though the jurors, once empanelled become the sole property of the system. After they were discharged, they were not allowed to communicate with anyone or discuss what caused them or motivated them to arrive at the conclusions, which resulted in the verdict given. Once a case is finished and the Jury have discharged their functions and duty, they become ordinary citizens again and are free to say what reasoning and logic they applied to the evidence to arrive at their verdict. Judges go too far in expressing their "views" and "comments upon the evidence." That is why the Jury is there. It seems the prosecution wants it both ways. If the Judge wants to control the reasoning of the Jury resulting in the verdict the Judge wants, then abolish the jury system and have trials by Judges only. One has to respect and admire the approach of the Courts of the United States of America. After a trial in the Courts in the U.S.A. jurors can be interviewed and are interviewed by the Press, television and other media regarding their views and reasoning upon which they based their findings and eventually their verdict.

All that leads me to this important development in the Shoukatallie Appeal heard both in the Federal Supreme Court of the Caribbean and the Privy Council of England. Both Courts had a really live and proper opportunity to bring the law up to date and more in keeping with good sense and sound reasoning. Two days after the 1.35 a.m. verdict of the Jury in the trial before Bollers, Ag. J., two Jurors came to my Chambers. They showed me the results of the physical injuries they suffered in the jury-room for wanting to abide by their oath and "a true verdict give according to the evidence." They told me they could not sleep. They were concerned and were being harried by their respective consciences. They could not give a guilty verdict. They held on to the end enduring two attacks with chairs by other Jurors who wanted to get home. Remember these men are laymen. They do not know the law or the practice of the law and their rights and privileges given to them by the Law.

After the 10.15 p.m. return to the jury-room, the majority of the Jurors, who by this time were mentally and physically tired and very hungry, said they will go back and tell the Judge that the majority wanted to return a verdict of guilty. In view of what the Judge said earlier "you must not be pig-headed," the majority of the Jurors started their blitzkrieg upon these two Jurors, no way connected to the accused and only being dictated to by their conscience. Two chairs were smashed during the assault on the two Jurors but they held on to their conscience. Then after some whisperings by the majority they told the two opposing Jurors that if we go back and tell the Judge we cannot agree, (remember it had to be a unanimous verdict) the Judge will send us back again and we will have to spend the whole night in this cell-like room. This was the mischief done by the Judge's exhortation to them at 8.40 p.m. ending at 8.49 p.m. when they returned to the jury-room.

The two Jurors instructed me that it was decided they were to return and tell the Judge that they cannot agree on a verdict and there is no way that will change no matter how long he intends to keep them empanelled without food, water or sleep. They made it clear to me that it was a verdict of not guilty and not the guilty verdict that the Foreman delivered to the Court. I listened without interrupting the two Jurors who were very upset and worried over what transpired in Court. I then ascertained that they were in no way connected to the accused. In fact, they told me they do not even know that part of Guyana where the incident was alleged to have taken place. They felt that the witnesses told lies and this was clearly brought out in cross-examination by the many discrepancies and irregularities.

I then advised them to write out their own statements in their own handwriting and have them sworn before a Notary Public. They decided to have this done. A day later, they came back to my Chambers with the statements. I again asked them why they were doing this. They both informed me that they had to live with their conscience and they made it clear after hours of deliberation that their respective consciences told them and dictated to them that they could not say that the men were guilty. There were in too many doubts in their minds for them to say "yes" to a guilty vote.

The two affidavits were then incorporated into the Grounds of Appeal to the Federal Supreme Court of the Caribbean. The Privy Council accepted the proposition that "No longer is any measure of coercion acceptable." Their Lordships in that Court "gave with one hand and took it back with the next." The Court readily saw the error in the summing-up of the trial Judge, Bollers, Ag. J., as it related to the *No. (2)* Appellant, Mahomed Ali. Their Lordships in that Court stated that in view of the non-direction by the trial

Judge they will allow the Appeal of Mahomed Ali and set aside his conviction and sentence of death. The Federal Supreme Court refused to admit the two affidavits and one wonders to this day, their real reason for so doing.

The Privy Council had a very unique opportunity to set the law right in so far as exhortations by trial Judges to Jurors are concerned and to examine the whole question of coercion. As a Barrister-at-Law, a Queen's Counsel, with fifty years of practice at the Bar and a Reviewer of the Law, I have the privilege and the right to disagree with certain decisions handed down. In practice, I may be bound by the decisions of the Privy Council handed down by Judges who are also Barristers-at-Law. However, Judges may have their own views and may see only one side of the coin. I am within my rights to say I disagree with the ruling of the Court. Professor G. C. Cheshire in his celebrated text on "Private International Law" encountered this problem and offered "constructive criticism" especially in the area of the Law relating to the "Decisions and Applications of Foreign Court Theory."

Let us see how the English Law was developed in this area of jury trials. In England, in olden times, there would have been nothing wrong in a Judge telling the Jury that they must agree and that he could not discharge them until they did agree, for that was, indeed, the law of the land. Lord Coke said that "a Jury sworn and charged in case of life or member cannot be discharged by the Court or any other, but they ought to give a verdict." Sir William Blackstone said that "When the evidence on both sides is closed, the Jury cannot be discharged till they have given in their verdict." Strong measures of coercion were adopted to secure a verdict. The Jury were not allowed to separate. They were kept in the jury room without meat, drink or fire (candle-light excepted) until they did agree. This was in 1670. Cockburn C. J. said "Our ancestors insisted on unanimity as the very essence of the verdict, but they were unscrupulous as to the means by which they obtained it." This was in 1866.

All the above is, of course, ancient history now. We have outlived those inhumanities. "Once the judge has finished his summing-up and the Jury given in charge of the bailiff, they are still not allowed to separate, but they are provided with refreshment and if need be, accommodation for the night in a hotel." per Lord Denning in the Privy Council hearing of this case I am writing on. This was the state of the Law in England in 1949. See: R –v- Neal. (1949) 2 All E.R. 438. I just stop here to pose this question: Was this done for the local Guyanese jurors empanelled in the Shoukatallie trial before Bollers, Ag. J? True enough they did have some refreshment and ice cream at 5:30 p.m. But at 10:00 p.m., they returned to the sub-standard jury room (no toilet facilities, no running water and no conveniences – just a wooden-table with twelve wooden chairs).

When the verdict was returned at 1.35 a.m. the next morning (June 3, 1960) there was no hotel room, no food or any comfort for the Jurors who had been under strain and stress from 4.50 p.m. Are the jurors of the then British Guiana less human than the jurors in England? What is accepted as "outlawed inhumanities" is not good enough for England but quite acceptable for the British Guiana Colonial Jurors. How could this be the Law? Or is this one standard intended for Englishmen and another standard for the Colonial British Guiana Jurors? Perhaps this is what Bollers, Ag. J had in mind. You know, the working class ordinary people are not on the same level as the professional upper class citizens!!!

As a Judge, did he feel that these twelve Jurors were not to be treated with the inhumanities of old England? After the verdict at 1.35 a.m. on June 3, 1960, I later learnt that many Jurors had to accommodate the many out-of-town Jurors who could not get back home. There was no available transportation as exists in the developed countries as England and the U.S.A. Two Jurors had to stay at a Police Station in North Georgetown until morning when the transportation system starts to operate.

If a juror cannot agree with the others, consistently with the oath he has taken, then it is his duty to differ and, for want of agreement, there will be no verdict. I agree there is nothing wrong with a judge telling a jury that they should try and reach a verdict, one way or the other. But to use the strong pejorative words, which the Judge used at 8.40 p.m. on June 2, 1960, in my view is unacceptable, wrong and coercive. This is what Lord Denning had to say in the judgment delivered by him in the Privy Council:

> *"He (the Judge) could only account for their disagreement (at 8:40 p.m.) by supposing that some of the Jurors were taking extraneous and improper matter into their deliberations or were being "pig-headed" about it. What motivated the Judge to think this way? The Jury were confused. Is it not a case that the Judge thought in his own mind that the men were guilty and that is the verdict he wanted? To say the least, the exhortation of Bollers, then Ag. J. was unfair, insulting and demeaning to twelve men – "good and true."*

One further conclusion I can arrive at and that is this, if this were a trial of an Englishman in England, the decision would have been different. That is my sincere view. Lord Denning admitted at the end of the judgment that it was a "strain" for the Jury, I agree, a physical and intellectual "strain" resulting in dysfunctional assessment and mental aberration of the Jurors.

This was in 1961. The Colonial days for British Guiana are over. There is a new approach to freedom and human dignity. Jurors are not treated in a casual and undignified manner. The community will not stand for it. I continued my practice. I found that my stature and reputation at the Bar were spreading and more often, I was being retained to argue matters in overseas jurisdictions. To date, I have completed three hundred and twenty-nine murder trials.

I have only ever had one adverse verdict in all my murder trials and that is the one I argued before the Privy Council in 1961. I am not being facetious, but, I do not think that the Privy Council decision is the correct one. You may hasten to say, "Well, you are saying that because they did not rule in your favour." Not really.

My English Professor at Law School, many scholars of the Law, experienced practitioners and the Reviewers of the decision all agree that it was a rather unusual decision, when a finding was made that there was no coercion by the trial Judge. All the authorities cited by the Appellant's Team of lawyers, the late Mr. Phineas Quass, Q.C. of the English Bar, Mr. M. P. Solomon of the English Bar and I and even the authorities on which the Court relied, established a case for coercion by the Judge. The difficulty is this: all assumptions, suppositions, conjectures and surmises by the trial Judge at the Jury trial, were woven into the authorities upon which the Privy Council relied.

The inhumanities that were outlined and once held improper were given recognition and condoned in order to find support for the coercive exhortation of Bollers, Ag. J at the trial in 1960. No wonder the report of the case and its findings are not noted in any of the leading practitioner's manual available today.

Appeals from Guyana no longer go to the Privy Council. Guyana now has its own final Court of Appeal. But one thing that remains on the credit column is the fact that the Shoukatallie decision settles once and for all times the then unsettled principles of law relating to accomplices and principals in the "first and second degrees" and accessories "after the fact." That is why the trial Judge lost sight of the legal principles and there was a complete non-direction by him in his summing-up on the question of "accessories after the fact." The Shoukatallie case will always be to me, one of the most exciting and rewarding cases I ever conducted, especially at that early era of my career at the Criminal Bar. Further, it was a decision from the then highest Court of

Appeal, condoning an injustice that was committed by the trial Judge.

Epilogue to Chapter 7

Some thirteen years after the Shoukatallie Appeal Case before the Privy Council, the Right Honourable Lord Denning, Master of the Rolls, visited Guyana. Lord Denning was born in Hampshire, England on January 23, 1899. To be exact his visit was from January 6 – 9, 1974. He was accompanied by his charming wife, Lady Denning.

I gave a talk on the then "Radio Demerara" in which I assessed and analysed suggestions and proposals put forward by that eminent English Jurist, Lord Denning, Master of the Rolls. I sent a copy of my Radio talk to Lord Denning. He replied to me in the usual Denning modesty and charm and stated, "I feel that I do not deserve in the least all the flattering things which you said, but I greatly appreciate it."

Lord Denning was at that time President of the British Court of Appeal. He came to us, inspired us, commended us, generated enthusiasm and left us. My first encounter with this pioneering jurist was in 1951 while I was a law student in England. I next met him in 1961 when he presided in the Privy Council in the Shoukatallie Appeal. As I have stated in the final pages of this Chapter on that celebrated murder appeal, I do not think that the Privy Council decision is the correct one. It completely places in the hands of a trial Judge too much power regarding views from the presiding Judge and the right to coerce juries by denying them food and accommodation, accompanied by long hours of deliberation in a sub-standard tropical jury room.

I was invited to most of the functions held in his honour. His remarkable memory left me spellbound having regard to the vast number of Appeals and cases that come up before him for his adjudication and the vast number of people he encounters on his many visits to various parts of the world. When Lord Denning and I met again at the University of Guyana Function on January 7, 1974, we discussed his reasons for coming to Guyana and then the conversation naturally drifted to Courts and Appeals.

I mentioned my appearance in the Privy Council in 1961, but not the name of the case. Lord Denning with quiet dignity just simply stated: "How well do I remember that case. It was the Shoukatallie murder Appeal. Mr. Manraj, you argued your case very well and I am sorry we did not accept your arguments." How elegantly put.

I replied, "My Lord, it is a leading decision on the law on 'accessory after the fact' and 'accomplices before and after the fact' but a sad confirmation of the Judge's coercive remarks and behaviour."

He smiled and said, "That is what makes the legal profession such a great profession."

In view of the fact that I had actually appeared before Lord Denning in the Privy Council, it was felt by the Guyana Bar Association (of which I was an active member) that I should perform the duties of liaison officer at this function and introduce him to the various members of the Guyana Bar present. I was delighted to do so. I knew that on January 6, 1974, when he arrived in Guyana, he was met by the then Chancellor of the Judiciary, The Honourable E. V. Luckhoo (later Sir E. V. Luckhoo), The Chief Justice, The Honourable H. B. S. Bollers (later Sir H. B. S. Bollers) and the British High Commissioner, His Excellency, Mr. W. S. Bates, C.M.G.

Therefore, Lord Denning had since his arrival already met Bollers, J. (Ag.) as he was in 1961, when he presided over the trial of the Shoukatallie murder case. I was with Lord Denning and Lady Denning and Mr. "Bill" Bates for a photograph to be taken. I saw standing nearby, the Prosecutor in the Shoukatallie murder case, Prosecutor Mr. J. Gonsalves-Sabola (later Sir J. Gonsalves-Sabola).

The Learned Lord Denning, (l) Dr. M. Shahabuddeen, Ph.D. (c) and A. Shakoor Manraj, Q. C.

Lady Denning (l), Lord Denning (c), and A. Shakoor Manraj, Q. C.

A. Shakoor Manraj, Q. C. (l), Dr. M Shahabuddeen, Ph.D. (c), and Lord Denning.

(L-R) Bill Bates, Lady Denning, Lord Denning, A. Shakoor Manraj, Q. C. and Sir Joseph Gonsalves-Sabola.

I should perhaps mention that in 1974, I was already a Queen's Counsel (Q.C.) having been appointed to that position in 1969. I asked him over to join our group and Mr. Bates had a photographer take a picture of the five of us – "Bill" Bates, Lady Denning, Lord Denning, myself and "Joe" Sabola. I have that photograph. One was forwarded to Lord Denning and he dropped me a short note, expressing his pleasure of having met the Shoukatallie team – trial Judge, Defence Counsel and Prosecuting Counsel.

Lord and Lady Denning left Guyana on January 9, 1974. Before he left, Lord Denning stated that he was impressed with the quality of the administration of the law and the way Judges and the legal practitioners he had met, carry out their duties. When asked about his view on the death penalty, he stated that his view on the death penalty was that "Capital Punishment" should be retained for "malicious deliberate killing."

In his own country, England, the death penalty has been abolished. Since Guyana became a Republic, no execution has taken place, clearly indicating that the death penalty has, for all practical purposes, been abolished in Guyana since 1966. Lord Denning was a very brilliant judge and his death in March 1999, has resulted in a severe loss to the intellectual development and concepts of the legal profession. For almost one hundred years, he was a beacon shedding light on many abstract and difficult problems in the Law.

Chapter 8

Results of Some Extraordinary Cases

"The English have a strong sense of law and order, but no respect for abstract legal principles as distinct from rules which have been applied in concrete cases." These are the words of Lord Shawcross, (formerly Sir Hartley Shawcross and Attorney-General of England, Member of the Council, International Law Association and former Chairman of the English Bar Council). He continues, "The English Constitution being unwritten, it follows that there are no guarantees of the personal freedoms. Yet, these freedoms are axiomatic and a person who is arrested has a right at once to be brought before a public court and to be tried for his alleged Offence."

Just a few points which I would like to make before I embark in *extenso* on this chapter which has given so much pleasure to write. The cases that actually come before the Court can produce many incidents and situations which would make even the most rabid, austere and stern individual succumb to hilarious convulsions.

The English legal system and procedure, especially in the criminal courts, are accusatorial rather than inquisitorial. The Crown Prosecutor must prove his case. Before trial and at trial, an accused person is stringently protected against any kind of inquisitorial procedure. It is not for the Judge to probe into the matter. He must hold the scales evenly and have regard to the legally admissible evidence presented to him.

A trial must take place in open with free access of the Press. All serious criminal cases have to be tried by a judge and a jury of twelve ordinary citizens. The Judge decides questions of law; he sums up the facts, but the ultimate decision on the evidence rests with the jury. The jury is the embodiment of the "reasonable man" who has played such an important role in the development of the criminal law.

Perhaps I can end this brief review of the procedure by putting it this way, "If the reasonable man, after hearing everything, has a reasonable doubt, then that reasonable doubt must be given to the accused." It is pertinent for me to state that in several classes of civil litigation too, like fraud or defamation of character, a party can, if he so desires, insist upon a jury trial.

Now let me get to the extraordinary cases and matters that have engaged my attention and my professional input. An East Indian immigrant came to see me in connection with preparing a Will. He could not read or write one word of English but his business acumen and intuition were outstanding and he amassed quite a fortune as a rice planter.

He owned a large estate and a rice-mill. He was very wealthy. His wife was also an East Indian immigrant. They had been married for over fifty years. At the time they went through a religious marriage ceremony as there was no legislation in force at that time for the religious marriages to be registered, thereby making it amenable to the law regarding legal marriages. They had in all ten children who were educated up to the primary school level.

He spoke a broken Creolese dialect of English. Having been born in British Guiana, I understood the Creolese which the immigrants spoke. He told me he wanted me to make out his "KAKAJ" (paper or will). He explained what he wanted. Then we came to the point where he wanted to leave some specific bequests for his wife. I asked him for his wife's name so I can make his intentions clear in what he called his "KAKAJ."

He looked surprised and told me that his wife name was MAI (meaning mother). He said everybody calls her MAI, including himself. Try as I did, I could not get him to understand that I realize that was her "call-name," but I wanted her proper name. He seemed rather annoyed that I would not accept her name as MAI. He told me that she was in the outer office. I now thought that I would solve the problem. I said to the old man, "Mr. Naraine, go to the door, call your wife and tell her to come in."

He immediately went to the door and without a second thought said, "Mai, come ya, Lawyer wan fo talk to you." ("Mai, come here, Lawyer wants to talk to you.") That was it. That is all he knew of his wife's name, "MAI." I asked him what he called her before they had any children and his answer was "Bet," a pet name for "Baytee," meaning a young lady. I asked Mr. Naraine for his Birth Certificate. He did not have one. I asked his wife what is her name and she told me "CHANDROWTIE." I had to put the brakes on. I could not go any further with the information I had. I told him to come back and bring his eldest son (who had finished primary school and ran the rice mill) with him.

From the son, I got the "white paper" (travel document) form issued by the Immigration Department showing name, date of birth and the immigrant ship on which his parents travelled from India to the then British Guiana. I was really surprised. Here, a man was married to his wife for over fifty years and did not know her name, but I later learnt that it was an established custom for the husband to call the wife "Mai" or "Mother," if there is a son or daughter, for example, Sugrim Mai (Sugrim's mother) or Parbattie Mai (Parbattie's mother).

The son, Sugrim, explained all this to me. He said his father conducted his business in Hindi and that he, Sugrim, found that his father, old man Naraine, was very thorough in keeping the records in order. Old Mr. Naraine told me that he never remembered his wife's name and never called her "CHANDROWTIE" during their fifty odd years of marriage. After I had collected all the relevant information, I prepared his WILL. He put his mark "X" and the Will was notarised.

He was a loving father and husband. He made ample provisions for his Dear "Mai" and his children and grandchildren. I never had another experience like this in my fifty years as a Barrister. Of course, many changes have taken place as British Guiana became more developed and Government established more available procedures to make things easier for the dwindling original East Indian Immigrants, many of whom elected to return to India on the chartered Immigration Ships that came periodically to British Guiana at the expense of the Colonial Office, to take the repatriates back to India.

But many remained, looked after their business, educated their children well and spent their lives in British Guiana. Then their children took over and there was a new generation of East Indians in Guyana, many of them entering the various professions, many more becoming Civil Servants, Teachers and Businessmen. Naraine and his wife, "MAI," were among those who remained in British Guiana and with their children's help, became very wealthy and successful businessmen.

~~~~~~~

The newspaper headline was "STORY OF FOUR MEN AND A COFFIN." The report went on: "A Magistrate was told an unusual story yesterday how a man, alive and well, was being taken home by four of his friends in a COFFIN."

The four men and the man in the coffin were out on a Saturday night spree. They had some drinks. All the men concerned lived at Bath Estate in the County of Berbice, British Guiana. As their evening of fun came to an end, they had to pass the carpentry shop of the estate. They had their own idea of macabre humour. They decided to take a roughly unfinished coffin from the carpentry shop and then one of the five men got in the coffin and lay down inside as if he were dead. His four friends decided to take him home; they were the so-called pall-bearers.
~~~~~~~

While they were on their merry journey, a local policeman saw what was happening and he became suspicious. He went up to the four men. They put down the coffin in the middle of the road and ran away and the policeman had a shock of his life when the so-called dead man inside got up to get out of the coffin to make his escape. The policeman himself, shocked at what he saw, also ran-off as if the Devil was behind him, he had never seen a dead man coming out of a coffin. These are the really stunning facts. I had to deal with them.

The next stage soon added to this rather bizarre case. The policeman stationed at the local police station recognized the four men and he laid charges against the four men fetching the coffin, with "stealing a coffin." That was the charge. The four men decided to retain me to defend them on this rather strange and unusual charge. They came to Georgetown, about sixty-nine miles from where the incident took place, to retain me. They told me exactly what happened. This was a novel case. I was beyond myself with laughter as the men told me what happened.

The one in the coffin, who accompanied the four to Georgetown, told me that he felt good being lifted home by his four friends, never mind it was in a coffin. Believe you me, I was really "in stitches." I asked them why they came all the way to Georgetown to retain me when there were lawyers in New Amsterdam, which is just across the Berbice River and very near to them. They responded that the Estate was pressing the case and the policeman felt he had to redeem himself after running away from the "dead man in a coffin" and they agreed that I could best represent them. They completed their statements and took care of my retainer, including travelling expenses all the way to the Fort Wellington Court Room, which is about three miles from Bath Estate.

The case was called up before the District Magistrate, Mr. Roopan Singh. The Police Prosecutor started the case. The Policeman gave evidence. The Police Officer told me that this was the first time he saw a dead man sit up in his coffin. I asked him what he did. His answer says it all, said he, "What I did, Sir? I never saw a dead man sit up in his coffin. I was so shocked. I ran like hell for a while and then I looked back and saw the man walking. I stopped. I then realized this was not a dead man but a live human being who had come out of the coffin."

The Court was over-crowded with curious members of the public (remember it is "open" Court and the public has access) to hear this unique and extraordinary case. The Magistrate had to remind the laughing spectators that they were in Court. The Prosecutor then called for his vital witness to identify the four men and the coffin (which was tendered as Exhibit "A"). The witness did not turn up in Court and the Prosecutor could not proceed. There was no reason he could give to the Court why the witness was not present in Court. I had a clear case to make "no-case" submissions. Was the wooden structure larcenable? I submitted it was not. Further, there was no evidence to establish that the men intended to "permanently deprive" the owner (no evidence of this) of the so-called coffin. Finally, there was no evidence that the structure was a coffin and was the property of Bath Estate. No one claimed or identified the coffin. In fact, it was just a wooden box.

The learned Magistrate accepted the submissions (he had no choice) made by me and the accused men were dismissed. In dismissing the men, the Magistrate told them that he had an inclination to order the four men to fetch the coffin (wooden box) from the Fort Wellington Courtroom to Bath Estate, a distance of about three miles. This was a very extraordinary case indeed and an extraordinary ending. The case stood me in good stead. Quite a few more substantial retainers came to me for appearances in that Court and the other Courts in Berbice County.

~~~~~~~
~~~~~~~

Larceny can be sometimes difficult to establish. I now turn to a Larceny case involving twenty-four kegs of paint. Again, I will go to the headlines in the newspaper reports:

1) "CLERK FREED OF LARCENY"
2) "KEGS OF PAINT UNIDENTIFIED – SO CROWN'S LARCENY CASE BREAKS DOWN"
3) "PAINT LARCENY CHARGE FAILS: ACCUSED FREED"

As I mentioned earlier in my book, this is not a legal text book but of necessity, there are occasions in my writing when, in order to make my point more intelligible, I must refer to the legal principles. The Law of Larceny has undergone many changes but the basic principles remain in force. "Theft…. involves four elements: (i) a dishonest (ii) appropriation of (iii) property belonging to another (iv) with the intention of permanently depriving the owner of it." This will suffice for the matters I am referring to in this Chapter.

In this case, a thirty-six year old clerk from a store in Georgetown, Guyana, was freed on charges of "breaking and entering" the Bookers La Penitence Bond, (at that time, one of the largest stores in Guyana) and stealing there from twenty-four kegs of paint and unlawfully receiving six kegs. This clerk had retained me to defend him. Originally three men were charged including my client, but after the preliminary inquiry, the Crown decided to proceed only against my client. As you will see, this case illustrates so graphically what I stated in an earlier chapter dealing with cross-examination. My client was eventually indicted and his trial came up before a Judge and Jury.

Cross-examination, I reiterate, is not a toy to be played with. It is not a procedure a lawyer must use to try to impress the gallery for ever so often, as I have seen in my long years at the Bar, an irresponsible and vociferous "fishing" cross-examination can sometimes reveal what the cross-examiner did not want, but he solicited the adverse evidence by his questioning and he is bound by the answers. One must know when to cross-examine and that is why it has been stated time and time again, that cross-examination in the hands of inexperienced counsel is a "dangerous weapon." I always emphasized this caution when I was lecturing on the Law of Evidence at several Universities.

I had the depositions of what transpired in this case at the Preliminary Investigation. I saw the weakness in the Prosecutor's case. They were having serious problems and difficulties proving identification and ownership of the alleged stolen property. At the trial, the person in charge of the bond could not identify the fifteen kegs of paint in Court. The Prosecutor did a very good job by fishing in shark-invested waters and tried to keep within the limits of the law on examination-in-chief. He had problems. The Bond Clerk could not identify the paint alleged to have been stolen. My turn came for cross-examination. Over the years, I had appeared before all the Judges of the Supreme Court of Guyana (formerly British Guiana) one time or another between 1954 and 1978 at jury trials and had on the opposing side as prosecutors, the most brilliant and highly talented minds in the Crown Attorney's Office. They used me and my cross-examination of the Crown witnesses as their barometer for an indicator to assess how their case was going.

When there is a "fight" or a "struggle" or a "wrestling" to attain Justice, nothing impaired my ferocious and consummate commitment to see that Justice, in my considered assessment must prevail. The Crown Prosecutor in this case was an experienced Prosecutor. I asked the Bookers Bond Clerk just two questions and sat down. I enquired from him how long he had been Bond Clerk at the Bookers Bond and secondly, whether he had any reason that would permit him to say that the paint kegs in question were the property of Bookers. To this last question, the answer was "No." I sat down.

That made my learned friend for the prosecution uneasy and the Judge's question, "Mr. Manraj, are you finished already?" was far more weighty than anything I could have said or done. I looked at the Jury. One learns after years of practice, to read the faces of the Jury. I saw "expectation" written across their faces.

The Prosecutor called his next witness, the Manager of Bookers Stores Estates Supplies. I listened carefully to every word he said. Every time, I raised my head, I saw the Jury looking at me with that querulous expression on their faces. The Manager said clearly and emphatically, "I cannot say that the paint in Court is the property of Bookers." The Prosecutor asked him if anybody else could identify or "claim the paint as the property of Bookers."

I rose to object to the question but before my objection could be heard, the Manager blurted out, "The only person who could identify the paint is the Clerk in charge of the Bond."

I sat down immediately. That bond clerk had already given evidence. He was the previous witness. I just asked the Manager one question to put the seal on the evidence he gave. He confirmed that the Bond Clerk was the only person who could identify the paint in Court.

After cross-examination by me for the accused man, my learned friend, the Prosecutor, properly stated to the Court that he had no further evidence to offer in respect to the identification of the kegs of paint before the Court.

The Judge explained the view that on the evidence adduced thus far, he did not see any useful purpose would be served in proceeding with the matter and commended the Crown Prosecutor on his frankness with the Court. The learned Judge stated that he knew the submissions I wanted to make and he would not call on me to address the Court. This is a signal honour. He directed the Jury to return a verdict in favour of the accused. This was done. Justice had triumphed. The accused left the Court in smiles. He at all times maintained, even under my most gruelling questioning of him when he came to retain me, that he did not steal the kegs of paint. As Defence Counsel, I expressed regret that a law applicable in the United Kingdom was not applicable in Guyana, as I would have claimed compensation in the circumstances of the case.

~~~~~~~

By 1965, I had established myself not only in Guyana but in other countries as well, as cases started coming in from many different overseas territories. A strange set of circumstances resulted in my being retained to do an Appeal before the itinerant Federal Appeals Court of the Caribbean sitting in Trinidad, in the West Indies. My father was returning from the Supreme Court Building to my Chambers then located at 15-16 Croal Street, Georgetown, just across from the Supreme Court Building. An East Indian gentleman with a travelling bag in his hand stopped my father and to my Dad's surprise, the gentleman asked him if he could direct him to the Law Office of Mr. Shakoor Manraj.

My father was very surprised. Of all the thousands of people crossing Croal Street and the other streets intersecting with Croal Street, he had to be asked to direct this man to my Chambers. My Dad said, "This is really unbelievable. I am Mr. Manraj's Dad." The man also expressed surprise at this rather fortuitous meeting. In due course, the man was eventually interviewed by me and both he and my Dad said it was one of the strangest meetings they ever experienced.

The gentleman was from Trinidad. He had a civil case against a very wealthy land-owner. He had retained several lawyers in Trinidad but had little success. The gentleman attributed this to the powerful landlord he had. He now had an Appeal against the said Landlord and the matter was to be heard in the Federal Appeals Court of the Caribbean.

After our interview, he retained me to travel to Trinidad and to appear for him and argue his Appeal. I had examined all the documents he had and the record of the
~~~~~~~

proceedings in the Court below (the trial Court) and I decided to accept the "brief," (a summary of facts and law-points of a case prepared for counsel – papers relating to the case).

All arrangements were finalized and I had to make arrangements to fly out to Trinidad. In Trinidad, I retained a junior member of the Trinidad Bar to appear with me and to take notes of my arguments. I clearly understood the anxiety and fear of my client when the Appeal was called up. For the wealthy landlord, the six best of the top-ranking lawyers were in appearance, many of whom I was meeting for the first time.

One of the lawyers in this formidable array of top-ranking lawyers was a colleague of mine during our student days in England. He had also reached the top of the ladder in our profession. Introductions were made and courtesies were exchanged but I must confess; it was one of the loneliest moments I encountered at the Bar. I was not afraid, just startled by this array of legal talent for the Respondent. As a practitioner in Guyana, I had audience to appear before the Federal Appeals Court sitting in any one of the subscribing territories.

I arrived in Port of Spain, Trinidad, three days before the hearing of the Appeal as I had to use the Law Library to get my authorities to support my arguments in Court. Much to my surprise, most of the authorities I wanted were not in the library. The junior I retained in Trinidad smiled. He said, "You know, Mr. Manraj, I am sure that the books we want are in the possession of the lawyers for the Respondent." (The person against whom the Appeal was brought.) This is an old trick. I had to seek the assistance of the Librarian. It took a lot of hard word and photo-copying to get what I wanted for the presentation of my arguments.

The Appeal was heard. The Court gave me a full opportunity to advance my arguments and to show that it was inequitable to have the lease revoked because of some very minor and unimportant breaches, far too minor, to be elevated to a "substantial breach" of the terms of the lease. After long hours of arguments on both sides, a stage was reached where a settlement between the parties appeared to be the best solution. Discussions took place and a settlement was agreed upon.

The Court expressed its pleasure over the agreement and felt that that was perhaps the best outcome for the parties as the Court's decision would have created extreme hardships whichever way the Court decided. My client was very pleased and he was most impressed over my stand in Court over the questions posed by the three Judges and my grasp of the facts of the case and the conciliatory attitude of the Respondent.

My client was an educated man and understood the proceedings fully and he was happy with the outcome. This was just the fore-runner. After this case was reported fully in the Press, I found that I was retained to appear in more cases in Trinidad, including two murder cases, both of which resulted in an acquittal for my clients.

~~~~~~~

I now move along to deal with a murder case that took me to Venezuela. These overseas retainers, much to my delight, kept coming in. I had come back to my office after a long tiring day in Court mostly spent doing some intensive cross-examination of some experts witnesses in a Theft and False Accounting case. Fraud cases are no "bed of roses" in which to appear.

I saw the clients who were waiting to see me. The last one was most interesting. My Secretary told me that it was a case to retain me to undertake the defence of a murder accused in Venezuela. The lady who came in to see me had come all the way from a place called Skeldon on the Corentyne Coast of Guyana about one hundred and forty-nine miles from Georgetown. This was in 1971.

The lady came in. She was a very simple lady and was obviously not very educated but was most polite and
~~~~~~~

unsophisticated. Her son was the only East Indian Guyanese sailor on board a merchant ship plying between the South American Republics and Europe. Many of the crew members were Afro-Guyanese and other coloured men from the Caribbean territories, Venezuela and Brazil.

Her only son was a seaman on board a boat which was in Venezuelan territorial waters off the coast of Caracas, the capital of Venezuela. He apparently had a quarrel with a coloured seaman, violence ensued in the course of which the son's assailant fell over one of the ship's rails to the deck below and died from injuries received. Her son was charged with murder and was in custody in Venezuela. This is all she could tell me.

She understood the fact that to retain me and cover all the expenses for me to go to Venezuela will cost her a lot of money. She told me she realized that, but she wanted me to appear for her son. At this period of my practice, my fourteen and a half years as Criminal Defence Counsel, I had completed one hundred and forty murder trials.

Arrangements were started the next day as I had to book hotel accommodation, secure air tickets and complete all the related plans for a trip overseas. I also contacted by telephone, the Guyana Ambassador in Caracas. He undertook to secure the services of a Venezuelan attorney (*abogado*) to appear with me as I was not fluent in Spanish. The dear lady was informed of every step of the arrangements. She agreed to pay all the expenses and my fees.

At that time, there were no direct flights to Caracas. I undertook to keep her informed of developments. You will see how Defence Counsel's life can, at times, become so complicated.

Just a relevant diversion. When British Guiana was part of the British Empire, Venezuela had made some claims that the Ankoko Island on Guiana's western border, belonged to Venezuela. This was hotly disputed and rejected by the British Government. When Guiana became independent, the Venezuelan Government again started its sabre-rattling claims to Ankoko Island.

The Guyana Government made it clear that it will not cede one inch of its territory to Venezuela and that Ankoko Island was part of Guyana. I was consulted by a large firm trading with Venezuela to write a legal opinion on the matter. To this date that firm is still trading with Venezuela. My radio talk which I made subsequently was the result of my research and my legal opinion. My client gave me permission to use my research information in my radio broadcast.

During my radio talk over the Guyana Broadcasting Service, I stressed that Venezuela was acting illegally and very undiplomatically. When the British were in Guyana, Venezuela never threatened Guyana with force to take Ankoko but, as soon as the British left, Venezuela started to flex her military muscles and claimed Ankoko Island to which she has no legal claim.

Apparently, a copy of my talk was sent to Caracas by the then Venezuelan Ambassador in Guyana. Having given you that background let us see what happened.

I arrived in Caracas on board a Venezuelan flight and when I reached the Immigration counter, I was denied entry and ordered to return to Guyana on the next flight. The Guyana Ambassador was at the airport to meet me. Eventually, he got to see me and questioned me about my being denied entry. I told him I have no idea of what is happening. He went to investigate. One knows what Government red-tape is like. No one could give the Ambassador any explanation.

I returned to Guyana and immediately went to our Foreign Affairs Minister, then Mr. S. S. Ramphal (later Sir S. S. Ramphal) and asked for an explanation. He told me to give him some time. Apparently he got through to his counterpart in Caracas and complained about the refusal to grant me, a lawyer, admission to defend a Guyanese seaman charged with the Offence of murder in Venezuela. Mr.

Ramphal knows me well. We were law students together in England. Soon, I was in contact with Mr. Ramphal and he told me that he will give me a letter to show the Venezuelan Authorities when I return.

I left again for Venezuela. I landed in Caracas. There was no incident. I was again met by the Ambassador for Guyana and was taken to the Embassy and then to my hotel. There was an apology from the Venezuelan Foreign Minister for denying me admission on my previous trip to defend a Guyanese seaman charged with murder in Venezuelan territorial waters. It was later discovered that the reason for denying me entry on the first occasion, was based upon my very pronounced and vocal criticism of the behaviour and attitude of the Venezuelan Government over Ankoko Island which they were claiming as part of Venezuela.

I met my client in Puerto Cabello. He seemed to be very relaxed. He was kept in custody but, a very honour-system form of custody. He was allowed to go out to the cinema with a prison attendant but best of all, there was next door to his detention centre, a very lovely young lady. She gave him cakes, cigarettes and a lot of food to make him comfortable. Apparently my client spoke the language fluently. To complete the story regarding this lovely young girl who befriended my client, let me add that she and my client got married after his acquittal and as far as I know, my client is still in Venezuela with the "love of his life."

In English Law, the modern test whether the force used in self-defence was reasonable is not purely objective. The jury has to consider what the accused himself thought. The old rule of English Law that a man attacked must retreat as far as he can, has disappeared. Thus, a defendant is entitled to rely on the plea of "self-defence" even though he is unable to show that he demonstrated by his actions that he was unwilling to fight. In this regard the law in Venezuela was more progressive in that the doctrine of retreat was not a component factor in the defence of "self-defence." My Junior Abogado advised that "self-defence" was an acceptable defence in criminal cases. To my mind, this principle did not apply at all. It is just that my client made a lawful and sensible move which resulted in the death of the deceased. These were the facts:

There was a quarrel between the deceased and the accused. The deceased was pummelling my client with blows. They were at the time on the second deck of the ship. My client slipped away. There was a stairway nearby and the deceased stood on one of the treaders of the stairway; he then plunged towards my client with an open blade and my client moved away from the rail. As a result, the deceased went flying over the rail to the lower steel deck. The deceased was seriously injured in the head. He died later.

The facts were that my client just moved out of the deceased's path and the deceased went head-long over the rail to the deck below. How could this be murder? If *A* is going to shoot *B* and the gun explodes and kills *A*, how could *B* be held responsible for his death? This was the defence and was supported by the witnesses under cross-examination. If my client had not moved away, he would have been fatally stabbed. The only charge brought against the accused was murder. The results were in accordance with good logic and common sense. The accused was acquitted. My client could not have thanked me more.

I phoned from Caracas. My client's mother was very pleased and grateful. I was met by the family on my return to Guyana. They thanked me profusely. I thanked my client's mother for giving me the opportunity to defend her son.

~~~~~~~

Follow me as I travelled around on my professional duties. My next trip abroad was to Jamaica. The time in between these overseas cases, I used to clear up the resulting backlog of cases. I was always given very much appreciated consideration and professional accommodation by the Judges of the High Court when I had to travel abroad on professional business.
~~~~~~~

My base practice was in Guyana until I left there in 1978 for Canada, where my practice assumed a more international dimension. My practice had become more complex with more difficult cases. I found that I had to give more of my time, skill and energy to fight every inch of the way to see that Justice was done. The path to Justice can sometimes be rough and uneven and strewn with pot-holes, difficulties, surprises and personal inconveniences.

When one begins a case, there can be so many twists and turns that were never anticipated by Counsel. But at all times, a seasoned Defence lawyer must be adaptable and able to adjust to new and unexpected evidence and circumstances. One cannot be stoically rigid to such a degree that he or she cannot adjust to the unexpected testimony that one gets from witnesses ever so often. To take this type of evidence and properly make use of it can sometimes cause consternation in the opposing camp.

Moving on, I had to travel to Jamaica to represent a wife in Divorce proceedings filed in Jamaica. The parties were Guyanese. They were married in Guyana and after two children were born, they all left for Jamaica where the husband landed a good job. Soon matrimonial problems arose based on the husband's philandering activities. Divorce proceedings were instituted by the wife. She returned to Guyana but the husband remained in Jamaica and eventually remarried.

The wife filed proceedings in Jamaica seeking maintenance for herself and support for the children. It was this case that resulted in my being retained by the wife and her relatives, to go to Jamaica. There she had filed proceedings. I appeared and it was rather strange. I was fully robed (wig and gown). The Judge said he needed some kind of evidence that the marriage certificate he had on the record, evidenced a valid and legal marriage in Guyana.

The Judge (whom I knew in England during our student days studying law) said, "Mr. Manraj, what better expert can I have than a Queen's Counsel to certify that the

Justice Amineen Edun, Jamaica, 1967.

Shakoor Manraj with his children, (l-r) Andrew, Anne, Marcina, Elizabeth and Michael.

Family is important to Mr. Manraj. Here he is surrounded by his nine grandchildren

marriage certificate is legal and admissible." He invited me to give the evidence as an Officer of the Court. I had to remove my wig and gown and I went into the witness box as a witness called by the Court and I certified that the marriage certificate before the Court was legal and admissible. The Judge was very pleased and adjourned the Court for a few minutes. He showed me to his robing room to re-robe.

This was a rather novel experience. I then returned to open Court and continued with my case. The matter was heard and an order was made in the wife's favour. The learned Judge was very liberal in the award of costs in favour of the wife. While I was in Jamaica, I was the house-guest of the late Mr. Justice Amineen Edun of the Jamaica Court of Appeal and the late Mrs. Gladys Edun, both originally from Guyana. Their second son, Andrew, later became my son-in-law, he having married my eldest daughter, Anne, in 1982. I also had the pleasure of meeting again with the late Sir Roland Phillips, who was earlier a Judge in Guyana. He was originally from Jamaica.

~~~~~~~

As I mentioned earlier, I was a Crown Prosecutor in the Ministry of the Attorney-General of Ontario, Canada. I returned to private practice in Toronto in 1988, after serving the Province of Ontario for nine years. In 1990, I appeared for an old client, who it was alleged, was in possession of cocaine. This was an important case and that is why I decided to write about it. The result was that the whole procedure of dealing with analyst certificates was streamlined. The law provided that those certificates or reports are legally admissible in evidence in Court, once certain procedures and conditions precedent are properly established.

In this case, the police officer testified that he took from my client a brown envelope containing a white powdery substance that looked like cocaine. He charged my client with having in his possession a prohibited substance,
~~~~~~~

namely cocaine. The police officer at the trial swore that he took the envelope with the white powdery substance to the analyst. He had sealed the envelope before he took the envelope to the analyst. He left the brown envelope with the analyst and about fifteen days later, he went back to the analyst department and uplifted the certificate which certified that the substance in a brown envelope that was analysed was cocaine.

The trial took place some six months after the police officer uplifted the envelope from the analyst department. This certificate was sought to be tendered through the police officer by the prosecution. I immediately rose up and objected to the admissibility of the said certificate. At that stage, the Court over-ruled my objection and continued with the evidence.

At the close of the prosecution's case, I submitted to the Court, presided over by a very pleasant and experienced Judge, that there was no case to answer. The Judge said that the certificate stated that on examination, the substance in a brown envelope was found to be cocaine. Of course, the Prosecutor interrupted to state that he proved his case to the hilt. When they were both finished with their cursory statements, I continued with my legal submissions.

I had defended many of these cases when I resumed private practice in Ontario, Canada and I did not have to look deeply to see the missing links in the prosecution's case. There was an obvious hiatus in the prosecution's case and a severe break in the chain of custody, control and possession of the envelope taken from my client. These were fatal to the prosecution's case. My submissions, for clarity, can be summarized as follows:

(1) There was no evidence before the Court that the substance taken from the defendant was the substance examined by the analyst and found to be cocaine.

(2) The vital chain of custody, control and possession by the police has been broken and that vital breach militates against the prosecution's case.

Bonita Manraj at the Hell Post Office on Grand Cayman Island.

Shakoor taking a relaxing stroll on Barrie Beach in Ontario, Canada.

Shakoor and Bonita on holiday on St. Simon Island, Brunswick, Georgia U.S.A

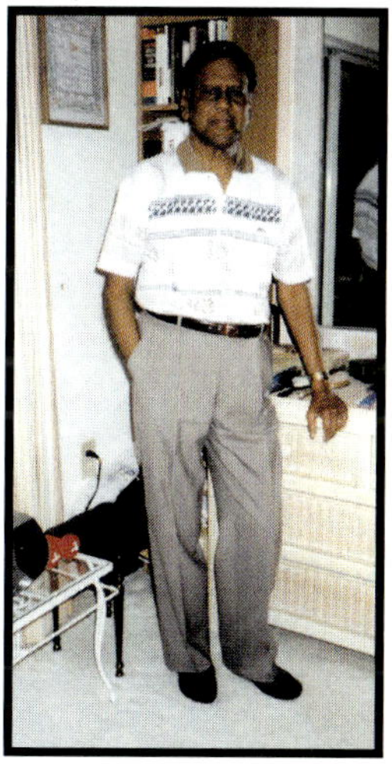

Shakoor relaxing in Canada (above) and at home in Florida (right).

Where was the evidence that the envelope tendered in Court containing the white powdery substance is the same envelope taken from the defendant by the police and that was the envelope that the officer took to the analyst?

There was no evidence that the envelope was marked and sealed with any Police seal at the time when it was handed over to the analyst department. This is vital. The prosecution has to connect the two things to make it admissible evidence. All we have here before the Court is that the analyst examined some white powdery substance in an envelope which was not identified by the analyst department by way of the departmental seal being affixed to the envelope and the date of the analysis.

All the evidence disclosed was that a sealed envelope with white powdery substance was taken to the analyst department to be analysed. Hundreds of such envelopes are taken to the analyst department each week. Each envelope having this white powdery substance inside to be taken to the analyst must have

(a) the police seal,
(b) the date when it was taken,
(c) the analyst department identifying work-number on the envelope and
(d) the sealed envelope with the analyst's seal when the said envelope was returned to the police officer.

This then establishes the chain of custody, control and possession by the police and analyst departments. This was the hiatus in the prosecution's case. It was fatal to the prosecution's case. But, it doesn't end there.

(3) The officer gave no evidence that after he uplifted the envelope from the analyst department, he took it to the vault in the police station for safe custody and it was kept at the police station until it was uplifted (some eight months after) to be brought to Court to be tendered in evidence.

The evidence must go further and state that no one had access to the envelope except the Senior Officer at the police station and that when he, the police officer, uplifted the envelope from the station, it was in the same condition as when he left it at the station for safe keeping. There was no tampering of the envelope. I reiterated my submissions forcefully that there is no connecting evidence before the Court to show that what was sought to be tendered, was the substance that was seized from the defendant and that is the envelope the officer took to the analyst and it is the same envelope he uplifted from the analyst, lodged it at the station and the same envelope is now before the Court. There is good reason for this connecting link to be traced at every stage and it must remain unbroken. I told the Judge that I had no intention of leading any evidence. The prosecution failed to prove its case. I closed my case.

The learned Judge then stated: "Mr. Manraj, the matter has now assumed a different complexion and does not appear to me now, as it first appeared when the prosecution closed its case." The Judge asked the prosecution if he had anything to say in reply. He quite properly stated that there is merit in my submissions and that the hiatus in the evidence is fatal to his case.

The Judge upheld my submissions and dismissed the defendant. No appeal was filed. The Judge then went on to advise the Prosecutor that in cases of this type, where the admissibility of the analyst report or certificate is being relied upon, then every step taken and condition precedent must be strictly proved by the prosecution, before the certificate can become admissible evidence. I felt very satisfied that Justice was done. The prosecution must always prove its case. The defendant was not invited to a picnic. His liberty was at stake. The defendant is innocent until proven guilty by the prosecution. That is the Law. Justice was done.

~~~~~~~
~~~~~~~

I started appearing in some important criminal cases in thc Turks & Caicos Islands in 1979. The Turks & Caicos Islands are a lovely group of Islands – Grand Turk, Providenciales (called "Provo"), South Caicos, North Caicos and a few more Islands that form the Turks & Caicos Islands. Grand Turk is the seat of Government. One travels from Island to Island by small planes. From Grand Turk to Providenciales is about thirty minutes flying time. There is an interesting tourist attraction on Providenciales. That is the Conch Farm. One has much to learn there. Providenciales is the Commercial Centre and most progressive of the Turks & Caicos Islands.

My practice in the Turks & Caicos Islands itself was something fascinating. In Guyana, I had a very efficient and dedicated Law Clerk named LLOYD RODNEY. At one time, he was the managing Clerk of the branch office I established at McKenzie City, about sixty-five miles South of Georgetown going up on the Demerara River on the right bank.

Lloyd was a keen student and when I was leaving Guyana to go to Canada, I was very instrumental in getting Lloyd Rodney admitted to the University of Guyana as a mature student. He then went to the Cave Hill Campus of the University of the West Indies in Barbados in 1980. He completed his LL.B. Degree in 1982. Lloyd then went on to the Norman Manley Law School in Kingston, Jamaica and was called to the Bar in Jamaica in November, 1984. Still moving on, he went back to Guyana and was called to the Guyana Bar in 1985. He went to the Turks and Caicos Islands in 1986. There, he started a very successful practice. He met his Dear wife, Leila, in the Turks and Caicos Islands.

We had lost track of each other, but Lloyd later told me that he was making enquiries as to where I was practising law. He had written to the Bar Council in England to find out if I was practising law in England. His efforts all proved unrewarding. Lloyd subsequently told me how he got in touch with me. One night, while he was in a Grand Turk

Restaurant/Bar, he heard a Guyanese man, in high spirits, saying to everyone that he had come to the Turks & Caicos to celebrate his freedom as he had just had his miserable marriage dissolved in Toronto. Lloyd asked him who his lawyer was and he answered (and I quote from Lloyd), "The best there is - Mr. Shakoor Manraj." Lloyd was elated. This is what he was looking for. He got my card from the man. Lloyd immediately contacted me and there was a new beginning.

Now, Lloyd Rodney is a prominent practising Barrister in the Turks & Caicos Islands with Chambers in Grand Turk and Providenciales. Even now as I write, Lloyd Rodney and his wife and family reside in the Turks & Caicos Islands and I still get important retainers from Lloyd to argue cases in the Appeal Court. On his current Letter Head this is what appears:

RODNEY AND ASSOCIATE ATTORNEYS

Lloyd Rodney, LL.B. CLE
Shakoor Manraj, Q.C., Senior Appeal Court Counsel, Etc.

Eventually, I was called to the Bar of the Turks & Caicos Islands in 1973.

~~~~~~~

In 1996, I was involved in a very long drawn-out case of Theft and False Accounting. These offences are called "hybrid" offences as they can be tried either summarily or on Indictment in the Supreme Court. In those circumstances the two accused persons charged were entitled to and should have been informed by the presiding Magistrate of their right to be tried by jury.

The Magistrate Court Ordinance states: "If both parties appear, the Magistrate shall cause the substance of the charge to be stated to the defendant and ask him whether he is guilty or not guilty. Provided, that the Magistrate shall not proceed to deal summarily with any charge of which the
~~~~~~~

accused person has a right to elect to be committed for trial before the Supreme Court, without first informing the accused of such right and ascertaining that he desires to be tried summarily."

The trial proceeded as a summary trial. It took a total of over three months to get all the evidence in. Expert witnesses were flown in from the U.S.A. and other overseas countries. The cross-examination was searching and in depth. After a long trial, the Prosecutor closed the case. There were no-case submissions that were made by myself and Counsel for the other accused. The submissions were lengthy and weighty and at the end of the submissions, the Magistrate without reflection over-ruled them. A fine was imposed and there was an order made for re-imbursement of the money that was alleged to have been stolen and obtained via falsification of accounts. Both accused persons were of high and respectable standing in the community.

Notice of Appeal was filed on March 19, 1996, at the Registry of the Supreme Court by Counsel for one accused person and by me on March 20, 1996, on behalf of the other accused. Both Appeals were against the respective conviction/sentence imposed by the Magistrate on March14th, 1996. This case was prosecuted at a high cost and considerable outlay of taxpayers' money.

The Appeals were heard by the then Chief Justice of the Turks & Caicos Islands. Both Counsel submitted that the Magistrate had not complied with the mandatory provisions of the Ordinance and all that followed were a nullity. In other words, the accused persons had to be told by the Magistrate of their right to a trial by jury. The Crown Prosecutor in the Appeal Court admitted that the Magistrate was in breach of the law and that the Appellants were not informed by the said Magistrate of their right to be tried by a jury.

The learned Chief Justice had to decide whether the "shall" in the Ordinance was "mandatory" or merely "directory." He considered many of the English authorities on the point. Where the requirement is mandatory, it must be strictly complied with and failure to comply with the mandatory provision invalidates everything that follows.

The Chief Justice finally concluded that the proceedings were a nullity as the giving of that information, that is, the right of an accused person to be tried by a jury, was a condition precedent to the validity of the proceedings that follow. Accordingly, both Appeals were allowed on June 23, 1998, because the Summary proceedings in the case were a nullity by reason of the fact that the learned Magistrate failed to inform the Defendants, or either of them, of their right to be tried by a jury on charges of Theft and False Accounting, which are "hybrid" offences, that is, offences which are triable either way. "It therefore follows," stated the Chief Justice, "that the convictions recorded on the Theft and False Accounting charges are quashed (set aside) and the sentence imposed in respect of each conviction falls away."

These cases were very important. In the first place the outlay of large sums of taxpayer's money could have been avoided had the learned Magistrate observed the law and applied it. Secondly, one does not trifle with the rights preserved for citizens. The requirement in the Magistrate's Court Ordinance is mandatory requiring strict compliance.

Thirdly, the reason is obvious and very important. A defendant, ignorant of his rights, may very well submit to a summary trial and then after conviction, when informed of his rights, appeal to the Supreme Court and contend that he would have opted for trial by jury, if he had been properly given the choice in the first place, by the Magistrate.

Justice is there to protect the strong, the weak, the poor, the rich and all persons who are entitled to her shelter, but were short-circuited in attaining Justice because of the error, mistake or oversight of the functionary entrusted to see that "Justice is done." I felt very happy at the result. No matter what is the financial outlay, Justice must be done.

One thing I feel obliged to state. A reader may feel that over fifty years I have been practising law and the cases that I have been reviewing in this book are not all high-profile cases. That is quite true. The choice of cases and the choice of the matters I have been reviewing and writing on are purely subjective. In the less flamboyant cases, you sometimes see more clearly the refinement of Justice and that the road to Justice could be rough and difficult, but in the final analysis, the true nature of Justice, fair play, good reasoning and maintenance of what is right is attainable, accessible and understandable. *Fiat Justitia semper.*

~~~~~~~

Now come with me to the Cayman Islands and the capital George Town. This is 1997. I was there on holiday, before I started going to Grand Cayman in the practice of my profession. My first legal retainer was in 1992. I was very much into Corporate Law at that time and I went to George Town, Grand Cayman, in my capacity as Legal Adviser to a large Development Complex that had banking business in that island. They treated me royally. I travel very much in my law practice but, in none of my overseas legal retainers was I ever treated and fussed over, like I was on my trip to Grand Cayman in 1992. It is a beautiful Island.

A wife in a divorce petition she filed in Grand Cayman in 1985 came to see me in Miami, Florida. She was the Petitioner. Her husband, the Respondent, came from a wealthy family and he himself had money. He was not very healthy. Fortunately, there were no children of the marriage.

An appointment was made for us to meet after dinner one evening at her hotel where she was staying. My wife Bonita and I went. "Discretion is the better part of valour." This was one of the many guiding principles of my life. I made it a rule of practice in my professional career to make sure that all females must be interviewed in my Law Chambers which was always staffed by competent and loyal secretaries and other office staff. If I am to meet with a
~~~~~~~

female client, as in this case in her hotel, I always made sure that my wife Mrs. Bonita Manraj went with me, or if this was not convenient, one of my female staff went along with me. Sometimes due to flight schedules, these rare meetings do become necessary.

So we met. She was a highly-strung individual and gave the impression that the whole world was her enemy. From my discussions with her regarding the age of her yet incomplete divorce proceedings, I gathered that she was the architect of the protraction of her divorce case due to the fact that once her lawyer could not do what she directed, that lawyer was incompetent and was fired. Some starting point!!! However, I tried to live up to the oath which I took when I was appointed a Queen's Counsel that I will always give the best advice I can, to those in need of it. I accepted the retainer as I was assured that my fees will be taken care of by the Supreme Court authorities. I had a lot of preliminary work to do and this necessitated two trips to Grand Cayman to do some research and get all documents in order for my Court appearance.

Eventually, I got through my preparation. The Divorce Petition was on-going for about twelve years due to all sorts of interlocutory applications and Summons being filed for redress at the slightest adverse ruling affecting the Petitioner. I went to the Court in Grand Cayman and the matter was held in the Judge's Chambers as certain proceedings for maintenance were affected by a multiplicity of Summons and Motions.

The Judge, a very charming man and studious incumbent of the office was acting as Chief Justice at the time. I started off by making my position very clear. I was shocked over the fact that this "bearded" matter was still incomplete after twelve years and I told the learned Judge that I was determined to see that the matter was brought to a stage of finality. It appeared to me that money demanded by the wife was the stumbling block. However, the matter was heard and legal arguments were heard.

The Court after hearing extensive arguments from Counsel on both sides and after sifting through some voluminous documentary evidence, on December 8th, 1997, finally gave judgment for the wife on December 19th, 1997 whereby a substantial sum of money was to be paid by the husband – respondent, who was in possession of the proceeds from the sale of a property situate in the heart of George Town, the capital.

That most hotly contested aspect of the matter was now completed on December 19th, 1997. Although I was invited by many of my professional colleagues and by the learned Judge himself, to stay over and spend a "Christmas in the sun" on an "Island in the Sun", I decided not to do so, as I had some very pressing and important appointments in Miami that called for my personal attention, before the Christmas holidays started.

I very reluctantly declined those kind and warm and tempting invitations to stay back for Christmas in Grand Cayman. At 6.35 p.m. the same day, I boarded my return flight to Miami. In my more then fifty years at the Bar, this was the most protracted matter still on the Court record, that I was ever retained as Counsel to complete. I was very happy to see it concluded without any further legal proceedings, namely an Appeal by either side.

But there is a lighter side to being retained to do cases in what are normally vacation paradises of the Caribbean. The next time someone tells you to "Go to Hell," don't be annoyed and get hot around the collar. Be gracious and say very kindly, "Thank you, my Dear friend; I can leave as soon as you give me the necessary monetary advances to facilitate my "going to Hell". That will surely stump the rude person who told you to go to Hell.

You see there is a place called "Hell" in Grand Cayman. It was once part of a submerged ocean bed, but now it is a tourist attraction. You would be amazed to see the very solid charcoal black razor sharp-edged rocks formations. It could surely be Hell. As one Governor of the

Island remarked when he saw it, "I can safely say that I have certainly seen Hell."

There is a platform built over the spot and tourists get a striking view of this place called "Hell." What is more interesting is this. You can buy post cards of the scene and have them posted at the Hell Post Office with the Hell Post Office post mark. That would more than satisfy your friends of your actual visit to Hell!!! Another tourist attraction is the turtle farm on Grand Cayman. You see whole development of the turtle from the egg right up to the baby turtle, which you are allowed to hold.

You see now, that overseas international law practice has its relaxing moments – but one has to make certain that duty comes first and then the relaxation kicks in.

Chapter 9

The Law Favours No One But The Innocent

You Are Innocent Until Proven Guilty

In the course of writing my memoirs and my encounters and experiences practising at the Bar, I am in duty bound to be up-front, careful and accurate. In this Chapter, I will take you through a proceeding where five very outstanding citizens of Guyana were charged with the serious offence of "seditious libel" – a very high sounding and grave breach of the law, which is most difficult to prove.

However, before I go into the matter fully, I feel constrained to lay the foundation to establish the reasons for what followed. In 1964, serious clashes developed, mainly due to an inter-union dispute for recognition in the sugar industry of British Guiana. Acres of sugar cane cultivation were deliberately destroyed. There were widespread conflicts between the rural Indians and the Africans who were in the majority in Georgetown, the Capital City. The Indians were planning a march to Georgetown. The march took place without any incident. The British Grenadiers were on alert. To prevent clashes and uprisings, England had also sent out members of the "Black Watch" Regiment to help to maintain order in the City and wherever their deployment became necessary. Hardly a day passed without an Indian or some other person supporting the political party of Dr. Jagan (PPP) being stopped and beaten in the streets of Georgetown.

The attacks on the Indians in Georgetown continued with increasing frequency. At this time, I resided on North Street, Georgetown just opposite the St. Rose's Convent at the corner of Church and Camp streets. One night just after dinner, I heard some loud screams coming from the Church Street area. I looked through my window and I saw three Indians being attacked by four Negroes.

It was a free-for-all, but the Indians were getting the worst of it. Passers-by learnt from previous experiences, to keep going and mind their own business. I thought for a moment and then telephoned the Governor, His Excellency, Sir Ralph Grey at Government House. Sir Ralph was an experienced, understanding and pleasant Governor and he and I had a very good relationship. In addition to being the Governor of Guyana, he was also a Barrister-at-Law. I got through to Sir Ralph and told him what was taking place just opposite my house. He was very concerned and told me that the "Black Watch" soldiers, who were sent out from England to assist, will be on the scene immediately.

They did arrive and serious injuries and perhaps murder were averted. I think some arrests were made by Police who arrived on the scene as well. En passant, I must mention that Lady Grey and my wife, Gladys, were known to each other and they got along well. In early 1965, my wife and I were guests at a "Cocktail reception" at Government House when Gladys started to feel very faint. She was pregnant with our fourth child. Lady Grey was very kind and assisted her, while I got our car and took her home. Later that same year, my second daughter, Elizabeth Sorayah was born. She now lives on Victoria Island, British Columbia, Canada, with her husband Ken and their two daughters.

The attacks in the city resulted in reprisals in the rural areas, especially on the sugar estates and so things were getting out of control. Things became very hostile, so much so that the riot squad had to be brought out to conduct the majority Indian legislators to and from the Parliament Building. This was the first major outbreak of racial violence in the city where Africans were attacking Indians. The early months of 1964 were a nightmare.

Things had reached such a dangerous situation that I thought the wisest thing to do was to send my English born wife (she died in 1976) and our three children at that time, Michael, Anne and Andrew, to England until things simmered down. I thought that alone, I could easier ride out this storm and serious upheaval and uncertain peace that were taking place in Guyana. It was a difficult time for Guyana.

The entire transition by Guyana from a former Colonial territory to an independent Guyana was marked by widespread fires in the city, riots, strikes and violence, all aimed at destabilizing the progress made by the Jagan Government to create an Independent Guyana. In 1961, the heart of the Commercial Centre of Georgetown was engulfed by an uncontrollable fire that was deliberately set.

Bookers Department Store, Bookers Supermarket, Fogartys, Sandbach Parker and J. P. Santos, to name a few large businesses, were completely consumed by the fire. The whole of Georgetown seemed to be ablaze. I personally had to evacuate my law office at 15 – 16 Croal Street near the Law Courts, because I felt that at any moment the building in which my office was, would soon be destroyed by the raging fire. I was fortunate to survive the conflagration (at least so I thought) and moved back into my office only to move once more when the fire took a turn again.

This time, I stayed away until the burning flames had completely subsided and the smoke had cleared. Life in Guyana during that time was no bed of roses – but I continued with my law practice. When things returned to some degree of normalcy, towards the end of 1964, my wife Gladys and our three children returned to Guyana. The two elder children, Michael and Anne, had started out school in West Worthing on the South Coast of England and they enjoyed it. They were all away for about nine months. My young son, Andrew, came back from England full of all the English colloquialisms to which he was exposed while in England. To this day, he still calls his hat his "titfa."

In March 1964, a New Indian Movement called the "Guyana All Indian League" (GAIL) was formed in Georgetown. A Press release of March 15, 1964 stated:

> *"This Organization was a non-political organization with its main object being to stimulate the Indo-Guyanese social and cultural life on a wide basis, so that a full and effective contribution could be made to the advancement of the country as a whole. It was also part of their mandate to restore racial-unity and to make fruitful representations on matters peculiar to the East Indian community of Guyana. The league recruited membership from among all Indians – Hindus, Muslims and Christians and entertained the idea of opening branch-offices all over Guyana. It was hoped that this movement would help immensely in developing an inter-racial consensus.*
>
> *The League appointed a Steering Committee comprising of Dr. Balwant Singh, Senior Government Pathologist and Bacteriologist as Chairman. This Steering Committee also included Mr. Doodnauth Hetram, M.A. LL.B. B.C.L. Barrister-at-Law, Principal of Queen's College, Georgetown and Lecturer in Classics at the University of Guyana and prominent City Practitioner, Shakoor Manraj, B.A. (Hons.) LL.B. (Hons.), Barrister-at-Law as Vice-Chairman of the League, Mr. Gool Khan, B.Sc. Chief Technologist at the Medical Laboratory as Secretary and Mr. Frederick Rampersaud, Barrister-at-Law, as the Treasurer. The Committee Members were also drawn from prestigious members of the East Indian Community and included Mr. C. Changur, Mr. Sam Sahoy, Barrister-at-Law, Dr. Jairam Bissessar, reputable medical practitioner and an experienced gynaecologist and obstetrician, Mr. M. M. Beram Singh, retired Civil Servant and trained first class*

teacher, Mrs. Maharanee Persaud, B.Sc., Sociologist and Hajee Ramjohn, a recognized Muslim social worker."

I cited this release to show that the Guyana All Indian League was made up of responsible, respectable and competent Indians to shoulder the responsibilities of the wide-ranging endeavours of the League. The attacks on Indians continued not only in Georgetown but also in the country areas where many hard-working Indians lived. The situation was becoming intolerable and seemed to be out of control... GAIL unanimously decided to issue a pamphlet headed "ATTENTION INDIANS" advising them "to go about their business without fear. Negroes beware! Stop your hooliganism and thuggery now. Citizens all show your disapproval before it is too late. This is a warning."

These pamphlets were printed by Mr. Jankie Persaud and were distributed throughout the city of Georgetown. Mr. Persaud was the proprietor of the Hindu Printery on Vlissengen Road on the East side of Georgetown. In the "rush and urgent" job that he took on, he forgot to put the name of the printer on the pamphlets. The Police after doing their checks with the Chief Security Officer eventually laid charges against Jankie Persaud.

The Police acted with admirable haste, which surprised everyone. On May 29, 1964 Dr. Balwant Singh, City Barrister Shakoor Manraj, Jankie Persaud, Gool Khan and Doodnauth Hetram of Queen's College, were charged by way of summons for three summary offences under the Newspaper Ordinance and one Indictable Offence under the Emergency Power Regulations of 1964.

Mr. Persaud was charged with printing a paper without the name of the printer. Mr. Gool Khan and I were summoned for dispersing a paper without having thereon the name of the printer. Dr. Balwant Singh and Mr. Hetram were charged with assisting to disperse a paper without the name of the printer. Then all five were charged that they, on

Tuesday, May 26th, 1964 at Georgetown, conspired together to publish a seditious writing, to wit, a pamphlet headed "Attention Indians" contrary to Regulation 18 (3) of the Emergency Power Regulations, 1964.

That was it. The full force of the law was invoked. It must be said at this early stage, that if any careful thought was given to the facts that the police were relying on to institute the charges, then any analytical mind, free-thinking individual, void of any political motivations, would have seen that the charges, save for the printing of the pamphlet without the printer's name and address, had no merit and could not stand up in a Court of law. The results eventually proved that. All the cases were fixed for hearing on June 24, 1964.

One interesting spin-off from the charges resulted in Doodnauth Hetram being admitted to practise law. He was placed on leave after the charges were laid. He had passed his Bar Final Examinations in 1962 but never proceeded to be "Called to the Bar" because of his teaching appointments. I decided to present his Petition for "Call to the Bar" so he can keep himself occupied by practising from my Chambers. His petition for admission to practise was heard before Mr. Justice Harry Bollers. My Dear Readers, you will recall he was the acting trial Judge in the Murder Appeal, which I argued before the Privy Council.

Mr. Hetram had such a distinguished academic career, that in keeping with the tradition of informing the Court of the academic background of the Petitioner, it took me fully forty-five minutes to inform the Court of his academic brilliance and his other qualifications that entitled him to be called to the Bar. The Judge, after listening to my presentation of Mr. Hetram's Petition stated that he hoped that Mr. Hetram's scholastic career would assist in raising the standard of the Bar. The Judge continued: "We need men like yourself to assist in guiding the younger practitioners." Hetram joined my Chambers and practised for a while before he resumed his duties at Queen's College.

On June 24, 1964 the preliminary enquiry into the Conspiracy charge where the five of us were accused of conspiring to publish a seditious writing on the pamphlets and distributing them on May 26, came up before City Magistrate, Eddie Gunraj.

There was an array of legal minds that appeared for us – all colleagues at the Bar. Every minute more and more lawyers were coming forward offering their services. The charges were so much without merit. Mr. B. O. Adams, Q.C. a brilliant lawyer and a (Queen's Counsel like myself) appeared for Mr. Gool Khan, Dr. Singh and myself. His instructing Solicitor was Mr. Laurie T. Persaud. Mr. Adams had as junior Counsel, Mr. W. R. Adams and Mr. P. Roopchand, (whose petition for Call to the Bar to practise his profession was presented by me in 1961 before the Chief Justice). Mr. J. O. F. Haynes, Q.C. (one of the ablest lawyers in the entire Caribbean region) instructed by Solicitor Mr. Dabi Dial (my high-school classmate) associated with Mr. J. R. Hope and Mr. Zaman Ali (I also presented his Petition for his Call to the Bar), all appeared for Doodnauth Hetram and Jankie Persaud.

When the case was called, Mr. Doodnauth Singh (I also presented his Petition for Call to the Bar) informed the Court that he was appearing for the Prosecution and addressing the Magistrate he said: "I would make an application that the particulars of the offence as described in the Information be amended by the addition of the following words after -- **Attention Indians**: "Go about your business without fear. Negroes beware! Stop your hooliganism and thuggery now before it is too late. This is a warning."

The Court enquired if the amendment was being made to include all the words of the whole pamphlet. Mr. Singh replied "Yes." Defence Counsel did not object to the amendment, which really was to add words to complete the entire statement in the pamphlet. The learned Magistrate granted the amendment.

After Magistrate Gunraj had granted the amendment, Queen's Counsel, Mr. B. O. Adams for Mr. Khan, Mr. Manraj and Dr. Singh, in a preliminary objection, argued that the accused were charged with a conspiracy to publish a seditious writing contrary to Regulation 18 (3) of the Emergency Regulations of 1964. Mr. Adams went on to submit that the prosecution would have to establish a number of ingredients as the pamphlet did not show a seditious writing or any offence under the particular section or any offence at all.

Mr. Adams invited the Court to look at the pamphlet and then cited legal authorities relating to the contents of the pamphlet. "Attention Indians," Mr. Adams submitted, seemed merely some advice for them to go about their business without fear. The pamphlet, he continued, had to be considered in relation to the circumstances as they exist in the country and all it said was, *"Negroes stop your hooliganism and thuggery."*

Continuing, B. O. Adams, Q.C. submitted that the words: "Citizens show your disapproval before it is too late," meant that citizens should pay heed to the existing serious situation. The words are not a threat, but merely intended to put citizens on their guard. The pamphlet seeks to show that the things that were being done were not right. In other words, "hooliganism" is not right in accordance with the law. Mr. Adams then gave the Court a definition of the word "<u>sedition</u>" – "agitation against the authority of a state; conduct or speech tending to rebellion or breach of public order." Mr. Adams submitted that the only heading under which this charge could be brought was to incite ill will between different classes of the sovereign's subjects. In other words, he pointed out, it did not amount to sedition. The pamphlet was really an attempt to cease violence and ill will.

It was submitted that what was said on the pamphlet amounted to be only a warning and the words conveying the warning in the pamphlet meant to "take heed." This was a warning and a warning is not a threat. Mr. Adams submitted that all the words meant was, "Be on your guard." That meant nothing sinister. If the Court was to view the pamphlet either according to the individual words or accumulatively as a whole, then, Mr. Adams submitted, the pamphlet was innocuous and was something to be commended. "On the plain English of the pamphlet," Mr. Adams concluded, "I am asking the Court to uphold the objection and discharge the five accused."

Queen's Counsel, J. O. F. Haynes for Mr. Hetram and Mr. Jankie Persaud, in supporting the submissions made by Mr. B. O. Adams, Q.C. said that the printing of a pamphlet of the kind was not a seditious enterprise within the meaning of Regulation 18 (3) of the Emergency Regulations of 1964. The matter was adjourned to Friday, July 10, 1964.

On the morning of July 10, 1964, the Police withdrew the charges against Dr. Balwant Singh, Doodnauth Hetram, Gool Khan and City Barrister, Shakoor Manraj. Superintendent of Police, Randolph Lambert, appeared on behalf of the prosecution. The Police, however, proceeded against Mr. Jankie Persaud. He pleaded guilty, as it was a fact that he had omitted to put the printer's name and address on the pamphlets.

He was not left alone. Mr. B. O. Adams, Q.C., Mr. J. O. F. Haynes, Q.C., Mr. W. R. Adams and Mr. Zaman Ali instructed by Solicitor, L. T. Persaud appeared for Jankie Persaud. My colleagues and I provided a powerful legal team for Mr. Persaud. Mr. B. O. Adams pointed out to the Court that the defendant, Mr. Jankie Persaud, readily admitted his guilt. It was the first time he had made such a mistake in not printing the name and address of the printer and he was sorry for what he had done. It was a real oversight and not a deliberate breach of the law. The Magistrate fined Mr. Persaud $25.00. That fine was immediately paid by the members of GAIL.

There was some humour in Court at the end of this unusual and exciting trial – exciting to the whole community having regard to the men who were charged. Mr. B. O. Adams, in lighter vein, addressed the Court stating that the Magistrate and the lawyers involved are all regular invitees to weddings, cocktail parties and functions at Government House and after a careful study of the relevant Ordinance, wondered whether many of the hosts who sent out printed invitations for the social events mentioned above, would not be liable to pay $25.00 for each invitation that they had sent out to guests. It all ended in a pleasant mood – the Magistrate himself observing that there are probably many printers who were not aware of their responsibility to put their names on bills and pamphlets to disclose the person responsible for the printing of them.

Let me just add this in lighter vein. I not only studied law and practised the law reaching the top of my profession as a Q.C., but, I have had exposure as a defendant and felt very happy to see how being on the other side feels. It made me feel that I have now been right around the circle, remember, I was in Canada, a Prosecutor. It is good to see all sides and angles of the conundrum. Justice is there for everyone. It is one thing to lay charges indiscriminately, but another thing to prove them.

When Criminal Defence Counsel has completed hundreds of criminal trials plus three hundred and twenty nine murder trials, he has to have the law in his veins. My colleagues of the GUYANA ALL INDIAN LEAGUE had entrusted to me the responsibility of putting together a first-class defence team of the best lawyers available. That I did. You have seen the array of lawyers I assembled.

There is a very old and trite adage that states "he who is his own lawyer, has a fool for a client." It is always the correct thing to disengage yourself from your legal problems. You see it subjectively. Let some one else trained in the law who has gained experience and competence, undertake to give you legal advice and conduct of your legal problems. He sees it objectively and with disengaged and dispassionate acumen.

Chapter 10

The Three-Man International Commission of Jurists in 1965

In the course of my extensive career, I have appeared in every type of legal procedure, enquiry and litigation that required the services, skill and in-put of experienced Counsel. That explains my appearances in Courts, Tribunals, Arbitrations, Enquiries, Commissions and Public Hearings investigating and probing the status and well-being of citizens and their employment opportunities.

Besides these activities, I also taught Law at University Level. I lectured on the law of evidence, the guidelines to successful cross-examination and the "hands-on" courses relating to "no-case submissions" and most important of all, addressing the jury. I also taught English Literature at High School and University Levels covering the period from the Norman Conquest to the decline of NEO-CLASSICISM, right on through to the break of Victorianism in the early 20th Century leading to the introduction of the NEW PROSE and DRAMA ERA. This latter discipline was my "major" study in my first Degree – my B.A. (Hons.) in English Language and English Literature.

The International Commission of Jurists came to British Guiana as a result of representations made to that Organization. The three-man Commission came to investigate the imbalance in the social and economic conditions and more especially, the imbalance in the employment opportunities available to Indo-Guyanese and Afro-Guyanese of the then British Guiana. I had in my presentation, to apprise the members of the Commission and outline to them in chronological detail, the history and development of the six races that comprised British Guiana's cosmopolitan population. In particular, my mandate was to deal in a specific manner with the Indo-Guyanese and the Afro-Guyanese, the two predominant races of the six races in British Guiana.

The East Indians (Indo-Guyanese) are descended from the East Indian immigrants who came from that vast sub-continent of India in 1838. The other five races are the Negroes (Afro-Guyanese) who are the descendants of the Africans who were brought from Africa, the Chinese, the Portuguese, the Europeans and the Amerindians, known as the indigenous people of British Guiana. This last group of people are called "BUCKS" or "ABORIGINESE." Not surprisingly, over the years, with this population comprised of six different races, a new breed of Guyanese, referred to as "MIXED" race, added to the interesting life that made British Guiana the "melting pot" of the world.

I submitted that the position occupied by each race in British Guiana had its origin in Guiana's historical and economic development. The position of the European (mostly from the mother country, the United Kingdom) in the Government services was as interesting a study as that of the Negro in the British Guiana Police Force and the nurses and employees in the Nursing profession of British Guiana. In order to present a comprehensive and historical picture, I went on to trace the development of the two dominant races, the Indo-Guyanese and the Afro-Guyanese in the country. At that time, the East Indians comprised 51% of the entire population.

The Afro-Guyanese "had the first break." The Negro adopted the way of life that led to a literary education. The role of the Christian Missionaries who came out to British Guiana was instrumental in moulding a more literary outlook of the Negroes resulting in their trek away from the plantations and their eventual conversion to Christianity. After the abolition of Negro slavery, they moved away from the plantations. They were not as plantation and agriculturally oriented in their outlook as their Asian Brothers and Sisters and there can be no doubt that educationally and economically, they were one generation ahead of the East Indians. It was not surprising therefore, that in time the Negroes found no difficulty in gaining entry into the Civil Service, the teaching profession and other spheres of activity where educational requirements were a prerequisite.

On the other hand, the East Indians who came to British Guiana as indentured labourers had to face a pattern of life, which, save for agriculture, was completely foreign to theirs. They brought with them the incidence of the caste system in the case of the Hindus and with the Muslims, the rigidity of their religious background.

When the indentureship of the East Indian immigrants ended, they did not have the necessary and basic liberal education to be assimilated into the various opportunities then available, that is to say, employment in the Police Force, the Guiana Civil Service, the teaching profession, the nursing profession and of course the legal, medical, dental, engineering and other professions. Not being able to find employment in those fields of endeavour, the East Indians took to agriculture, not only as a means of self-employment, but also as a source of more lucrative development. It is only by an examination and complete appreciation of these facts, that the respective social and economic development of the Indians and the Negroes in British Guiana can be understood.

I continued the presentation of my submissions and went on to focus the attention of the Commission on the commitment of the East Indians who worked hard and long hours and lived frugally, thereby acquiring some measure of economic competence and stability. The thrifty East Indians used part of the products from their farms for their home use and marketed the rest and coupled with the family labour force, profited substantially from the family input on the farms – rice cultivation and agricultural products cultivation.

The frugal Indian not exposed to the nightlife and other social activities accepted by the Negroes, used his money to buy land and small estates and then established the co-operative farm and family unit, centred on his acquired land. The old adage that "land is power" was so relevant. Land is the basis of economic power and strength. The East Indian built his home, with the family help available, on the land and lived with his family from off the land and on the land.

At all times, I focused my attention on the fact that the International Commission of Jurists had come to British Guiana to study and understand the development of the position of these two predominant races in the country and to study the work-force imbalance in the employment of East Indians in the basic areas of employment. These facts had to be set out with historical clarity. It was cheaper for the East Indian to live the pattern of life explained above, than it was for his Negro counterpart. The resultant feature of this early and pragmatic life-style and the basic strength of the family unit was that when the question of education arose, the East Indians who had lived a frugal life, had the money to pay for primary, secondary and advanced education.

Once that forward movement gained momentum, there was no stopping the East Indians. Their children had the advantage of a good local-based primary education, the benefit of a developing secondary education and from there went on to become doctors, lawyers, dentists, engineers, teachers and civil servants and at last they began to identify themselves with the activities and development of British Guiana.

But it took the East Indians three generations to be in a position where they could hold their own against all comers, educationally, economically, socially and culturally. It is a clear historical fact that the East Indian had made gradual and unabated progress, while the Negro, "who had the first jump" rested on his laurels. It is apparent that the development of the Indians, in contrast to the almost static position of the Negro, could be attributed to the differences in the life-styles, customs and up-bringing of these two predominant races in British Guiana.

I went on in my presentation of my arguments before the Commission to advert their attention to the fact that the "imbalance" in employment opportunities had its roots in the different historical routes travelled by the two basic races in British Guiana. What was responsible for one particular race being predominantly employed in a particular occupation? There was definitely an imbalance in the distribution of the races in the various fields of employment.

I then proceeded to illustrate to the Commission the incidence of certain requirements in certain areas of employment, which precluded certain individuals in the Guyanese racial mix from securing employment in those particular areas of endeavour. The Police Force had certain regulations with respect to "height" for prospective entrants into the Force. This clearly operated against the indigenous Amerindians members and Chinese members of the population. They are by nature a short people with a smaller body frame than the Afro-Guyanese or Indo-Guyanese. This prevented the Amerindians ("Bucks") and the similarly built Chinese from getting into the Police Force. The East Indians at first were not interested in going into the Police Force and that is why the British Guiana Police Force was predominantly made up of Afro-Guyanese.

Originally, the same thing happened in the teaching and the nursing professions. Almost all of the nurses in the early days of the Nursing Profession were female Afro-Guyanese. These facts clearly indicated that there was a very serious "imbalance" in the distribution of the races in some important areas of employment. The Commission was invited to investigate these facts and make the necessary and relevant recommendations that the offending regulations, which prevented the Amerindian and the Chinese Guyanese from gaining entry into the Police Force, be speedily removed.

I am happy to state that steps were eventually taken to remove the "offending height requirements" for entry into the Police Force. It took some time for this reform to show its effect on the racial integration of the Police Force. I was pleased to see young Amerindian and Chinese police recruits on the streets of Georgetown after the regulations were revised. This was the answer to the two questions:

(A) What was responsible for one particular race being in predominance in a particular field of employment?

(B) Was there an "imbalance" in the distribution of the races in the various sectors of employment in the then British Guiana?

In the beginning, there was a literary test to get into the Nursing profession. Added to this fact was the disinclination of the East Indians, due to their cultural background, to send their daughters to work as nurses, especially where night shifts were part of the work schedule. That also changed as Guiana progressed.

Today, the races are all well represented in all the fields of employment. The two main Banks of Guyana in the early days showed an open discriminatory attitude in the hiring of Bank employees. Only European, Chinese and Portuguese girls were employed in the two Banks. You never saw a dark-skinned person working in the two main Banks that were in operation in Georgetown in the early days before the "Guyana Industrial and Economic Revolution" which came about through political pressure from the political parties that highlighted these practices in their political manifestoes.

Today, due to the exodus from Guyana of most Chinese, Portuguese and Europeans, all the Banks have Bank-staff drawn from the available Indo-Guyanese, Afro-Guyanese and Amerindian members of the population.

In winding up my arguments before the Commission, I pointed out that "direction of labour" is a very dangerous concept. There must be complete freedom of choice when it comes to one's choice of employment. I told the

Commission that in theory, all occupations are open to all Guyanese and once the conditions were satisfied, one can gain employment. However, the field had to be levelled having regard to the physical stature of some Guyanese. But whatever reforms resulted in the removal of irregular and unfair practices, it still left the cancer of "imbalance" brought about by political nepotism, political patronage and disguised discrimination.

The Republic of Guyana is today a different place. Guyanese are in control of their own destiny. One has to remember that a "people get the Government they deserve." In a Democracy, the people have a vital role to play in the Government they want and changes demanded by the Electorate result in achieving the goals, the people feel is best for them.

At the conclusion of my submissions and representations, I really felt a glow of complete satisfaction. Each member of the Commission in a flow of ornate language thanked me for my useful and in-depth arguments and presentation, which each member emphatically stated will help them immensely in formulating their report. I thanked them for their gracious and kind comments.

My appearances and arguments before the International Commission of Jurists were given full coverage over the broadcasting stations and an avid press. The press Reporters excelled in their publications reporting fully, comprehensively and accurately what I actually submitted to the Members of the Commission. They were also complimented by the Members of the Commission.

My appearances before the International Commission of Jurists had its far-reaching results in my further service to Guyana. I was appointed the Chairman of the Quarry Workers Commission of Enquiry and several other Commissions of Enquiry set up to inquire into the Social and Economic conditions of the workers of Guyana. In the last one I presided over, was as Chairman of the Restaurant Workers, Conditions of Work and Wages Inquiry. It proved to be very advantageous to the entire restaurant industry in Guyana as wages and working conditions were reviewed.

Shortly after my appearances before the International Commission of Jurists, I was retained by the majority shareholders in a large successful company, which was seeking to merge with another successful company conducting similar business. The shareholders were sceptical about this move and wanted to know much more than what was actually published about these new proposed merger proceedings in Guyana. I was retained to advise and guide them through the merger. In the first place, I had to study the "Aims and Objects" Statements of the Company and having satisfied myself that the merger was not *ultra vires* the powers as set out in the Memorandum and the Articles of Association, I advised that the merger was legal and very beneficial to the shareholders.

At that time, mergers were in their infancy and quite novel in Guyana. However, today, mergers are commonplace in the commercial world. Little did I realize then, that in the very near future, mergers were to become "the going thing" and they now dominate the local and international commercial environment. Mega-mergers are now frequent occurrences. It is difficult to keep abreast of the terms and conditions of the mega-mergers that are currently in place. Mergers have served business well and one studies with interest, the reorganization that takes place once the merger is established. The human factor is important and companies that merge try very hard to avoid violent "shake-ups" involving old, loyal and experienced employees.

Chapter 11

It Wasn't Law All the Time

There Were Extra-Legal Activities Punctuated By Hilarity

After 1966, there were many changes in the political, social and economic climate of Guyana. As an Independent State within the Commonwealth, Guyana had to send her own Diplomats to England and other Commonwealth Countries as well as to other sovereign nations around the world. Mr. L. F. S. Burnham, himself a Queen's Counsel and a distinguished Barrister-at-Law, was the then Prime Minister.

He recruited capable Guyanese to represent Guyana abroad. One of the first appointments was that of Lionel Luckhoo, Queen's Counsel, as High Commissioner to London, England. Lionel Luckhoo was knighted by Her Majesty the Queen and became Sir Lionel Luckhoo, Q.C. A word about the brilliant Luckhoo family: an uncle, the late Mr. J. A. Luckhoo, at that time K.C. (King's Counsel as the reigning Monarch was a King) was an eminent Criminal Defence Counsel. He eventually became a Judge of the High Court and acted as Chief Justice on several occasions. He had two sons, both Barristers, J. A. Luckhoo (Junior) and Ronald Luckhoo. The Junior J. A. Luckhoo eventually became Chief Justice of Guyana and was knighted and became Sir Joseph Luckhoo, C.J. and his brother Ronald, (we practised law together on the East Coast Circuit) eventually was appointed a Judge of the Court of Appeal of Guyana. That is a short background sketch of that branch of the Luckhoo dynasty.

The brother of the Senior J. A. Luckhoo was E. A. Luckhoo, also a lawyer. He qualified as a Solicitor in 1899, the first East Indian Solicitor in Guyana. His brother Joseph Alexander Luckhoo (the Senior J. A. Luckhoo) went to England and passed the Bar Final Examination in 1912, thus becoming the first East Indian Barrister-at-Law in Guyana. Edward Alfred Luckhoo, the Solicitor, had three very famous sons – Edward Victor, Lionel Alfred and Claude Lloyd Luckhoo.

These three sons were three "giants" at the Bar. They all excelled in the profession. Professionally and socially, I was very close to them, especially Sir Lionel Luckhoo. When I started practising my profession in Guyana, I worked very hard and long hours. I caught the eye and attention of Lionel Luckhoo who became a Queen's Counsel many years before I was appointed a Queen's Counsel and he assigned many cases to me to conduct. Lionel, "LIO" as he was called, was a fine orator, was possessed of a good sense of humour, logic, reasoning and above all, he was an eminent and brilliant lawyer as were his brothers, Edward Victor (called EV) and Lloyd, who was the leading *turfite* in Guyana. Lloyd loved the sport of horseracing. Edward Victor Luckhoo was knighted and became Sir Edward Victor Luckhoo. He eventually became Chancellor of the Judiciary. He acted as Governor-General of Guyana after the sudden death in London of Sir David Rose, until Guyana became a Republic on February 23, 1970. It was in this capacity that Sir Edward signed my Letters Patent issuing out of Guyana House informing me of my appointment as Queen's Counsel on December 31, 1969.

Sir Lionel Luckhoo was awarded the honour of K.C.M.G. and was appointed Guyana's High Commissioner to the U.K. One of Lloyd Luckhoo's sons, Eddie, practises law in Guyana. Lloyd took up residence on the Island of Antigua in the Caribbean. All three of the Luckhoo brothers have passed away. I want to record the professional ties between Sir Lionel and myself.

Professional Ties with Sir Lionel Luckhoo

At this time in my career, more and more, I appeared in cases with Sir Lionel, who was mentioned in the Guinness Book of Records as the *"most winning lawyer"* in the world. He appeared successfully in over ***four hundred*** murder trials. Very early in our professional relationship, Lionel mentioned to me that I had all the qualities and potential of being appointed a Queen's Counsel.

It is a tradition of the English Bar, that junior Barristers use a blue bag in which to put their robes and wigs when travelling or going to Court. Queen's Counsel, on the other hand, are privileged to have a red bag. The tradition goes further that when a Queen's Counsel carefully estimates the degree of competence and experience of a Junior Counsel who is eligible for the appointment of *"Silk"* (Q.C.), because of the silk robes he wears when he becomes a Q.C. (called *"taking silk"*), the senior Queen's Counsel gives his red bag to that Junior Counsel.

I had the great honour and privilege of appearing with, and at times for, Sir Lionel Luckhoo, Q.C. on many occasions. In 1966, when he left to go to London as Guyana's High Commissioner, he gave to me his "Red Bag." When in London, we kept in touch with each other and whenever he came to Guyana, we saw each other. I was appointed a Queen's Counsel on December 31, 1969. Even today, I still have Sir Lionel Luckhoo's Red Bag, which is elegantly inscribed, "From LAL To ASM" in white silk needlework. Whenever I have to travel to practice away from my office location, I always use that Red Bag. It is sturdy and stands up to constant use. I shall always remember the late Sir Lionel Luckhoo, Q.C. He was a terrific and legendary Criminal Defence Attorney.

Although all three brothers have passed away, I shall always cherish the deep professional ties I had with these three legal luminaries and will never forget the many happy social events that we had the pleasure of attending. It was always a very special event whenever we met at Lloyd's son's (Eddie's) home in Georgetown for the celebration of some event. It was so much fun, that on one occasion, when the Reverend Gentleman was called upon to say a prayer for Eddie on his birthday, he started to pray for Edward Victor, Eddie's uncle and we had to put him right by way of gentle undertones, that it was Eddie's birthday and not EV's birthday.

In 1966, Sir Lionel Luckhoo was appointed Guyana's High Commissioner to London. In June of 1966 the Guyana Bar Association, of which I was an active member, held a cocktail reception at Queen's College to honour Sir Lionel. Glowing tributes were paid to Sir Lionel and fellow Queen's Counsel, J. O. F. Haynes, was most eloquent in outlining Sir Lionel's sterling contribution to Guyana. In the course of the evening, Sir Lionel addressed the lawyers present. It was an enjoyable evening. I mentioned earlier that Sir Lionel was possessed of a fine sense of humour.

Once, Sir Lionel told us of a passenger ship that encountered difficulties not far from shore. The Captain of the ship hurriedly called an Emergency Meeting of all the crew and passengers. The Captain said that the only way the ship can be saved is for it to be secured by towline to the shore. He called on volunteers to swim with the towline to shore and secure the ship.

After repeated calls for volunteers, three passengers came forward – a doctor, a priest and a lawyer. Everybody applauded. The towline was tied around the waist of the doctor and after prayers, he was thrown overboard. He swan valiantly for a while, but then sharks came and attacked him and he vanished. The priest said a prayer. A towline was tied around his waist and he was tossed overboard. A similar fate befell the valiant priest. The feisty lawyer stopped and said, "Give me a towline." He tied it tightly around his waist and plunged overboard.

Everyone stood in awe. The lawyer started to swim towards the shore and surely, the sharks came to him, but, this time, instead of attacking the lawyer in the now bloody water, the sharks started to swim along with him, with the towline around his waist. Everyone kept asking what is happening. An old retired lawyer standing on the deck with the passengers said, "Nothing surprising, just plain professional courtesy." You got it. Sir Lionel had everyone doubling up with laughter. The evening continued.

Then, just when Sir Lionel was coming to the end of his witty and enjoyable address, he said, "I want to tell a story for the benefit of our younger brethren." A rather young lawyer defending his first murder case, decided to do something very unprofessional. He could not bear the thought of a conviction of his client for murder and the consequence of the death sentence. He got around bribing a man on the Jury to stand firm and see that a verdict of manslaughter is returned. The case was committed to the Jury. They took a very long time to deliberate and finally arrived at a verdict.

The Jury returned to Court and delivered a verdict of *not guilty* of murder but *guilty* of manslaughter. The lawyer was elated. When the Jurors left the Court, the lawyer ran to the Juror and said, "My friend, thank you, did you have any difficulty?"

"Difficulty?" said the Juror. "I had a hell of a job. The other eleven Jurors wanted to acquit your client." This one brought the house down. That was Sir Lionel Luckhoo, Q.C. He came. He practised. He conquered. He is missed.

Stump the Panel

The Dominoes Club of the East Bank of Demerara wanted two new trophies for inter-clubs competition of the region. The executives of the Demerara Dominoes Association asked the then Mayor of Georgetown, Mayor L. F. S. Burnham, to donate one of the trophies. He did. They then came to me and made a similar request. I also complied with their request. The trophies were called the "Burnham Trophy" and the "Manraj Trophy." It was a pleasure.

The presentation ceremony of the trophies took place at the Bagotstown Village Council Hall before a large gathering including the President of the Demerara Dominoes Association. Mr. Burnham and I addressed the gathering. The competitions were run on a "knock-out" basis and were supervised by the Demerara Dominoes Association. Mr. Burnham and I addressed the appreciative audience and saw the trophies handed over to the proper authorities for safekeeping.

As I stated in my opening words of this Chapter, "It wasn't Law all the time." Despite my very busy and demanding practise, which took up most of my waking hours, I was forced to find time for other non-professional activities. Since my student days, I was assiduously connected with radio and broadcasting. I delivered commentaries over the radio; I hosted the Saturday Night Radio Show "Off the Record." In this programme, I played the records I liked or the music, which I identified with places I visited, with reasons for my selections. This was a one-hour programme on the leading Radio Station, "Radio Demerara" in Guyana.

I was a member of the Panel on the "Stump the Panel" programme heard every Tuesday night on "Radio Demerara" from 7.25 p.m. Other members of the panel were Bill Carr of the University of Guyana, Cicely Robinson and Elinor DaSilva. The four of us provided a lot of fun and the programme was very highly rated.

After some time on the air, I became the Moderator of the programme. However, by far the most popular programme I had the pleasure of airing over "Radio Demerara" was the morning programme called "Analysis." Here, I selected some contemporary and controversial political, economic, social or religious topic and analysed the dialectics of the propositions and issues and went on the air with my analysis of my views and conclusions.

This was by far the most popular radio programme in which I was involved. Politicians sought my advice on my analysed views and many times adopted my arguments. On one occasion when my colleague, Mr. Burnham (he was called "Odo" by all his closest friends and colleagues) was dealing with the Middle-East Oil Crisis, he asked me to see him at the Residence to discuss my conclusions. At Queen's College, Bishop's High School, many of the other secondary schools and even in the lower schools, students were directed to listen to my "Analysis" Programmes heard at 7:25 a.m. on Friday mornings and then write their views on what I said. I was really pleased and thrilled doing this programme. I prepared my script as if I were preparing an address for a very highly critical jury. In time, I offered gifts of fountain pens to the students who really submitted the best essays of my "Analysis."

Add to this the social occasions where I was asked to be present – Weddings, Birthday Parties, 25th and 50th Wedding Anniversaries. At these occasions, you can be certain that I will be called upon to "say something." Other Radio programmes included interviews and panel discussions. It was a full life then and now.

Several times, I am asked by people how did I find the time to do what I did – including three hundred and twenty-nine murder trials and my appearance before the Privy Council of England. Truth to tell, I cannot answer that question except by offering two motivating aspects of my life – I love what I do and do it with gusto and I have always lived on four hours of sleep Monday through Saturday. Sundays (when free from commitments) were my "catch up" days when I enjoyed the luxury of six to seven hours of sleep.

JOE CHIN'S TRAVEL SERVICE PRESENTS STUMP-THE-PANEL

This is the panel that is seldom stumped on the "STUMP THE PANEL" programme heard every Tuesday night 7.25 over Radio Demerara. Members are (from LEFT): Bill Carr, Cicely Robinson, Elinor DaSilva and Shakoor Manraj.
(As it appeared in the Guyana Graphic, March 27, 1969)

Informal talk by Sir Lionel *High Commissioner to London, Sir Lionel Luckhoo on Tuesday night gave an informal talk to members of the Guyana Bar Association at Queen's College. A glowing tribute was paid to Sir Lionel by fellow Queen's Counsel, J. O. F. Haynes for his sterling contribution to the country. Members of the Association later entertained Sir Lionel at a cocktail party. Picture shows the audience enjoying a wise-crack from Sir Lionel. Next to Sir Lionel is Mr. J. O. F. Haynes.* ***June 2, 1966***

However, Sunday nights it was in my library to go through my work for the week ahead. I always observe one rule unfailingly and that rule is – Never go to Court unprepared. Even at this time of my life when I go to social functions I meet very often many people who tell me, on introduction, that they never met me before but heard of me through my programme “Analysis” over “Radio Demerara”, or they read of my cases in the press.

~~~~~~~

The question had been raised often times in Guyana and other Commonwealth Countries whether young lawyers graduating from Law Schools should be allowed to enter the field of practice without any “pupilage” (some practical work in a lawyer’s office or any Court experience under the guidance of Competent Counsel). This very hotly debated subject was causing much concern over the newly admitted members of the legal profession.

Since 1968, this question of “pupilage” has been very much in the forefront in respect of young lawyers entering practice. The case of “pupilage” and legislation regulating it was considered by Sir Kenneth Stoby, Chancellor of the Judiciary in Guyana. Sir Kenneth explained back in 1968, “during the young barrister’s period of study, he need not enter a law court or a lawyer’s office and yet he becomes a fully qualified barrister. This means he is completely unsuited to represent clients until he gets some practice. The remedy for this is legislation in each territory compelling a young lawyer to spend a year in chambers either in this country or any territory in the West Indies.”

I was asked as a senior practising lawyer to comment on these remarks by Sir Kenneth Stoby. That is why when I present the Petition of young law graduates to be called to the Bar to practise their profession, I always made it clear that they will have to spend some time in my Office to gain some practical experience.
~~~~~~~

My comments on Sir Kenneth's trite remarks were these: "In England, pupilage is an established institution in the Legal Profession. To my mind, pupilage is to the Legal Profession what internship is to the Medical Profession. There is no substitute for practical experience. A lawyer, to my mind, matures in learning, professional confidence and professional conduct at the Bar, as his practice increases and expands.

Theory is all very well and good in its place but it seems unfair to the general public that its members should have inflicted upon them, a barrister who, though brilliant in Law School, has no experience of Court procedure, preparation of cases and presentation – not to mention actual conduct in Court. The Law is now a very complex study and it is my view that pupilage requirement should be introduced in Guyana by Legislation as that would help immensely to produce more experienced, responsible, capable and professionally conscious members of the Bar".

Some Universities in the United States of America have introduced courses called "hands-on courses" where capable and experienced practitioners teach and demonstrate practical courses like preparing addresses for juries, the fundamentals of effective cross-examination and how to conduct one's self in Court and the correct professional relationship as between counsel and counsel. More young men and women are leaving law schools today much better prepared for practice than were their colleagues who started practice several years before them.

The best type of humour in Court is spontaneous humour. There was a defendant called "Rampat." He was noted for his battered felt hat, which was a must, no matter where he went. He was not very literate but was very kind and respectful to all. He liked his "bottle." He was not violent or rude and the police really liked him, as he was always ready as he went along his unknown business, to help them direct traffic. He felt he was doing a great service in helping the Police Officers in their onerous task of keeping traffic flowing.

Nobody knew where Rampat lived, but almost every morning you will find him in Court charged with either "disorderly conduct" or "loitering" or "being under the influence of alcohol in a public place." The presiding Magistrates in the three Georgetown Magistrates Courts knew Rampat well – he was always respectful, saluting and enquiring if they needed any help with their brief cases as they went to their cars. Truthfully, I liked the old rascal. He hurts no one. He lived in his own world, but the thing that everyone liked about Rampat was his courtesy and willingness to help. He did not know much English. Everyone was either "Boss," "Sir" or "Missie."

One morning Rampat appeared in Court No. (1). (I had a matter in that Court that morning) and Rampat was in Court. He was charged with disorderly conduct. Apparently, he was being annoyed by some youths and he lost his cool.

The Police arrested him for Disorderly Behaviour. The Magistrate came on the Bench and shortly after, Rampat's matter was called. The Magistrate read the charge to him and asked him how he pleads. As usual, he entered a plea of "Guilty." He never gave the Prosecutor any trouble in having to lead evidence. After the Prosecutor outlined the facts to the Court, the Magistrate decided to lecture to Rampat about a change in his life-style. Rampat stood before him with his battered felt hat in his hand. The Magistrate upbraided Rampat and this is how it went:

Magistrate: "Rampat, you are here again."
Rampat: "Yes, please Boss."
Magistrate: "When are you going to pull yourself together?"
Rampat: "I am all right Boss. I never give you trouble."
Magistrate: "Rampat, every single morning you are before the Court charged with one

Even at home, there is still much work to do...

...but every once in a while, Bonita and Shakoor enjoy a special evening out together.

It wasn't law all of the time. Here Shakoor is Go-Cart racing in England.

At home in Florida, Shakoor relaxing by playing a tune on his harmonica.

offence or another. You are not a criminal; you are charged with petty offences, not serious offences like stealing or assaulting anyone, or offences of that nature. Don't you feel ashamed of yourself?"

The Magistrate held up Rampat's convictions sheet.

Magistrate: "Every morning you are here in Court, aren't you ashamed? Aren't you disgusted with yourself? What have you got to say?"

Rampat: (Fumbling with his battered felt hat in his hands) "Boss, you no deh hay in Court every manin, too? You no shame ah you self?" (Translated, it reads thus, Boss, you are here in Court every morning too. aren't you ashamed of yourself?)

The lawyers, the Prosecutor and all the people in the Court went hysterical. The Court Orderly called the Court to Order. When order was restored, the learned and understanding Magistrate continued:

Magistrate: (Smilingly) "Rampat, you should be glad that I am here every morning to look after you. But today, enough is enough. You have to change. If you ever come back before me, I am going to send you to jail. Do you understand what I am telling you?"

Rampat: "Yes, Boss, me na ga come back." ("Yes Boss, I will not come back.")

When a lawyer decides to write his memoirs after fifty years of active practice, he is confronted with many internal organizational problems, selecting decisions and the interests of the reading public. If I were to set about to write on all the thousands of cases in which I have appeared, it will result in an almost impossible and unachievable task.

One must be selective and use one's discretion. The whole exercise is a subjective one. I must write about cases and matters, which I feel, would interest the non-legally trained readers, as well as the legally trained ones. This decision is aimed at getting across the selected cases and supporting materials, in a manner that preserves the true context of the matters being reviewed. The selected materials must bring to the readers' attention and understanding, the practical and legal difficulties that confront a practitioner and his ability to resolve those difficulties.

The matters selected must also bring to the readers' attention, the achievement of the end product and goal at all times, that is, the attainment of JUSTICE – sometimes illusory and sometimes achieved by some unusual, surprising, humorous and circuitous routes. I feel I must in duty bound, satisfy those standards that I have set for myself. Doing this, sometimes justifies the injection of some permissible humour that ever so often arises in court proceedings especially when that humour emanates from witnesses' reactions, behaviour and utterances.

I will now deal with a case in which I appeared for the Defendant. It was a Civil Action. The Plaintiff, to whom I shall refer as the City Property Agent or "CPA" for brevity, was a very successful City Real Estate Agent. His business was very wide covering sales of properties not only in the City, but also in other parts of the Country. First, Mr. CPA was the living example of the old maxim: "He who is his own lawyer, has a fool for a client."

I also refer to this case to illustrate the second point, that is, in trying to save a lawyer's fee in a civil action, one can lose quite a lot, as Civil law is not as cut and dried as the Criminal law. There are far more intricate and complicated legal rules and principles involved in civil law than in criminal law. One does not master these principles of civil law by being one's own untutored legal adviser. Not knowing the law, can result in losing your case, with the consequent Court Order that you pay the costs incurred by the other party.

The third point this case illustrates, is that trying to be a lawyer without any knowledge of court procedure and observance of the traditions of the Bar, the individual can become very abrasive or rude to the Court even though the Court is trying to assist him by putting him right on legal rules and principles. You will see how these points unfold as I get into this case which I purposely selected from the hundreds of civil matters in which I appeared either for the Plaintiff (the person who brings the action) or the Defendant (the person defending the action).

The CPA sued a businessman for commission due on the sale of lands at a place called HUBU in the County of Essequibo in Guyana. I appeared for the businessman, Abdool Majeed, then head of Abdool Majeed and Sons (1959) Investments Ltd. This was quite a reputable firm. I was their legal adviser. This matter has a fascinating history. It came up for hearing before Mr. Justice Akbar Khan. The CPA asked the Court to award him $2,000.00 being the commission due on the sale of lands, which he had sold for my client. At this hearing, my client was very ill.

In open Court, I informed the Court that Mr. Majeed was suddenly taken very ill and could not be present in Court. In the trial, the Defence filed would indicate that his presence was necessary. In view of this, I respectfully asked the Court that the case be taken off the list to be re-fixed for trial. I informed the Court that I had in my possession a Medical certificate from a competent and reputable physician indicating the nature of the sudden illness of Mr. Majeed, my client.

The CPA, appearing in person, objected to the application on the ground that Mr. Majeed had admitted liability in the defence, which I had filed, on his behalf. Mr. Justice Khan, trying to help the CPA to understand the pleadings in the Defence filed, told him that in the Defence there was no admission that $2,000.00 was owed but there was an admission that the CPA was owed $660.00 being three percent of the sale of the land for $22,000.00. This sum of $660.00 was lodged in the Registry of the Court on instructions from me to Mr. Majeed. The Judge told the CPA that he was entitled to uplift that sum of money. Now comes the part of the behaviour of an untrained person, not qualified at the Bar to practise law.

The CPA started shouting to the top of his voice that all this is "nonsense" and he wanted his "costs" for the day. As a member of the practising Bar and an Officer of the Court (as all members of the practising Bar are Officers of the Court), I upbraided the CPA and advised him not to speak to the learned Judge in that tone and manner. Let me digress for a few seconds. A member of the Bar appearing for the CPA would have addressed the Court in the following similar or like words, " My Lord please let it be on the record that if you propose to grant the adjournment, then I am respectfully asking for Costs for today in any event." That is how it is done.

There is one other point to clarify what I said earlier about "understanding the pleadings in the Defence filed." Here the Defence pleaded was a written agreement between the CPA and the Defendant. The Plaintiff at trial was attempting to vary the rate of the commission due to him on the sale price of $22,000.00 at the agreed rate of three percent, making his commission $660.00 which sum I directed my client to pay into Court.

Here, in this case, the CPA was trying to rescind the contract on the one hand and vary the contract on the other hand. These are difficult and intricate concepts and principles of law, which constantly engage the attention of the Supreme Court sitting in its Civil Jurisdiction. The illegality of the contract was not pleaded by the Plaintiff CPA. There was no application to vary the terms of the original contract.

The learned Judge was explaining to the CPA that on the Pleadings, without trial, he is entitled to judgment of the $660.00 lodged in the Registry of the Court. I have always said that I feel happiest when I have qualified lawyers appearing against me. That is where the joy in practice is, when one has done the necessary preparation and the procurement of the binding authorities on the point. Very humbly, I state, this is where my strength and my success at the Bar were established.

The CPA was a hostile and highly-strung man. He kept on raising his voice and without any justification shouted at the Judge, "If you adjourn this matter, make certain you fix a date when I can attend Court." This was uncalled for. All Judges, if they are going to grant an application for an adjournment by either party, always make certain that there is agreement between the parties or their lawyers of the date to be fixed.

I felt the Judge, up to that time, was very patient and showed great restraint, but after this last rude and uncalled for and crude remark to the Judge by the CPA, the learned Judge ordered him to leave the Court immediately. Said the CPA who was most rude, "I shall leave your Court, but I will return."

Do you see what I mean my Dear Readers? That is not how Court procedures are conducted. The CPA was his own enemy. As his own lawyer, he was foolish. As a litigant, he allowed his abrasive attitude and his obvious bad manners to ruin his day in Court. I will deal with this matter right on down to its final adjudication. All the way the CPA acted in a stupid and unmannerly manner. He was his own enemy all the way to the Judgment of the Court of Appeal.

The next Act in this developing Drama was about three months later. The matter came up before Mr. Justice Bollers, now a permanent Judge. In the Privy Council Appeal (See Chapter 7 ante), he was an acting Judge. Mr. Justice Bollers went on to become Chief Justice of Guyana and he was knighted by Her Majesty the Queen and became Sir Harold Bollers.

At the hearing before Mr. Justice Bollers, the CPA circus behaviour became more convoluted and disgraceful. Firstly, he objected to Mr. Justice Bollers hearing his case because, as he said, "His Lordship had a private conversation with Mr. A. Shakoor Manraj, with respect to the case." More of this appears below in the Judgment of Sir Kenneth Stoby, Chancellor of the Guyana Court of Appeal.

Justice Bollers over-ruled the objection and began to take evidence in the case. At this stage, the CPA (Plaintiff) asked for judgment because, he submitted, the Defendant did not plead any "denial in his Affidavit of Defence." Quite correctly, the Judge over-ruled the motion to get judgment. The Defendant in his evidence said the agreement with the Plaintiff was the usual one, whereby he agreed to pay him three percent of the purchase price of the property and not $2000.00 as is claimed by the Plaintiff. In pursuance of this agreement and acting on his Counsel's directions, he had deposited $660.00 in the Registry of the Court, but the Plaintiff has refused to uplift the money.

The hearing of the action continued the next day. I submitted that the Plaintiff had failed to discharge his burden of proof before the Court in establishing that he had introduced a purchaser to Mr. Majeed for the sale of the property at Hubu, Essequibo. Earlier, the Plaintiff had asked Mr. Majeed whether his Company had passed a resolution authorizing the sale of the property. If the Defendant had said "No" that was the end of the Plaintiff's case. The Judge refused to have the question answered.

The Judge, very properly, told the Plaintiff that he was not represented by a lawyer and that he, the Judge, would not sit there and allow him to ask those very unsuitable and dangerous questions without advising him. The Judge went out of his way to assist this unrepresented Plaintiff by telling him that he was destroying his own case. The whimsical, abrasive and unappreciative Plaintiff walked out of Court, saying he was withdrawing from the case – mind you, he is the Plaintiff. How complicated can things get?

You have not yet heard the end of this irresponsible, abrasive and vindictive Plaintiff. The Plaintiff appealed. The matter was heard in the Court of Appeal in its first sitting since its creation. The Court was presided over by Chancellor of the Judiciary, Sir Kenneth Stoby, Mr. Justice E. V. Luckhoo (later Sir E. V. Luckhoo and Chancellor, succeeding Sir Kenneth Stoby) and Mr. Justice Guya Persaud. I appeared for the Respondent, Abdool Majeed and Sons (1959) Investments Ltd. The Plaintiff – Appellant was again the destroyer of his own case and again appeared before the highest tribunal of the land, unrepresented by Counsel.

Try as I may, I cannot properly *précis* this unanimous powerful judgment of the Court of Appeal delivered by Sir Kenneth Stoby. The Chancellor rebuked the Plaintiff – Appellant for making disgraceful allegations against a Judge. The Plaintiff – Appellant (the CPA) stated that a certain agreement which was necessary for his case had disappeared, adding that when the agreement was tendered at the trial, he saw the Judge take it and put it in his pocket!!! How mischievous and malicious could the Appellant get! I immediately sprang to my feet and objected strenuously. I informed their Lordships that the Agreement in question was never tendered in evidence. The Respondent had it in his hand. I saw no need to tender it. The Judge never touched the document. The statement by the Appellant shows how wicked he is and it seems he is suffering from severe delusions and mental aberration.

The Chancellor, in the Judgment of the Court continued,

"We have heard what you (the Appellant) had to say on this first ground of Appeal and we have heard what Mr. Manraj had to say to this Court about the truth of the matter. This Court does not propose to permit you to make disgraceful allegations against the trial Judge. We are not going to have it and if you proceed with that line of argument, we will refuse to hear your Appeal. We propose to expunge from the record those allegations you have made."

After listening to further unmeritorious and strange grounds of Appeal, The Appeal Court through the Chancellor dismissed the Appeal and he said in his judgment:

"Litigants must learn to respect and to trust their Judges. It is impossible for a Judge not to have conversation with counsel. It is something that happens all over the civilized world. As a Judge walks down the Court corridors, counsel tells him good morning or stops to pass the time of the day. There is nothing wrong with that. When a Judge sits on the bench, he sits to hear the issues in the case involved. He is not concerned with people. For an individual to come before this Court and assert that because counsel asked for an adjournment in Chambers, that makes the Judge biased, is a disgraceful thing to do. It is something THIS COURT WILL NOT TOLERATE."

A simple question of fact was involved in the Appeal. The Plaintiff (CPA) alleged that he had entered into a contract with the Defendant company that if he sold the property in question belonging to the company, he would be paid $2,000.00. The company on the other hand stated in their Statement of Defence and gave evidence that the contract was for payment of a commission of three percent if a certain price was achieved. The Judge heard the evidence on both sides and came to the conclusion that the contract was for the payment of three percent commission and dismissed the case.

It is usual for applications for adjournments to be made. Such applications are made in open court so that the other side would have an opportunity of being heard on the application. When both sides had been heard, the Judge will decide whether or not he would grant the adjournment."

The Court of Appeal dismissed this most unmeritorious appeal. I cited this whole case to place before you, Dear Readers, the ramifications of the law and to illustrate that every man has access to all the Courts of Justice. All the law demands is that that access must not be abused or used as an instrument to vilify and denigrate those who administer the Law. Justice must be protected from those who would like to destroy her image of fair play and unbiased judgment.

I spent my spare moments when not practising Law, with the youths. I was very interested in youth work and I felt if they knew that grown-ups were interested in their problems, their aims and their ambitions, they would be more responsive to adult participation in their spare-time and their activities. I always tried to let them see that they are all responsible citizens and thus, the leaders of tomorrow.

I lectured to youths of all denominations at the Y.M.C.A., the International Youth Organizations and the many other youth-oriented Associations. I always hammered home the point that they are the masters of their own destiny. I encouraged them to find out what was within them, what they wanted to do in life and what specific branch of learning appealed to them. They must not be afraid to make up their minds and once they have decided what they would like to do as their life's calling, go after it, pursue all the relevant learning and instructions available and achieve their self-realized goals.

The response was always encouraging and many of the youths I had the pleasure of guiding, became teachers, professors at Universities, doctors, lawyers, scientists, businessmen and women, civil servants and qualified agriculturalists, mechanics, engineers and politicians. I always felt very happy when one of my young brethren came in to see me to let me know how he or she is progressing. I taught them what I preached and I practised what I preached. I was committed and dedicated to the practice of my profession and I allowed nothing to deter me from my goals and my aspirations.

Time to Practise What I Preach

When I returned to Guyana in 1954 to practise my profession, the then Attorney-General, the Honourable, Mr. Frank Holder, (later Sir Frank Holder, Chief Justice of British Guiana) was very kind and invited me to join the Attorney-General's Chambers as a Crown Counsel (Prosecutor). This was not what I had in mind for myself. I knew that my real interest and potential lay in practising law as a private practitioner. I respectfully told the Attorney-General that I would rather stick to my private practice. He did not take that very kindly and asked me if I felt that the A.-G.'s Chambers was not good enough for me.

I told the Attorney-General that he is wrong in his assessment of my choice and my decision. I knew what I wanted. I knew what my goal was. I knew the road I had to travel to achieve my goal. In the short time that elapsed before the Attorney-General became the Chief Justice of Guyana, I had already established a successful practice and I had the pleasure of appearing before him on several occasions either as Counsel for the Plaintiff or Defendant. He was very generous in his comments in open Court about my conduct at the Bar and my dedication to the Law.

Later on, as I established myself at the Bar, but shortly before becoming a Queen's Counsel, I was approached by the then Chief Justice to accept an appointment as a Judge of the High Court. I again "stuck to my guns" and respectfully declined the invitation. I was not yet prepared to leave the practising Bar then, or any time afterwards.

When Mr. L. F. S. Burnham became the Prime Minister, he told me that he was looking for a capable and suitable person to go to India as Guyana's High

Commissioner and he asked me to accept the appointment. This was before December 1969. I did not want anything to interfere with my eligibility to be appointed a Queen's Counsel. I told Mr. Burnham that I would not give up my practice to accept the position he was offering me. Although he assured me that I had already qualified myself from my standing at the Bar, to be appointed a Q.C., I declined the offer and thanked him for that confidence he reposed in me.

I had my own thoughts on the matter and I wanted to be in practise when the time came for me "to take silk" (to be appointed a Q.C. – Queen's Counsel.). The Prime Minister and I appeared in many cases together and he was not very pleased with me, but I succeeded in convincing him that I am not inclined to change my course and the achievement of my goal, by interrupting my practice at the Bar. He told me that he understood how I felt.

A rather difficult situation arose after 1969 when I was appointed a Queen's Counsel. The portfolio of Minister of Local Government became vacant through the resignation of the then incumbent of that portfolio. I was again asked by the Prime Minister to join his Government and take over the vacant Ministerial position. A different consideration had then energized my life.

I was up front and I told the Prime Minister in a frank and polite manner that I felt that I wanted to continue to practise at the Bar as a Q.C. I felt I owed it to myself but above and beyond my personal feelings, I felt I had a duty to all my countrymen to continue serving them as a Senior Supreme Court Counsel. I had already defended up to that point of time, one hundred and twenty-five murder trials. I enjoyed my work and I felt I owed it to myself to spend my energy and time in doing what I enjoyed most in my life – practising at the Bar.

Chapter 12

Murder Cases from Guyana Racial Riots

My Youngest Defendant ~ The Herstelling Murder Case

Herstelling is a small village about six miles South of Georgetown on the East Bank of the Demerara River. It is near the Providence Magistrate's Court where I practised in my early days at the Bar.

My client was just nineteen years old. He was charged with murder of a cake-shop proprietor. I had as my junior counsel associated with me, Mr. Aubrey Bishop, who subsequently became a respected High Court Judge. The State Prosecutor was Mr. Michael Quail, who I had the pleasure of introducing to the Bar by presenting his Petition to be admitted to practise law.

The case for the State, simply put, was that the accused pelted a full bottle of beer at the deceased. It was alleged that the bottle hit the deceased in the abdomen thereby causing a rupture of his enlarged spleen, resulting in his death. The Jury was an intelligent jury and from the questions asked by the Foreman of the Jury, it was clear that they were following the evidence carefully.

There were many contradictions that were established under my cross-examination. The witnesses gave many versions of what actually took place and some admitted that they saw the deceased collapsed as he stretched to take down a bunch of keys. In addition to the discrepancies established in the cross-examination, the defence relied heavily on the testimony of Dr. Leslie Mootoo, the pathologist who conducted the post-mortem examination on the body of the deceased.

His evidence was clear and put the prosecution in some difficulty. Dr. Mootoo stated that he found "two abrasions on the body of the deceased in the region of the spleen." I cross-examined the pathologist and his evidence was clear. I had put to him the allegation of the State that the accused had pelted a full bottle of beer, which struck the deceased in his abdomen thereby causing a rupture of the enlarged spleen of the deceased. Dr. Mootoo was emphatic and positive that the alleged beer bottle could not have caused the abrasions that he found. Part of my cross-examination went as follows:-

Mr. Manraj: "Dr. Mootoo could the deceased have ruptured his already enlarged spleen by falling and hitting himself on the abdomen in the region of the spleen?

Dr. Mootoo: "That seems more consistent with the two abrasions I saw. The answer is yes."

Mr. Manraj: "Were the abrasions lateral or vertical?"

Dr. Mootoo: "They were lateral abrasions consistent with the deceased hitting himself on a hard surface when he fell, resulting in the abrasions I found on the body of the deceased."

Mr. Manraj: "Given the fact that the deceased had an enlarged spleen, could that have been ruptured if the deceased hit himself on a hard surface in the region of the spleen when he fell down?"

Dr. Mootoo: "That seems very consistent with the injuries I saw."

Mr. Manraj: "I thank you, Doctor."

I glanced at the Jury. I knew then, after several years studying the facial expressions of jurors and their body language that I had created enough doubt for me to ride home on an acquittal. There was no re-examination of the pathologist by the State Counsel, Mr. Quail. The State finally closed its case. Without any hesitation, I rose on my feet and submitted that there was no case to answer.

The State had failed to prove conclusively that the cause of death was due to the alleged act of the accused. I canvassed very forcefully the evidence of the Pathologist. The two abrasions on the body of the deceased in the region of the spleen could not have been caused by the beer bottle. It was clear that the deceased collapsed when he stretched and probably over-reached and strained himself as he tried to take down a bunch of keys.

The Judge, Mr. Justice Frank Vieira, over-ruled my no-case submissions and sent the case to the Jury. This Judge usually adopts the stand that the Jury should decide on the facts of the case even if those facts are so much at variance with evidence adduced from the various State witnesses. The Judge sent the case to the Jury after he gave them directions about manslaughter and told them to consider the lesser charge.

I addressed the Jury fully. I always feel that my duty is not to leave out anything that is favourable to the defence and never leave anything to chance, thinking that the Jury will consider certain obvious weaknesses in the case for the prosecution. I told the Jury in clear language that this was neither a case of murder nor manslaughter. The evidence adduced by the prosecution did not support either offence. It was made clear to the Jury that the beer bottle alleged to have been thrown by the accused, did not cause the abrasions.

The defence was that the accused did not pelt any bottle at the accused. The deceased died from the rupture of his enlarged spleen after he collapsed and fell to the ground as he stretched to take down a bunch of keys. I told the Jury about "reasonable doubt" and addressed them on the fundamental ingredients of what amounts to a "reasonable doubt." I concluded that quite apart from the evidence of the pathologist there were too many inconsistencies in the evidence that could lead them to have serious doubts about the validity of the case for the prosecution.

If they are in that state of mind where they are in doubt as to what transpired on the day in question, then the prosecution has failed to discharge the onus of proving the guilt of the accused beyond a reasonable doubt and in such a situation the law is that that benefit of the doubt must be given to the accused. I addressed the Jury until I felt I had touched the reasoning of every member of the Jury panel.

The Prosecutor, according to the Criminal Offence Ordinance then in force in Guyana, always has the last word. That is the reason why defence counsel must vigorously address the Jury on the points the prosecution may raise and defence counsel must demolish them in his address to the Jury. There is another side to the tactics of doing that. If and when the Prosecutor addresses on those points, the Jury will already have heard of them and the severe weakness or invalidity of those points.

After the Prosecutor concluded his address, the trial Judge started his summing-up. It was fair and balanced. I could not quarrel with the Judge's final remarks: "Members of the Jury, you have been in Court throughout the whole of the trial and you have heard all the evidence adduced in Court by Defence Counsel and the Prosecuting Counsel. You have heard what the pathologist said from the witness box. I have directed you on the law relating to murder.

I have explained 'malice aforethought' to you. I told you how the law treats manslaughter. You are now in a position to weigh the evidence and allocate the weight you think you ought to give to the entire evidence in the case. I have given you a careful direction on what your duty is, once you have a reasonable doubt. I explained to you what in law amounts to 'reasonable doubt'. Now the time has come for you to consider the evidence and then return your verdict." I thought this was a good and proper way to end the summing up. I commend this type of summing up to younger Judges who, try to sway the Jury by injecting ad nauseam their own biased views. Justice is for the State, as it is for the Citizen.

After a reasonable deliberation, the Foreman of the Jury in open Court delivered the verdict of the Jury – "Not Guilty of Murder" and "Not Guilty of Manslaughter" – I think that was the only proper verdict that could have been returned. "Justice has prevailed." Those two little words – powerful, the most eloquent and mellifluous sound to the ears of the accused – now set free.

This particular case gave me a remarkable feeling of elation. So far, I had won every murder case I was privileged to defend. Here, I defended the youngest accused charged with murder. He was one of a family of eight. Sewpattie Kalso could not hold back her tears of joy as she embraced her nineteen-year-old son, now set free. Some other female relatives joined the mother as she wept for the freed man. They were very emotional in their thanks to me and, as I usually do, I told them to go across to my Chambers and I will meet them there, as I had to go to the robing room to change. Sometimes I would walk across to my Chambers from the Supreme Court fully robed.

What really moved me in this case is the depth of love and devotion of this dear lady – the mother of the accused. Each time she came to Georgetown, she would make it her duty to come to my Chambers. If I am busy or out of my Office in Court, she would wait with the patience of Job, until it was her turn for me to see her. She would come into my Chambers and greet me with profound respect and feelings expressed in very motherly terms. She would only ask me to tell her again that her boy is going to be all right and that I will do my utmost to send him home. That was music to her ears when I reassured her of my assessment of the case. She would leave my Office just telling everybody as she was leaving: "Mr. Manraj just spoke to me and my boy is going to be all right."

I was really moved by the confidence she placed in me. The accused was no less grateful. After his acquittal, whenever he had to come to Georgetown, he would always come in to report to me how he is progressing. Sometimes, a lawyer can really be moved by the gratitude and loyalty of satisfied clients. No fee in the world can buy that. The next morning, splashed right across the front page of the most widely circulated newspaper, appeared this headline:

"MOM WEEPS AS YOUNG SON IS FREED OF MURDER"

Riots in Guyana

While on this topic of murder cases, I want to add here something about the very many murder cases I defended during the racial uprisings and rioting in Guyana. This period marks the lowest ebb and most violent era in the history of Guyana always described as the "Garden of the Caribbean." The Police Force could not cope with the uprising and violence and troops from England had to be brought in to help to enforce Law and Order. What was once described, as the "melting pot of the Caribbean" because of the harmony that existed between the six races of Guyana, became the "coal-pot of the Caribbean" – marked by heated and brutal racial riots between the two leading races – the Indo-Guyanese and the Afro-Guyanese.

The predominantly Afro-Guyanese Police Force charged many Indo-Guyanese on the mere accusation by Afro-Guyanese, with the capital offence of murder. This was particularly widespread in the Buxton and Enmore areas on the East Coast of Demerara. A similar situation arose in the McKenzie City area, which is on the Demerara River about sixty-five miles South of Georgetown. This area was predominantly an Afro-Guyanese stronghold. About eighty percent of the work force in the bauxite mining areas was made up of Negroes. They carried out a massacre on the small East Indian population living and working in the area.

The important aspect of this unfortunate part of our history, is that when it came to the selection of a lawyer to represent the many Guyanese who were charged with murder, the "race" card was not played. During this sad period of extreme violence emanating from the country's social, political and economic evolution, I appeared and defended as many as two hundred murder cases. Some of these cases were dismissed on submissions by me at the close of the prosecution's case, that there was not sufficient and proper identification of the accused person. The others went on to full trial. Here is where penetrating cross-examination of defence counsel is a real asset.

In many of these cases, there were serious irreconcilable conflicts in the evidence flowing from the simple fact that many of the so-called eyewitnesses were never at the scene and did not really see what happened. These false witnesses went into the witness box and swore to testify to tell the "truth, the whole truth and nothing but the truth, so help me God." As I write, that was the oath they all took. I am reminded of the very apt word my very learned friend, Professor Alan Dershowitz, of Harvard University used in his brilliant and well-written book "Reasonable Doubts" on the O. J. Simpson murder trial. He called this act of swearing to testify to tell the truth and then lie -- *"testilying."* One is struck by the ease and complacency that the witnesses in the "riot" murder cases I am presently discussing *"testilied."* It was a really rewarding experience to have to cross-examine these "false witnesses" who swore on oath that they saw everything. The cross-examination brought out the truth that they really saw nothing and were just paid witnesses of convenience, called to testify.

It was good for me as Defence Counsel. Many of these cases eventually reached the Jury. It was a painful exercise to go through the evidence of each witness and highlight the parts of their evidence, which conclusively showed that they could not have been speaking the truth when they stated that the accused was the person who committed the crime.

They were obviously giving "padded" and untruthful evidence. I won these "riot" murder cases by probing and investigating thoroughly the original reports made by the various so-called eyewitnesses at the Police Station or to the Police Constable on the scene. I cannot possibly write on all the murder cases arising from the unrest and rioting, in which I appeared. I am just writing my memoirs and not a report on each case.

I will just give one example to illustrate the points I am making. In this case, under review, the report at the Police Station showed that the informant had told the police officer on duty, that the man who committed the murder was a medium-height, brown-skinned East Indian named "Sonny." That informant, who subsequently became the main witness for the prosecution, told the police that he knew "Sonny" very well. He lives in the area.

My investigations revealed that Sonny had removed from the area when the rioting started and went to work on the West bank of the Demerara River. I was able to get the name of his employer and when contacted, he assured me (supported by time book and wage slips counterfoils) that on the day of the alleged incident "Sonny" was at work in his rice mill. The documents I saw were the regular records kept by the employer in the course of his business. There were no erasures or insertions on the list of the employees who worked on that day. Sonny was not at the murder scene when the deceased was fatally wounded on the head. He was at work far away from the scene.

About three weeks after the witness had made the original report, he was asked to return to the Station. He then told the Police at the station after he was informed by the Officer on duty that Sonny was not at the scene of the accident, that the man who hit the deceased was Harripaul. He lives in the area. Well, Harripaul was charged with the murder of the deceased. He was the accused in the dock (the prisoner's box). In Guyana, murder accused are not granted bail so that Harripaul was in custody for about nine months before his case came up for trial. In a way, the time awaiting his trial came in very useful as I was successful in getting all my investigators working and the facts derived from their investigations disclosed that the new name given at the Police Station was given three weeks after the first report. Therefore, Harripaul was substituted for Sonny. Just like that.

The witness gave his evidence but no mention was made of the fact that he had gone to the Police Station three weeks after his original report and changed the name from Sonny to Harripaul who was sitting in the dock accused of murder. Here is how the cross-examination unfolded:

Mr. Manraj:	"Mr. John Blakey, are you also known as "Damage?"
Mr. Blakey:	"How you know that?"
Mr. Manraj:	"Don't let us start off on the wrong footing. I ask the questions. You answer them. If you do not understand a question put to you by me, tell His Lordship, or easier yet, just ask me to re-phrase or repeat the question. Just let us get our respective roles right. Now then, are you known as 'Damage'?"
Mr. Blakey:	'Yes, Sir. My friends call me that."
Mr. Manraj:	"How many times did you go to the Police Station in connection with this matter?"
Mr. Blakey:	"Only one time."

Mr. Manraj:	"Are you certain? Think again."
Mr. Blakey:	"Only one time."
Mr. Manraj:	"Do you know Sonny?"
Mr. Blakey:	"Yes. He lived in the area."
Mr. Manraj:	"Did you report at the Police Station when you went there to report what you claim you saw, that you saw Sonny hit the deceased on the head?"
Mr. Blakey:	"I never told them that."
Mr. Manraj:	"What did you tell them?"
Mr. Blakey:	"I told them I saw an East Indian man hit the deceased on the head and he fell down."
Mr. Manraj:	"Did you know the name of the East Indian you mentioned to the Police?"
Mr. Blakey:	"No, I do not know the name of the person."
Mr. Manraj:	"Did you call the name of anyone when you reported the matter at the Police Station?"
Mr. Blakey:	"I did not call any name."
Mr. Manraj:	"Do you recall however, making a report of the incident at the Police Station?"
Mr. Blakey:	"Yes."
Mr. Manraj:	"Do you know the accused?"
Mr. Blakey:	"Yes."
Mr. Manraj:	"Did you know the accused's name when you went to the Station on the first occasion?"
Mr. Blakey:	"Yes, Sir."
Mr. Manraj:	"Did you go back to the Police Station about three weeks after you made your first report?"
Mr. Blakey:	"Yes. The Police told me they wanted to see me and I went."

Mr. Manraj:	"Did you, on that second visit, tell them at the Station that it was not Sonny but Harripaul who hit the deceased on the head?"
Mr. Blakey:	*No answer.*
Mr. Manraj:	"Did you hear the question? Please answer it."
Mr. Blakey:	*No answer.*
Mr. Manraj:	"Do you remember telling the Sergeant on duty at the Station that you made a mistake about the person you named in the first report?"
Mr. Blakey:	"I cannot remember, Sir."
Mr. Manraj:	"If I show you the first report, would you recognize your signature at the bottom of the report?"
Mr. Blakey:	"Let me see it." (Witness is shown the report and his signature.) "Yes, I see my signature at the bottom of my report."
Mr. Manraj:	"Look in the body of the report, do you see the name *SONNY* in that report?"
Mr. Blakey:	"Yes."
Mr. Manraj:	"What do you see above *'Sonny'*?"
Mr. Blakey:	"I see *'Sonny'* scratched out and *'Harripaul'* written above."
Mr. Manraj:	"Now, having seen that, do you agree with me that you told the Police three weeks after that it was not *Sonny* but *Harripaul*?"
Mr. Blakey:	"It happened a long time ago. I cannot remember."
Mr. Manraj:	"But do you see your initials *'JB'* just above the insertion of the name Harripaul?"
Mr. Blakey:	"Yes, Sir."

Mr. Manraj: "When was that signature affixed or put on the report, the first or the second visit?"
Mr. Blakey: "On the second visit."
Mr. Manraj: "Mr. Blakey, do you know why your friends call you *Damage*?"
Mr. Blakey: "I never asked them."
Mr. Manraj: "I thank you Mr. Blakey. No more questions."

One must know when to stop. I got all I wanted. The Prosecutor tried to re-examine the witness, but I was forced to object to many of the questions he asked, as they were leading questions. The Prosecutor, in re-examination of the witness is not permitted to ask leading questions (which are questions that suggest the answers). Further, re-examination is only limited to questions that arise from my cross-examination. If the Prosecutor wants to ask a question that does not arise from my cross-examination, he must ask leave of the Court. All of my objections were upheld by the learned trial Judge. I gathered from what I was seeing that the prosecution was in disarray.

The Prosecutor then called his last witness, the Police Officer who took the statement given by the accused, Harripaul, when he was taken to the Police Station. In that statement, which was tendered in Court, the accused told the Police Officer that he was not present at the scene of the murder, he did not strike the deceased at any time, never had any quarrel with the deceased and that he was innocent of the charge. The defence did not challenge the statement and there was therefore no *voire-dire*. (Proof that the accused gave the statement voluntarily). Just to show that my client was most co-operative with the Police, I cross-examined the Police Officer as follows:

Mr. Manraj: "Officer did you have any trouble or difficulties with the accused when you asked him to go with you to the Police Station?"

Witness: "No Sir, he was most co-operative."

Mr. Manraj: "Did the accused hesitate or object to giving you the statement?"

Witness: "No, Sir."

Mr. Manraj: "I thank you, Officer. You have been very helpful."

It is always good policy to say something kind to a police officer when he gives straightforward and truthful evidence.

The prosecution closed its case. In all, including the Government pathologist, nine witnesses were called. I did not make any no-case submissions as there were some facts, which in my considered opinion, the Jury needed some time to deliberate. The Jury, comprising of seven Afro-Guyanese and five Indo-Guyanese were following the case intently. Not for one moment did the "race card" enter my mind.

I have clocked up a lot of exposure to and experience of all types of jurors and my gut feeling is, that regardless of any racial prejudices a person may have, when he or she goes in the jury box and each one swears on his or her religious book – be it the Holy Bible, the Holy Qur'an, the Geeta or the Torah – that he or she *"shall well and truly try and true deliverance make between the State and the prisoner at the bar whom I shall have in charge and a true verdict give according to the evidence. So help me God,"* then a different frame of mind and sincerity to the oath each took, become the pre-occupation of the Jurors and they sincerely apply themselves and focus their conscience to the task of returning a verdict, true "according to the evidence."

I addressed the Jury until I felt I had brought to their attention all the salient features of the defence and the obvious unreliability of the main prosecution witness. I did not have any difficulty. I could see that I had penetrated their thinking. I closed my address by asking the Jury to let Justice be done and free the accused. The Prosecutor replied. He tried as best as he could, to destroy the defence. In doing this, he paradoxically and unwittingly destroyed his own case. He finally asked the Jury to find the accused guilty of murder.

The learned Judge, to my mind, had a more difficult task in his summing-up. He did tell the Jurors that their decision must of necessity depend upon the weight they placed on the main state witness John Blakey. The learned Judge gave the Jury a full and careful summing-up of reasonable doubt.

In this particular case, the learned Judge showed commendable restraint in not offering or injecting too much of his own views into the summing-up. He made it very clear to the Jury that if they were uncertain, if they had any reasonable doubt, they had one duty only and that is to return a verdict of not guilty. On the other hand, if they are satisfied that the prosecution had proved its case "beyond a reasonable doubt," then and only then, they can convict.

The Judge asked both the Prosecutor and me if there is any point either of us wished him to dwell on. Both the Prosecutor and I informed His Lordship that his summing-up was full and covered all the points. The Jury then retired to consider their verdict. It was not surprising to me, in view of the evidence before them, that they returned under one hour and returned a verdict of *"Not Guilty."* Justice had triumphed. Justice was done. Justice remained triumphant and unadulterated. My client was most relieved and his expressions of thanks and appreciation were deep and sincere. I had already told him at the beginning of the case, that I believed in his innocence.

Chapter 13

Less Complex Cases

Provide Relaxation And Humour

It sounds somewhat contradictory that my full and busy law practice could be relaxing. It sounds somewhat contradictory – a paradox – doesn't it? Most of the cases in which I appear are complicated, difficult and weighty matters like murder cases, cases of rape, fraud, perjury, manslaughter, burglary, indecent assault, bigamy, receiving stolen property and those types of cases, usually ending up before a jury for trial.

On the Civil side, the cases are of a different type – not the spectacular types of criminal cases that would come under the Criminal Jurisdiction of the Supreme Court. Cases like breach of contract, specific performance, tortious liability and matters invoking the Equitable Jurisdiction of the Civil Court, are not as appealing to the general public as the criminal cases. It has been said by the most experienced practitioners, that a "Barrister does not know any law until he masters the principles of Civil Law." The Criminal Law practice is flamboyant. The Civil Law practice is more remunerative in the long run, but less ostentatious.

This is so true. Many members of the Bar who were leaders at the Criminal Bar, eventually shifted gear and ended up as brilliant and wealthy civil law practitioners. I must admit that I enjoyed the best of the two worlds. My leaning however was always towards the Criminal Bar.

In the Magistrates Courts things move more expeditiously and the summary offences trials are more speedily concluded by the Magistrates. The Divorce Court of the Supreme Court has jurisdiction over Matrimonial matters and the lists are made up of defended and undefended divorces and related procedures. Undefended divorces are easy to decide. When there are children of the marriage to be considered, usually agreement is reached before trial, as to the father's contribution to the welfare and upbringing of the children. These cases really bring to the forefront the whimsical behaviour and weaknesses of the spouses and the transient and ephemeral nature of matrimonial behaviour in this well-worn institution called "marriage."

My examples will show you what I mean in my preceding paragraphs and how quickly matters move along in the Magistrates Courts and the undefended Divorce cases heard in the Supreme Court. Let me start in the Magistrates Court.

"Justice Delayed Is Justice Denied"

Six men were charged indictably of the felonious wounding of a British soldier with intent to maim, disfigure or disable him. These men were on a very serious charge – one Indian, three Afro-Guyanese and two Chinese.

The injured man had recovered and left for England. The matter came up for the 7th time before the Court and all the Police Prosecutor could inform the Court was that he was not in a position to say whether the injured man would be returning to Guyana to give evidence in the case. My clients – all six of them had a very good defence. I had to tell them to be patient and see what is happening. However, on this the 7th appearance in Court, the Police had the audacity to request another postponement.

I was quick on my feet and addressed the Court as follows: "Your Worship (Magistrate), I do not normally object to applications for postponement by the Police. On several occasions I am forced to make applications and I have to give good reasons. Here, the Police are not in a position to say whether the injured man will ever be coming back to Guyana. Justice is not an open-ended virtue. I am respectfully asking that the matter be struck out and my six clients be set free. What is my reason? One only has to go back to the basic axiom in jurisprudential reasoning and submit that 'Justice delayed is Justice Denied'".

The learned Magistrate agreed with the submissions and discharged the six men. They were so pleased and delighted. I was so satisfied. Justice was done.

"The Silk Pyjamas Suit"

Jimmy was married to a very lovely lady. He worked very hard at a night job which paid him more than he would have earned doing the same job in the day time. He had a respectable home, ran a car and was at peace with the world, his wife and his life. For three years everything was the epitome of marital bliss.

Soon Jimmy noticed that an old school mate started to visit the home. Soon neighbours began to drop some funny remarks to Jimmy about working all night and sleeping all day. On a few occasions his wife, Nora, mentioned to Jimmy that his friend had called and he spent a few minutes with her. That was the understatement of the century. Jimmy, a very sensitive man, come to realize that something was not right. Whenever he tried to make love to his wife, she would tell him that he is working very hard and he needs his rest.

Things got worse and soon the potential co-respondent started to park his car on Jimmy's bridge each week night around 10.00 p.m. and would leave early in the morning. You could say what you like, "people will talk." An old retired Police Officer living next door to Jimmy told him what he was seeing and what was happening. I do not know how you, the reader, feel about it, but it happened. Would you have done what the old officer did?

As Jimmy told me, "I was lost. The bottom of my world had fallen out. I felt betrayed both by my wife and my friend" (who by the way was also married). What explanation he gave to his wife about being out of their matrimonial home all night does not concern me. Jimmy went "into a shell." He decided to act. He left home as usual one evening after saying "by" to his wife. There is a window just at the top of his stairs and he could gain access to his home through this window. He unbolted the window before he left the home. He got in his car and drove off as usual.

About four hours later he drove back in the direction of his home, but he left his car about one block away from his home. Of course, his friend's car was parked in front of Jimmy's house. It was now about 11:00 p.m. Jimmy took off his shoes, walked up the steps, opened the window making sure not to make a sound, got in his house and went to the bedroom door, pushed it open, simultaneously putting on the light switch.

There was the evidence. In bed was Jimmy's "Dear Nora" with Jimmy's friend. Jimmy was mad, not so much at what he found, but because his friend was wearing Jimmy's silk pyjamas suit that his mother had given him for his last birthday. Jimmy ordered the man out of his house. Jimmy later told me that he was prepared for this and vowed that there would be no violence. He calmly told his wife that he is giving her exactly one hour to leave his home. If she failed to do so, then he will go berserk. She was glad to get out. She left.

The next morning Jimmy came in to see me. He had made arrangements to get some time off. I could not fully interview him then as I had to leave for Court. I gave instructions to my Managing Clerk to take a full statement from Jimmy. Everything was done. I filed Jimmy's Divorce Petition alleging adultery and citing his friend as the Co-Respondent. The usual hearing procedures were followed. Neither the wife nor the co-respondent took any part in the proceedings. No entry of appearance or answer was filed. In short, no appearances were filed. The matter was undefended.

Soon, the matter came up before His Lordship, the Chief Justice. I presented the Petition to the Court via

Jimmy, who gave evidence from the witness box. The Chief Justice listened very attentively and congratulated Jimmy in open court for being so cool and level-headed and exhibiting commendable restraint. The Chief Justice granted the Petition and allowed the Divorce.

The learned Chief Justice asked Jimmy if he wished to say anything. Jimmy very pensively said, "Yes, My Lord. I am still very hurt, but the thing that hurts me most is the fact that not only was <u>my</u> friend in <u>my</u> house, in <u>my</u> bed with <u>my</u> wife, but worse of all, he had on <u>my</u> silk pyjamas <u>my</u> mother had given to <u>me</u> as a birthday gift".

That was it. The lawyers, the other litigants and the people in Court and the Court Officers could not suppress their laughter. The Judge adjourned the Court for a few minutes. He later told me he had to go to his Chambers to get over the sardonic humour. It was one of the most bizarre cases he ever did.

"Tailor Apprentice Freed"

An eighteen year old tailor apprentice was freed by His Worship, Mr. Churuman, because the prosecution failed to establish any one of the essential ingredients that constitute the felony of breaking and entering and larceny.

I defended the young man. The defendant was charged with stealing shoes and socks worth more than five hundred dollars when, the police alleged, he broke and entered the Bata Shoe Store. Five witnesses testified for the prosecution. All the evidence established was a certain amount of suspicion cast on the defendant, who was seen near the store by the watchman.

There was no evidence that any of the items alleged to have been stolen, was ever found in the possession of the defendant. My submission was neatly put in a nutshell. I stated the well-known and accepted doctrine that "Suspicion upon suspicion can never amount to criminal liability" applied. The Court agreed. My client was dismissed. Justice had prevailed.

"Damages Awarded For Dog Bite"

A young seamstress, hair-dresser and caterer was on her way to Church one Sunday morning. As she passed the house of her neighbour, his dog ran out of the yard through the open front gate and bit the young lady on the left leg. The owner came out and gave her forty dollars in an envelope.

The wound eventually became septic and the resulting illness caused her much suffering and financial loss. She was very embarrassed by the scar left by the dog-bite on her leg. The seamstress sued for damages. I appeared for her. The owner of the dog was also represented by Queen's Counsel. The matter was heard and the Court awarded the seamstress four hundred dollars as damages and commented that the wound was not that bad and was on the inner side of the left leg.

There was the funny side of this episode. The owner of the dog remained after the case was finished and when he came out from the Court, he stated that the dog was sensible and intelligent. It did not bite the young lady on the outer side of the left foot, but on the inner side which is not easily visible to the public!!!

~~~~~~~

Now back to the Chief Justice's Court. Much of my Supreme Court cases in the Civil side, in the Divorce and Matrimonial Jurisdiction were before the Chief Justice who did the bulk of the civil work. These cases I am reviewing in this chapter will show the flight and all-embracing nature of my practice.

Still, my colleagues continue to ask me how did I find the time to do any other work than the three hundred and twenty-nine murder cases that I completed successfully, plus my appearance in London before the Privy Council. The
~~~~~~~

only answer that comes to my mind is that I loved what I was doing and never grew tired appearing for clients to defend their rights in Court.

"Reasoning Of Women Not Understandable"

Per Chief Justice, Sir Joseph Luckhoo

The Chief Justice said he could not understand the reasoning process of women, when the wife of a police constable defended a divorce petition filed by her husband. The wife gave evidence before the Court of her husband's cruelty. She recalled a night when she met her husband and another woman walking arm in arm on a road near the matrimonial home.

She told the Court he gave her a serious beating in the presence of the other woman and left her lying injured on the road. How in these circumstances, can a woman want to defend and resist a Divorce Petition brought by her husband? That also baffles me!!! I would have thought that in order to preserve her rights, she would have filed an "Answer" and a "Cross-prayer" seeking divorce from her incredibly cruel husband. But an old lawyer once said to me in my younger days at the Bar, "My Dear young friend, don't ever try to understand the workings of a woman's mind". I never do.

"Blind Horse Deal"

A woman, who sued a vendor for damages because she was sold a blind horse, won her case. The purchaser sued for damages in the Magistrates Court because she claimed that the horse she bought for her son to use with his cart was unfit to do the work as it was blind. The vendor countered with the legal defence of "caveat emptor" – "let the purchaser beware" (i.e. he or she buys at his or her own risk). I appeared for the vendor.

The Magistrate said he did not think that the purchaser was properly advised and gave her back fifty dollars from the purchase price. This is what I prefer to call rough and ready Justice. The purchaser had the horse for six months, used the horse and then brought the claim to recover money on the ground that the horse was blind. The purchaser called no witness (e.g. a veterinarian) or any one else to prove that the horse was blind. The vendor denied that the horse was blind.

"Don't Kiss Him While He Drives"

Many of my cases and my Appeals at all levels have resulted in clarifying and elucidating the many principles and rules of law which have been under serious review for many years. This is one of the many achievements that goes to make a practitioner an outstanding member of the Bar. Of course, a very busy and lucrative practice, coupled with a reputation for being an excellent advocate, a piercing cross-examiner and a great jury lawyer all go to give a practitioner the qualifications to be appointed a Queen's Counsel and Leader of the Bar.

Above all, one must have an unblemished record of integrity and professional rectitude. The above head-note came from the judgment delivered by the Court of Appeal on an Appeal by the Police against the decision of Mr. Clifford M. Baburam, the Magistrate who heard the case and ruled in my favour. The police appealed the decision. My client was a passenger sitting in the front seat of a car driven by one Deonarine. My client, Roopchand, was under the influence of liquor. As they reached a corner, Roopchand shouted, "turn here man" and pulled the steering wheel towards the south thereby causing the car to hit the traffic island.

This case became the leading case as to what constitutes being the "driver" of a motor vehicle. The prosecution closed the case brought against Roopchand who was charged with dangerous driving – an offence requiring *mens rea* as opposed to strict and absolute liability offences.

I then submitted very strenuously, that Roopchand was not the driver of the car, Deonarine was. The wrong person is before the Court. Roopchand, my client, could only be made to answer a civil liability claim as steering plus other controlling factors of a motor vehicle would have to be in place before a person can become the driver of a vehicle. The other controlling factors were missing.

The learned Magistrate agreed with the submission and held that Roopchand was not in law driving or was a driver at the time when the motor car ran into the traffic island. The Police appealed and the Appeal was ably argued by Mr. M. Shahabudeen, then Crown Counsel, now Dr. M. Shahabudeen, Ph.D. a member of the International Court at The Hague. He and I were at Law School together in London. He argued that the steering wheel is a vital instrument of control and whoever took control of the wheel was the driver. A girl who kisses her boy-friend or husband or male friend while he is driving his car can find herself in serious trouble, as by kissing him, she could cause him to lose control of the car, which could have ended up in an accident. Roopchand was charged with the following offences:

- Being the driver of a car while under the influence of liquor;
- Driving in a manner dangerous to the public and
- Not being the holder of a licence in respect of which a policy of insurance was in force in relation to the user.

The learned Magistrate, Mr. Baburam, appreciated and accepted my no-case submissions and found that there was no case for Roopchand to answer. The Full Court presided over by Chief Justice, then Mr. Joseph Luckhoo (later Sir Joseph Luckhoo) and Mr. Justice Guya Persaud did not agree with my arguments and allowed the Police Appeal.

I then appealed to the Federal Court of Appeal of the Caribbean. Sir Stanley Gomes, the Federal Chief Justice and the other Federal Appeal Court Judges allowed the Appeal and found that Roopchand was not in law, the driver of the motor car at the time it struck the traffic island. The decision of the Caribbean Court of Appeal was a great victory for me and further enhanced my reputation and practice in that jurisdiction as well as at home.

"Two Men Cannot Support One Child"

You know a very busy practitioner can find relaxation in simple cases in the Magistrates Courts. The headline in the Newspaper, "TWO MEN CANNOT SUPPORT ONE CHILD" was enough to arouse the interest of the reading public. I enjoyed appearing in the case. I had done quite a lot of these types of cases in my early days at the Bar, so it was a change from the formal and more demanding practice we encounter in the Supreme Court.

Mary brought a complaint under the Bastardy Act of Guyana seeking support from William for a child she bore him. The complainant, Mary, was represented by Counsel and I appeared for William. As I stated before, I am always most happy when I have to appear in matters where both parties are represented by lawyers. I feel somewhat uneasy when I am appearing against a person who is not represented by Counsel. I have known where on occasions, I just had to advise the lay person against whom I was appearing, not to ask certain questions, the answers to which would be detrimental to his case.

The Court usually tries to be of some assistance to unrepresented litigants, but, I find from my experience, that this is not fair to the Magistrate and the Client who is represented by Counsel. After all, the Magistrate has to make findings of fact and determine questions of law involved in the case and all too often the Magistrate, who is a trained lawyer, goes too far and from his conduct shows where he is leaning. It is always best when both parties are represented by trained lawyers. This is one of the main reasons why I have always supported Legal Aid to deserving litigants and given freely to other social and religious organizations which set aside some of their funds to help needy clients with their matters before the Courts, especially domestic proceedings.

To get back to my Magistrates Court matter. I admitted that Williams was the father of the child. I, however, indicated to the Court that although paternity was admitted, I intended to advance legal arguments to show that William was not liable to maintain the child in the circumstances of this particular case. The learned Magistrate was a highly qualified Barrister and I always feel at home when I have to argue law before properly qualified and experienced Judges and Magistrates.

I submitted that in Guyana even though a woman is the mother of the illegitimate child, if she subsequently married and the child was living with her and her husband, then the putative father of the child is not liable to maintain the child, for the basic principle in law is that two men could not be responsible for the support of one child. I went on to submit to the Magistrate that it was against public policy.

Magistrate:	"Mr. Manraj, I am sure you will make submissions on the international law aspects of your legal arguments."
Mr. Manraj:	"I am pleased you have mentioned that, Your Worship. It is clear you are following the development of the legal arguments I am advancing. It is interesting to compare the situation in Guyana with the similar type of situation occurring in France. In France, several men could be made liable for the maintenance of an illegitimate child, once the mother can prove that these several paramours had sexual intercourse with her during the relevant period that can affect gestation".

Mary's lawyer, Mr. Alvin Holder, a pleasant and capable lawyer, readily conceded that my submissions were meritorious and that I had stated the law correctly, "in my usual meticulous style." He went on to inform the Court that the child is being cared for by its maternal grandmother. But before considering the question of maintenance for the child, I ended my submissions this way:

Mr. Manraj: "In view of the provisions of the Maintenance Act of Guyana and the Bastardy Act, it must be clearly understood that no married woman living with her husband could make a separate application for maintenance for an illegitimate child so long as she continues to live with her husband".

The learned Magistrate thanked me for coming to her Court. Some pleasantries were exchanged and Mr. Holder and I then discussed the question of the maintenance for the child. This was not difficult as the standards were established very clearly by the Appeal Court in earlier matters.

"Now, Back to the Supreme Court"

Headline:

"WIVES MUST HELP OUT TOO,"
says the Chief Justice.

On an application by a wife for alimony pending the hearing of a divorce petition, the Chief Justice observed that a husband must support his wife, but went on to say that unless "the wife is ill or infirm, she just cannot sit down and do nothing and expect the husband to maintain her solely".

I appeared for the husband. Here is the part of my cross-examination of the wife, which prompted the Chief Justice's remarks.

Mr. Manraj: "Would you like to work and help out?"
Wifc: "No."
Mr. Manraj: "Would you like to help your husband who is working very hard to make the house comfortable?"
Wife: "No."
Mr. Manraj: "Why?"
Wife: "I do not know why, I just don't like to work."
Mr. Manraj: "What do you do all day?"
Wife: "I look after myself and listen to music."
Mr. Manraj: "Why did you get married?"
Wife: "I wanted a husband to work for me and look after me."
Mr. Manraj: "Are you ill?"
Wife: "No."

It was at this stage that the learned Chief Justice said, "Mr. Manraj, I am not cutting short your cross-examination or directing your course of action, but this wife must be told that wives must help out too, but unless she is ill or infirm, she just cannot sit down and do nothing and expect the husband to maintain her solely. In this case, if all her expenses are to be met by the husband, then there would be nothing left for the children and running expenses of the home."

I did not cross-examine the wife any further. I had already made my point. She created astonishment in the Court. In another undefended divorce petition, a wealthy legislator and cattle-rancher ended his two-year old marriage to his pretty brunette wife, who, he told the Court married him for his money.

I appeared for the husband who told the Chief Justice, before whom he got his marriage dissolved, that his wife told him as he reprimanded her for her indifference towards him, "I only married you for your money, not for love. I do not love you." This marriage had its sad moments.

The husband was sixty and the wife was twenty at the time of their marriage. Despite the thousands of divorce cases I have conducted – both defended and undefended, I always have a feeling of disappointment when I am confronted by cases of loveless marriages, but entered into just for the sake of material gain, financial security or status upliftment. Those marriages are immoral and the contracting party entering a marriage with those hidden horizons has a perverse view of marriage and its sanctity.

My client was very wealthy. The young wife had gone to England to give birth to her baby – a son, who was named after the father. On her return to Guyana, her attitude became "cold, indifferent and unconcerned." Attempts were made at reconciliation but to no avail. The wife actually assaulted her husband. Eventually, I was consulted. Divorce proceedings were filed by me for and on behalf of my client. When the proceedings were over, my client, who was a very practical businessman and politician, thanked me and stated very simply, "You know Mr. Manraj, I paid a high price to experience a loveless marriage and an unwarranted invasion of my generosity and my kindness."

To continue with what I call the "run-of-the-mill" cases, it appears that I was not alone in finding some relaxation despite a wide practice which allowed us like-thinking Barristers to accept those types of cases. How vividly do I recall appearing for a husband, the petitioner in a very keenly contested Divorce Case. Appearing for the wife was fellow Queen's Counsel, B. O. Adams, a very competent and successful practitioner. There are times when I go into

Court and feel as if I am going into a class-room at University to lecture on a particular topic.

This is what happened in the case, which was in the newspaper headlined as:

> *"THREE FORMS OF RELATIONSHIPS BETWEEN MAN AND WOMAN SAYS MR. SHAKOOR MANRAJ, Q.C. COUNSEL FOR THE HUSBAND IN DIVORCE SUIT"*

Mr. Adams and I had discussed the case before the Judge came on the Bench. We reached a settlement. When the Judge came into open Court, I reported to him that Mr. Adams and I had arrived at a settlement in which the wife would not continue to defend the petition and the husband would therefore be entitled to a decree nisi on the evidence before the Court. On the question of permanent maintenance, Mr. Adams for the wife stated that the husband had agreed to give her a monthly allowance.

I then informed the Judge, Mr. Justice Churuman, that the *"dum sole et casta clause"* (during and while the wife is single and pure and chaste) must be added to the Order. For my readers, that was the usual clause which simply means that the husband will pay the agreed maintenance, so long as the wife remained a single woman and chaste. The wife's counsel asked the Court to make an Order that included only the *"dum sole"* clause which would mean that the husband will pay the maintenance to the wife so long as she remained a single woman. I could not agree to this.

Here is where I saw myself as the lecturer in law to the Court. I submitted most respectfully to the learned Judge, that in Guyana there were three forms of relationships that existed between man and woman. One was a legal marriage registered in accordance with the provisions of the law and the second was a "religious marriage" whereby the priest just married the parties in "the eyes of God." This marriage was not registered and therefore was not legal.

Thirdly, the plain and simple practice of a woman "taking up with a man" better known as a "common law marriage", which resulted in the expression "common law wife". I continued by stating that though the wife may remain technically a single woman in the sense that she was not legally married to anyone, yet she is living as man and wife in a common law relationship.

Finally, I submitted to the learned Judge that if the wife "takes up" with a man earning about two hundred dollars a month (in Guyana), it would really result in her drawing maintenance from her ex-husband and pooling it with the earnings of two hundred dollars a month of her current partner, thereby resulting in a figure to which she was not entitled to draw, based on the earnings of the ex-husband. This was not the rationale which was behind the payment of maintenance to the wife. For all these logical and legal reasons, I was asking that the Court Order include the *"dum sole et casta"* clause.

The learned Judge stated that he accepts and fully agrees with the points I submitted and there could be practical difficulties arising from the situation outlined by me if he were to ignore the submissions I made on behalf of the husband. The learned Judge said that he does not accept Mr. Adams' argument that only the "dum sole" part should be inserted in the Order he is about to make. Accordingly, the Judge granted the husband dissolution of the marriage on the ground of malicious desertion by the wife and went on to add in the Order of Court that the permanent maintenance from the husband be paid to the wife, so long as she remains a single and chaste woman – *"dum sole et casta."*

~~~~~~~
~~~~~~~

Where an Ordinance or Act clearly states that Regulations governing the provisions of the said Ordinance or Act are to be published in the "Official Gazette", then this "subsidiary legislation" as it is called, must be proved to show compliance with the substantive Ordinance or Act. I have seen ever so often young practitioners come into Court and enter a plea of guilty without checking to see if there are really any Regulations that were in fact passed.

Unfortunately, these young and inexperienced lawyers just take it for granted that once the charge is laid, it must be right and correct, as the Police would not lay charges that do not exist in the law books of the country. They are so wrong at jumping to this irrational conclusion. I see it happening ever so often. Some of the younger practitioners are grateful for advice given to them by senior members of the Bar. Others who don't care to listen, often lose their case if the Magistrate does not see the legal point involved and depends upon the learning of Defence Counsel to guide the Court at all times.

Let me illustrate what I mean about "subsidiary legislation" must be identified and proved or at least have the relevant section of the named Regulation inserted in the charge. The citizen is entitled to know what charge he is on and not left to guess what is the authority for the prosecution of the offence. The headline in the Daily News read:

"ATTEMPT TO SELL ID PAPER: 3 FREED.

MAGISTRATE UPHOLDS LEGAL SUBMISSIONS

BY A.SHAKOOR MANRAJ, Q.C."

Three young men were charged by the Police with having attempted to sell an "Identity Paper" in the name of "Harold James" an elector, in contravention of the Registration Regulations. (Note: No section of the Regulation or the Substantive Ordinance or Act was mentioned). The men came in to see me and retained me to appear on their behalf.

The matter was called up before Magistrate Dhan Jhappan for trial in the Georgetown Magistrates Court, No. (1). The prosecution led evidence and I declined to cross-examine the prosecution witnesses. It tickles me to see how very uncertain and disturbed Prosecutors get when I do not cross-examine their witnesses. They know from past experience that "something is in the works."

At the close of the Police case, I submitted there was no case to answer as:

- There was no evidence before the Court to show that the Identity Paper was a document contemplated in the Regulation to be an Identity Paper.
- No evidence before the Court showing that the defendants attempted to sell the Identity Paper within the meaning of the law.
- The main witness called by the prosecution to whom it was alleged that the three defendants had offered for sale the ID document, failed to identify the three defendants.

The Court, presided over by an experienced Magistrate, had no difficulty in accepting my submissions, dismissed the charges and set free the three defendants. Justice was done. One cannot assess the inestimable joy that fills my heart when Justice has been done. That is what I dedicated my professional life to accomplish.

Headline:

"EVENING POST NEWSPAPER VINDICATED:

GMC LIBEL ACTION FLOPS"

Finally in this chapter I want to deal with a case that was keenly followed by all other media in Guyana. The

"Evening Post" newspaper reported it as it is – no frills, no dressing, just the facts as they came out in Court. The Guyana Marketing Corporation (GMC) brought an action against Peter Taylor & Co. Ltd. publishers of the "Evening Post." I had the great honour of shouldering the responsibility of being their legal adviser for many years.

The GMC was claiming substantial damages for libel which they alleged was falsely and maliciously published in an article in the "Evening Post" under the caption: "Cold rooms don't work, so FOOD GOES BAD". In their Statement of Claim, the GMC had urged that by reason of the words in the article, "they were severely injured in their credit and reputation and had been brought into public scandal." I filed a Defence on behalf of Peter Taylor & Co. Ltd. denying that the words were published falsely or maliciously and also *inter alia*, set up the defence of fair comment.

The GMC then brought a Summons in Chambers before His Lordship, Mr. Justice Bollers (later Sir Harold Bollers) asking that the part of the defence where the defendants had denied that the words were published falsely or maliciously, be struck out.

I, on behalf of the Defendant Company, argued that the pleading was a denial of the allegation made by the GMC in their Statement of Claim. I further submitted that the Defendant Company was relying on the defence of "fair comment" and that they therefore were justified in filing the Defence in the way it was worded. Still going into the very depths of the "Law on Libel," I further submitted that the plaintiff's (GMC) contention was untenable and that if the Defendant attempted to raise any other defence, the plaintiff would certainly object.

His Lordship, Mr. Justice Bollers, reserved his decision until the morning. Then he delivered a written judgment. In difficult points of law arising in Civil cases, it is always best to have a written judgment. His Lordship stated in his judgment that such a pleading as filed by me on behalf of the Defendant Company was permissible providing that one of three defences was raised namely, privilege, justification or fair comment. The learned Judge therefore dismissed the Plaintiff's application and the Summons and awarded costs in favour of Peter Taylor & Co. Ltd. and Mr. Peter Taylor. It gave me great pleasure to tax my Bill of Costs. This was not an easy case – but careful study led to Justice being done for all the parties in the matter.

This is how I see myself – an Officer of the Court, a Senior member of the Bar, a practising lawyer, advancing every point of law and fact I could make on behalf of my clients and assisting the Courts to administer Justice. This is how my fifty years at the Bar were spent. It paid off handsome dividends. My professional standing at the Bar, was and continues to be, very high and that is recognized by all the Judges before whom I have the honour to appear.

Chapter 14

Husband "Gets Even" With His Ex-Wife

Taking Children Outside Of the Jurisdiction of The Court

I have always maintained that Divorce cases do not have to degenerate into open warfare between husband and wife. There must have been some chemistry existing between them, when the "I love you" vows were exchanged. It is sad enough when couples get divorced especially when there are children to be considered and are caught in the cross-fire.

This has caused me some concern and that is why in my fifty years at the Bar, I have always endeavoured to make the Divorce proceedings proceed as smoothly as possible, without rancour, enmity, hate and spitefulness dominating the procedure. Perhaps, I am being too idealistic. How can one subdue the inherent hatred one spouse has for the other, who committed adultery so publicly and flagrantly as to bring shame and cause wounded feelings to the other spouse? Even the son "Hamlet" in Shakespeare's Tragedy, assessed his mother's behaviour with these caustic words: "Let me not think on't; frailty thy name is woman". ("Hamlet" Act 1. Scene ii, Line 148). This is even though his mother, the Queen of his deceased father, the King of Denmark, married Hamlet's uncle within a year of the King's rather suspicious death.

As I proceed, Dear Readers, you will see how involved reprisals can become. In this case under review, the husband came from Madeira. He was Portuguese. He set up business in Georgetown, the capital of Guyana and soon became a very successful horologist with an elite clientele. The wife was a pretty young Portuguese girl who worked as a Secretary in a large firm in Georgetown. Eventually, the horologist and the Secretary got married and everything was heavenly for a while. They had three children. Then the honey and milk turned sour.

The wife came to see me regarding the break-down of the marriage. There was no hope of reconciliation. I filed a petition for Divorce on behalf of the wife. The Divorce was heard and the wife was given custody of the three children of the marriage with reasonable access, on appointed days, for the father to see the children of the marriage.

So far things were moving pretty normally until the ex-husband, on one of his access days, vanished with the three children and took them to his homeland, Madeira. The wife was seriously affected by this dishonest move on the part of her ex-husband. The wife was under severe trauma and became very hysterical as she told me what happened. I had to calm her down and when she was composed and able to listen to me, I told her there is nothing to worry about. I will file proceedings to get the children brought back to Guyana. That was easier said than done. But I set the law in motion and it prevailed.

I filed proceedings before the Chief Justice, Sir Joseph Luckhoo, asking for an Order of Court to compel the husband to return the children to Guyana and within the Jurisdiction of the Supreme Court. The Supreme Court in law is the "guardian of all minor children." I further asked in my application for the Learned Chief Justice to declare that the ex-husband was in "Contempt of Court" as he had brazenly violated the Order of the Court giving him access to the children, who were born in Guyana.

It was a serious violation of the Court Order, as by removing the children out of the jurisdiction of the Court, he was attempting to render the Court sterile of its inherent powers. But the Court does not lose jurisdiction and do nothing about it. The Chief Justice made an Order for the children to be returned to the wife immediately and the assistance of "Interpol" ("International Police") was sought and obtained.

The wife armed with this Order of Court left Guyana and went to Madeira, some two thousand, five hundred miles away, to get back her children. The Majesty of the Law must prevail at all times.

Mr. Manraj:	"And did you bring back the children?"
Wife:	"Yes, Sir.
Mr. Manraj:	"How much did you spend in all?"
Wife:	"More than seven thousand, five hundred dollars, of which, my ex-husband has not paid me back a cent."

The children are all now in the custody of their mother, but that is only the first part of this episode. The husband purged his contempt and had to give very substantial monetary security before regaining access to his children in Guyana. Let us call this Act I, Scenes I & II. Now for Act II.

The city horologist, the ex-husband, about one year after served a Contempt Order on his former wife based on these following facts. On a day when he had access to the children, accompanied by a policeman and another witness, he drove his car to some distance away from the wife's residence. He sent the two men and they asked the mother for the children. She quite correctly refused to hand over the children as she did not know the two men who were strangers to her. The ex-husband then went to Court asking the Court to find that his ex-wife had disobeyed the Court Order which provided that she will allow the father access of the children on appointed days.

The husband was represented by Mr. B. O. Adams. Again we were on opposing sides. This happens ever so often when Senior Barristers find themselves on opposite sides in high profile cases. I again appeared for the wife with Mr. Oliver Valz as my instructing Solicitor. I submitted very forcefully to the learned Judge, Mr. Justice Arthur Chung (he later became the first President of Guyana) that the mother of the children had to seek the assistance of the International Police in Madeira to rescue her children who were whisked out of the country and what is worse, out of the Court's jurisdiction, by her ex-husband.

She was therefore and understandably so, very distrustful of him and refused on the day in question to hand the children over to the two strange men. I further submitted that it was not a case of the mother of the children disobeying the Court Order, but a case of her being fearful of handing the children over to two strangers whom she never saw and did not know.

She was afraid of a repetition of her ex-husband's conduct and attitude. She feared he would flee the country with the children and take them to Madeira again. I told the Court that up to the present time, he had not reimbursed the money she spent to go to Madeira a year ago to recover her children. I ended up by saying to His Lordship, the Judge,

> "My Lord, this is not a case of contempt or flouting the relevant Court Order. The mother acted properly and must be commended for her wisdom. If the father had come himself for the children and the mother had refused to allow him the access which he was entitled to in law, then the mother would have been in a very difficult situation. This is not the case. The Order did not state that she must hand over her children to strangers on their representations that they had come to collect the children for the father. Why did he not go and collect the children? He was in his car, which was parked some distance away from my client's residence."

I asked His Lordship to dismiss the ex-husband's contempt proceedings. He is just trying to be vindictive to his ex-wife.

Mr. B. O. Adams, representing the ex-husband, stated to the Court that the "brutal" fact of the matter was that up to the time of the service of the Contempt Order, the children had never been to their father's home. He went on to state, much to my surprise, that the father might have had very good reasons to take the children to Madeira. Mr. Adams contended that the wife flouted the Order of Court regarding access to the husband and that was contempt of Court. I did not reply to these rather strange and untenable submissions by my friend. I felt I had covered every aspect of my case sufficiently.

Mr. Justice Arthur Chung dismissed the ex-husband's application and stated *inter alia*, that he found the businessman to be very vindictive towards his ex-wife. The husband was asking the Court to commit his ex-wife to prison for contempt of a Court Order following the sad occasion of their divorce proceedings which ended about one year ago.

The Judge said that he was not satisfied that the case went beyond a reasonable doubt. He said he could not see the ex-husband gaining anything by his ex-wife's imprisonment. He told the ex-wife that she must be careful because the Courts have the power to commit to prison those who flout the Court's Order. It is a very satisfying feeling when a Judge acts in accordance with principles leading to Justice being done.

Where else must one turn to attain Justice in a civilized and orderly society? Below the statue of Justice are these words, which I cited earlier: "Defend the children of the Poor and Punish the Wrongdoer." In today's evolving society Justice defends all children either of the poor or of the rich and that is why the welfare of all children is of paramount importance to the Court. This will be illustrated in the next matter which I will deal with in this chapter.

Before starting to write this book, I did a lot of "ground work" and surveys of the types of material in which the reading public is genuinely interested. As a result of my researches, I decided to give my readers a "mixed bag" of cases and matters I appeared in during my fifty years at the Bar. One thing that I was delighted to discover was this. The reading public is not interested in hearing only about murder cases and other types of criminal infractions, but were very eager to hear more of my experiences in civil claims, proceedings to protect rights and interests, juvenile matters and most important of all, the human factor, so very vital in a domestic relationship.

It would have been easier for me to write about my successes in the three hundred and twenty-nine murder cases in which I appeared and defended successfully. That is just "cut and dried" reporting. But I can quite understand when I was told by the many members of the public, parents and social workers to whom I spoke in public libraries, University libraries, workshops and generally, that they would like to learn more about the human conduct and behaviour in Court, in contractual relationships e.g. marriages, custodial proceedings and proprietary rights. Of course, there is always an eager interest in cross-examination of witnesses and witty and sometimes heated interchanges and exchanges between Bench and Bar. I hope that overall, my humble efforts in this book, will reflect the interest of my prospective readers of all classes and tastes and walks of life.

Just a few introductory remarks before I deal with what was headlined in one of the daily newspapers:

"MUMMY WEEPS IN COURT AS DADDY GETS THE SIX CHILDREN OF THE MARRIAGE"

The Supreme Courts of all countries are the "Fountain heads of Justice." One reads about the "Royal Courts of Justice" in London, the "United States Supreme

Court" and "Supreme Court Judges." "Justice" flows from the Court. The various Judges are the Guardians of this "Justice." In a special reference to children, there seems to be a singularly binding vinculum between the Courts and the welfare of all minor children.

Flowing from this, we have the developing responsibility that the Supreme Court is the "Upper Guardian" of all minor children. It is under this principle that the Supreme Court appoints itself as Guardian of all minor children who then become the WARDS of the Court. People who contend that their young children are theirs and they can do what they want to do with their children and the Court cannot interfere, are SO WRONG.

In cases brought before the Court by Child Welfare Officers and a host of Social and Religious Organizations that are deeply committed to the welfare and well-being of minor children, the Supreme Court Judges have been vested with the authority to make Orders of Court, affecting the welfare and the best interests of the young children and their guardianship.

Mummy Weeps; Daddy Gets the Six Children

The first matter I dealt with in this chapter, was one in which the Court awarded custody to the mother of the three children of the marriage with access to the father. Usually, this is the general practice – custody to mother with access to father. But all too infrequently it happens that the mother is denied custody. In this case that I will be reviewing, let me show you what happened.

My client, Mr. Jashus Young was legally married to his wife Bibiana and there were six children of the marriage. At the time of the custody proceedings the children were thirteen, twelve, eleven, nine, seven and six years old – five girls and one boy, the seven year old. Mr. Young was a Telecommunications' Technician and worked with the Telecommunications Department. Mr. Young had brought

Divorce proceedings for dissolution of the marriage. The children were with the mother. He lost his divorce petition for dissolution of the marriage. It must be mentioned that the wife had filed an Answer to the husband's petition and cross-prayed for a Divorce on the ground of the husband's misconduct with his housekeeper.

The Divorce Judge found that the allegation was not proved. The children and mother lived apart from my client but he sent regular sums of money for his children. He had a good paying job, technicians always get good salaries. The husband saw his children regularly and they always complained to him about their mother's cruelty to them and her rather frequent disappearance at nights from the home leaving the children alone.

The children said to their father, "Please take us. Mommy does not treat us well. We are left at home at nights." The eldest child, aged thirteen, was "big sister" to all the children and she told her Dad that sometimes they had to wear the same dirty clothes to school day after day as their mother told them she was too tired to wash their clothes. What was really the last straw was when the children turned up at the father's house looking (to use the words of my client) "dirty and starved." The eldest child complained that the mother would curse them and beat them with her shoes and slippers.

The father came to see me and brought the children with him. He could not find the mother. I listened to all that was said and before I could say anything, the father said to me: "Mr. Manraj, these are my children. I love them all – my one son and five little girls. I want custody of them. I have a house with all the amenities and I can take care of them."

From what I heard from the father and the children, I had to concede that he has a very good and tenable response to the wife's application to the Supreme Court for an Order giving custody of the children to her. I proceeded to file that Answer to the wife's application before the Supreme Court. The father had taken the children to his house and provided for them. They were well treated and on the morning of the trial they looked clean, bright and happy. The trial was before Mr. Justice Guya Persaud. The mother was represented by Counsel, who did not seriously dispute the contents of the father's affidavit in support of the answer filed by him.

The trial started. The mother presented her case saying in essence that as mother, she was entitled to custody of the children of the marriage. The father then presented his case and told the Judge about the mother's treatment of the children and what he saw with his own eyes, of the mother's neglect of the children. I had him tell the Court about his job, his earnings, the regular schooling of the children, his supervision of them and their home-work and all the relevant facts to support his answer to the mother's application. The father was prepared to give the mother reasonable access to the children. The eldest child Loretta, only thirteen, was called by me to give evidence. I therefore had to elicit evidence in chief. This is how it went:

Mr. Manraj:	"Loretta, how old are you?"
Loretta:	(Barely audible) "Thirteen years old."
Mr. Manraj:	"Loretta you will have to speak much louder than that so that His Lordship, the Judge, can hear you. I can hardly hear you. Please speak as loudly as when you are on the playing fields at school. Do you hear me?"
Loretta:	"Yes, Mr. Manraj."
Mr. Manraj:	"When last did you see your mother."
Loretta:	"About a month ago."
Mr. Manraj:	"Do you see her in Court today?"
Loretta:	"No, I did not look across to the other side."
Mr. Manraj:	"Do you love your mother?"
Loretta:	"No, Sir."
Mr. Manraj:	"Why do you not love your mother?"

Loretta:	"She always cursed me and my sisters and brother. For the least thing, she would beat us with her shoes and slippers. She called us bad names."
Mr. Manraj:	"Would you please tell the Court, Loretta, what were the bad names?"
Loretta:	(A little pause) "She called us dogs. She called me and my sister sluts. She told us that Daddy will make sluts of us."
Mr. Manraj:	"Do you understand what is meant by the expression or word 'slut'?"

Before she could answer, the mother's lawyer, the late Mr. C. V. Wight, got up and objected to the question put by me to the witness.

Judge:	"Mr. Wight, what is wrong with Mr. Manraj's question?"
Mr. Wight:	"My Lord I object because it is leading the witness."
Judge:	"Mr. Wight I would like to think that a lawyer of your experience would know by now, what is a leading question. All Mr. Manraj is asking the witness is whether or not she understands what is meant by the expression or word *'slut.'* Your objection is over-ruled. Mr. Manraj, please continue with your examination in chief of your witness."
Mr. Manraj:	"Thank you, My Lord. Loretta, I repeat the question: Do you understand what is meant by the expression or word 'slut'?"
Loretta:	"Sir, I think it means a bad woman."
Mr. Manraj:	"Loretta, do you love your mother?"

Loretta:	(Between sobs) “No. I love my Daddy. We all love Daddy.”
Mr. Manraj:	“Please tell the Court why you love your Daddy.”
Loretta:	“He loves us. He cares us. He gives us food. He sees to it we are kept clean. He helps us with our schoolwork at home. He is always enquiring from us about our school and teachers.”
Mr. Manraj:	“Well Loretta, would you want to go back to your mother?”
Loretta:	“No, Sir.”
Mr. Manraj:	“Could you tell us why?”
Loretta:	(Still sobbing). “She kicked me two times.”
Mr. Manraj:	“Where did she kick you?”
Loretta:	“On my legs.”
Mr. Manraj:	“Do you know why?”
Loretta:	“When Daddy went to England on a Telecommunications scholarship to study, Mommy used to go out most nights and especially on Saturday nights, leaving us alone.”
Mr. Manraj:	“How do you know she used to go out?”
Loretta:	“Because I would see a car come and Mommy will go inside and the car will drive away. She did not come back until morning time.”
Mr. Manraj:	“What happened to you and your sisters and brother when your mother stayed out?”
Loretta:	“Sir, we were all afraid. We had no one to look after us. I used to lay awake and cry until Mommy returned.”

Then followed the cross-examination by Mr. C. V. Wight. As I said earlier, an incautious cross-examination could be disastrous. A young witness usually tells the truth. If, as some lawyers do and try to prepare their witness, experience has shown that it is dangerous to do that with young witnesses. They cannot be coached easily to tell untruths. I think the old saying is: "From the mouths of babes you get the truth." Suffice it to say that the cross-examination confirmed that young Loretta was a truthful witness.

Several times, Mr. Wight suggested to Loretta that she was coached by her father to give the answers she gave to me under examination-in-chief, but, Loretta become more convincing when she replied to one of these suggestions: "Sir, I do not lie. Mommy lies. She told us a lot of lies when all of us asked her why doesn't she come home and spend the nights with us. We are only small children." I just called two more witnesses. After all the evidence was in before the Judge, then both lawyers addressed the Judge in closing arguments.

In my address to the Judge, I submitted that the only questions before His Lordship were the question of custody and secondly, which one of the parents should be given custody of the children. I cited several legal authorities to show circumstances relating to custody and what are the guiding principles of law. The Judge then adjourned the matter for his ruling. The ruling was delivered the next day.

The Judge refused the wife's application for custody. The mother, Bibiana Young sat in Court, her eyes filled with tears as the Judge delivered his decision in favour of the father, Jashus Young. I was present in Court. The learned Judge went on: "The plaintiff and the defendant (father) were wife and husband and the children mentioned in the application were the lawful children of the marriage. I am not concerned whether the father had deserted the mother, but I am concerned with custody and custody alone and I am only to give legal effect to the provisions of the Law on this particular aspect of the law. In any event, my mind is not swayed one way or the other by the wishes expressed by the children who testified. The application by the wife was based on the alleged misconduct of the father with his housekeeper but I found from the evidence, that the allegations had not been proved.

Where a common law jurisdiction was being exercised, unless the right of the parent was diminished by reason of misconduct on the part of the parent, or by some statute affecting such rights, then it seems to me, that the right of the parent to the custody of the child was absolute and the Court would have to give the child over to the parent.

In the circumstances, having regard to my findings on the fact, I must refuse the order the mother asked for. I have taken into account the existing amenities which the children enjoy at their father's house, as against the absence of any such amenities at the mother's residence. The wife's application for custody of the children is dismissed. I therefore make the Order giving custody of the six children to the father."

I feel that Justice was done. The learned Judge clearly stated the yardstick which is used to consider the welfare and well-being of young children. The Court, at all times, must act in its faithful discharge and performance of that sacred trust – The Supreme Court is the "Upper Guardian" of all minor children. In both of these cases, Justice was done. From any reasonable and moral approach of the two cases considered in this chapter, Justice was done. The recipients here were young children. A wrong standard can cause inconceivable harm and distress to a young child. That is a development no reasonable and caring individual would want to happen.

Chapter 15

Never Judge A Book By Its Cover

Facts Of A Case Take On A Different Appearance

At first blush, the facts of a case as set out in the police charge sheet can appear difficult and very strong against the defendant, but after investigation, research and closer, patient examination, things take on a different appearance. Never judge a book by its cover. Please read on, dear reader and you will see what I mean.

I had just returned from the Bahamas where I had appeared in a lengthy and intricate civil action involving title to land and trespass to land. Judgment was given in my favour. My clients were very pleased. Now is the time I thought that I would take a little break and enjoy a few days at home, catching up on domestic correspondence and all the things my wife, Bonita, looks after for me while I am away. My wife takes care of a multitude of important matters while I am away on overseas cases, or out of state or out of town cases, or sometimes just very busy in Court.

Hardly had I settled in to what I saw as an earned mini vacation, when I received a phone call from an old acquaintance, Neville Chand, who presently lives in Providenciales in the Turks and Caicos Islands. Neville is a fine gentleman. He left Guyana to go to the Turks and Caicos Islands on promotion in the Police Force of those Islands. When I started travelling to the Turks and Caicos Islands on special retainers several years before, we had the pleasure of renewing our friendship. We used to meet very often when we were both in Guyana. I knew him and some members of his family – not all of them. In his phone call,

Neville told me that he wanted me to appear for his son, Kasodatt, in New York.

He told me that his son will contact me and give to me all the details and the relevant documents. The very next day, April 26, 2001, I received from Neville Chand, twelve sheets of photo-copied documents. He had come to Miami on business and brought the documents with him. On April 30, 2001, Kasodatt Chand phoned me from New York. He told me that he had retained a lawyer in New York, Mr. Leonard Ressler and he told Mr. Ressler that I will be appearing with him in the case as Senior Counsel. He said to me that Mr. Ressler was very pleased with this arrangement.

He had never met a member of the English Bar or a Queen's Counsel before. Kasodatt assured me that Mr. Ressler was very anxious to have me on board as Senior Defence Counsel and that if it becomes necessary, he would present my Petition for Call *pro hac vice* to the New York Bar conferring upon me, special permission to appear in and conduct the case. This was very re-assuring news as I always have to make sure that this requirement is met when I go to practise in overseas or in any other jurisdictions. Things were moving swiftly. All the domestic arrangements regarding fees, travelling and accommodations were worked out to my satisfaction. It was just at a stage now where I must start studying the charges and decide what steps we will take.

In a short while I will set out fully what were the charges laid against my client, Kasodatt Chand, who now runs a very successful international trucking service. Eventually copies of the charges and disclosures from the New York Police were forwarded to me by my client. I was glad to wade into them. On the face of the documents I had in front of me, it seemed to me that this was a rather serious and difficult matter, especially having as its locus, the City of New York. But this was a "first blush" impression.

First, let me outline the events of the early evening in question. It appears that my client and some of his friends were in a bar on Sunday night, November 12, 2000 having some week-end drinks. The bar was crowded. It was a popular and regular "spot" for the residents of the area. In the course of the evening, an altercation arose in the bar between some revellers. My client objected to the high-handed action taken by the resident "Bouncer" and before you could say "Jack Robin," my client was thrown out of the bar. This incident is important. You will see the importance of this incident at the very end of the case. See if you could be Sherlock Holmes and work out how this incident will become very important to my client who admitted that he was thrown out of the bar by the Bouncer. There were certain incidents that were alleged to have taken place outside the bar and it is in relation to these alleged incidents that charges were laid against my client, Mr. Kasodatt Chand. What were the charges and the Police case?

The Police charged my client who, "while acting in concert with another, aiding and abetting another, and/or being aided and abetted by another, committed the offences of:

- The defendant, acting in concert with another, did, with intent to commit the crime of murder in the second degree and to cause the death of another person,
- Engage in conduct which attempted to cause the death of such person or a third person,
- With intent to use the same unlawfully against another did possess a loaded firearm outside his home or place of business,
- With intent to cause physical injury to another person, causes such injury to such person or to a third person by means of a deadly weapon."

These were the particulars of the charges. The Statement of the Offences all stated in the Penal Law (PL) is as follows:

- "Attempted Murder in the second degree.
- Criminal possession of a weapon in the second degree- an armed felony offence.
- Criminal possession of a weapon in the third degree – an armed felony offence.
- Assault in the Second Degree – an armed felony offence."

The above discloses the "Statement of Offence" and the "Particulars of Offence." Just a note of interest at this point: you will see how ponderous is the language of the "Particulars of Offence" and how equally vague is the language in the "Statement of Offence". But these later on did ground my attack on the whole proceedings and my submissions to halt and arrest any proceedings in this matter. The best is yet to come. I must now go through the facts on which the police were relying. This is very important as you will connect these facts with the submissions I made materially affecting the whole of the State's case against my client. These are the facts on which the Police were basing the prosecution:

"The deponent (that is, detective Perlene E. Kaalund – this parenthesis is mine) is informed by an eye witness, Herman Espinal, that on November 12, 2000 at approximately 2:15 a.m. at the vicinity of …, said witness observed his brother, the complainant, Jose Espinal, engaged in an altercation with the defendant (Kasodatt Chand) and another male. The complainant did then flee the location by getting inside a vehicle, driven by another male, going towards his (complainant's) home. The said eye-witness, (Herman Espinal) observed the defendant and another male entering a green Thunderbird car and started following the vehicle in which the complainant was riding.

Eye-witness states that when the complainant arrived at his home, the vehicle in which he was travelling stopped and the complainant exited. Defendant's vehicle also stopped. Defendant came out of his vehicle, pointed a hand-gun at the direction of the complainant from a distance of about twenty feet and fired a shot from the said hand-gun. The complainant (Jose Espinal) immediately after the shooting, re-entered the vehicle which he had just exited and asked the driver to flee the location quickly. This he did. As a result of the shooting, the complainant sustained gun shot wounds about his shoulder and more specifically, an entry wound about the rear area of the shoulder and an exit wound about the front of the shoulder accompanied by bleeding and substantial pain. The above-described wounds required treatment at a local Queen's Hospital and follow up treatment with oral medications upon being discharged. This was for a period of about ten days."

Now let me pause here for a moment. If nothing else was forthcoming, what would you say? The case against the defendant on paper looks very bad for him and no doubt many readers would say that "without a doubt" the defendant is guilty. But when we go further and examine the evidence and the method involved in securing the evidence, a different scenario is established pointing to the weakness and flaws in the prosecution's case. Constitutional rights are enshrined in most written Constitutions for the protection of the citizens of the country.

The Courts are there to see that constitutional rights are enforced and protected. These rights do not exist *in vacuo* (in empty space, in a vacuum). The Judges who sit in the Courts are not walking law libraries. That is why legal practitioners are there to defend, to translate and to transform these abstract constitutional rights into a reality, into something that has meaning, where the rights of the citizen are concerned. It is an inviolable trust that is placed in the hands of lawyers, especially Criminal Defence Attorneys to see that rights which are in place to protect the citizen, must be applied by the Court and so see that "Justice must not only be done, but must be seen to be done." Then and only then can a civilized society say that Justice has triumphed and fairness has been meted out to the citizen.

With these standards and principles firmly embedded in my mind, I set about examining the case against the defendant and the manner in which the evidence was obtained. Only evidence which is properly and legally obtained can be adduced in evidence. For example, hearsay evidence is not usually admissible. There are many exceptions to the hearsay rule. One has to examine those exceptions to see if they are properly applicable to the offending inadmissible evidence.

As I started my research and investigation of this case, several strange facts left me very perturbed. Kasodatt Chand was taken into custody on November 30, 2000 on the facts mentioned earlier in this review of the case. Bail was set in the amount of two hundred and fifty thousand dollars. On December 26, 2000 Mr. Leonard Ressler filed a Writ of Habeas Corpus seeking the release of the defendant or in the alternative, reasonable bail for the defendant. Mr. Leonard Ressler is a very competent, capable and meticulous lawyer and his supporting facts filed with his Application for Writ of Habeas Corpus were very adequately and effectively summarised.

While in custody, my client Kasodatt Chand evinced great ingenuity. He was severely restricted in the supply of writing material. He had a pen. That was his only "weapon." He used the Gideon "Holy Bible" in his cell to record his inner thoughts and the developments taking place with respect to his matter. When I met him in New York for the first time on July 8, 2001 at JFK Airport at 4.30 p.m., I found him to be a very pleasant, caring and disciplined individual.

Something told me there and then that the allegations against him are out of place. Somewhere, somehow, something was not right. After so many years of active practice at the Bar, one gets a "hunch" that something was not right – something that just did not "gel". I also had the pleasure of meeting his wife, Alicia and their daughter, Felicia, a lovely little girl, who at the time was just about two years old. She was a pre-mature baby and could not walk and was “wheel chair bound.” First impressions can be at times very important. That night, in my Hotel room, I read every piece of information that was handed over to me including the notes made in the Holy Bible. I saw clearly then on a factual assessment, that my client was not guilty and I started my preparation of the case with a definite commitment to see that Justice is done.

That very night I read the copious notes made by my client in the Holy Bible. My colleagues tell me I have a photographic memory. Every aspect of his account in the Holy Bible of what happened in the bar and afterwards became deeply embedded in my memory. On July 11, 2001 I returned the “Holy Bible” to my client and told him to keep it in a safe and secure place. On July 9, 2001 at 3.00 p.m., I met Mr. Leonard Ressler in his law office for the first time. He is a very pleasant man and reminded me very much of my Law Professor in Equity at Law School in England.

We “clicked” and I knew then that our representation of our client will be successful. I discussed with Lenny Ressler all the weak links in the prosecution’s case. It reminded me of what I always and unfailingly tell the jury in the closing part of my address that “a chain is as strong as its weakest link.” Examine that aphorism. It is one hundred per cent correct. I discussed the question of trial dates with Leonard Ressler and even when I returned to Florida, I continued discussions with him of not only the weak links in the prosecution’s case, but the fatal and incurable errors in the case.

By August 14, 2001, I completed my lengthy legal opinion and assessment of the case and I wrote to Ressler a long letter with my legal opinion featuring prominently in the communication. I saw from the documents in my possession, that all the Felony charges were withdrawn or at least no evidence will be offered by the State in all the Felony charges. The charge of Assault was substituted. This is a misdemeanour. It was suggested that the defendant pleads guilty to this misdemeanour. This my client could not do as he maintains that he never assaulted Jose Espinal. The evidence that the State hoped to adduce in Court in this regard, bristles with evidentiary difficulties with respect to its admissibility.

You, dear readers, will see the reason when I deal with this aspect of the case a little later on in this chapter. The only violation committed by Kasodatt on the night in question (that is, November 12, 2000) was disorderly conduct.

Regarding the Misdemeanour Charge

The State has a weak case and would encounter severe evidentiary difficulties to prove this case. Identification is the pivotal issue in this case. The defendant is saying he did not commit this offence of assault with the gun. His defence is an alibi. Now let me outline why the prosecution's case is so very weak and cannot succeed.

1. The eye-witness, Herman Espinal, said he saw the defendant enter a GREEN Thunderbird and followed the complainant Jose Espinal.
2. The defendant owns a Blue Thunderbird car. This vehicle was inoperable since October 27, 2000. Proof of this was supplied to the Police. It is ridiculous and most of all, ludicrous to state that the defendant does not know the colour of his own car. The fact is that on the night in question, the defendant was driving a RED NISSAN SENTRA. This is where the prosecution's case started to crumble. The man the prosecution was after, was the man who drove off in the GREEN Thunderbird. This was the statement of the State's eye-witness, Herman Espinal.
3. On the question of identification of the defendant, it is significant that the complainant was involved in a face to face altercation with the defendant; yet, the very complainant could not identify Kasodatt Chand, the defendant. Very important indeed.

4. The identification line-up took place outside of the presence of learned Counsel (Mr. Ressler). The request was made by the defendant for Counsel to be present. Mr. Ressler was there. He offered to be present at the Identification Parade. He, Mr. Ressler, was representing Vickram Chand, the brother of the defendant. Mr. Ressler was barred from being present at the identification parade. Why? What is the reason to prevent Mr. Ressler from being present? Is it that preparations were being made by the police for some "testilying"? This is the word used by Professor Alan M. Dershowitz in his beautifully written book "Reasonable Doubt" (referred to in an earlier chapter of this book). Why prevent Mr. Ressler, a competent attorney, from being present at the identification parade? It is clear as a matter of law, that the evidence regarding identification would be inadmissible. This case is crumbling rapidly.

5. Vickram, Kasodatt's brother, is alleged to be the accomplice of Kasodatt. Vickram stated from the very outset that neither he nor his brother, Kasodatt, had been involved in any altercation with any Hispanics that evening at the bar. Vickram stated that Kasodatt had left the bar earlier on the night in question and was at home at the time of the alleged incident. Vickram, it must be noted, was arrested but released due to insufficient evidence.

6. The defendant had left the scene of the alleged incident and drove ANOEP K. DHAWTAL home around 1:30 a.m. Kasodatt then drove home and stayed at home. He was not at the scene.

7. A wife's credibility cannot be impeached, simply because she is the defendant's wife. She is a competent witness. Kasodatt's wife, Alicia, is the main witness to his alibi. She states *inter alia*: "I was at home on the morning of November 12, 2000 with my child and Kasodatt arrived home that morning between 1.15 a.m. and 1.30 a.m. and he remained at home for the rest of that morning and until the afternoon of November 12, 2000. During the hours of 1.30

a.m. until the afternoon of that day, (November 12, 2000), I was constantly in his presence."

I mentioned earlier that I will be dealing with some other important aspects of the case later in the chapter. I will do so now. It is the law and it must be obeyed, that when a person is taken into custody, he must be told of his MIRANDA rights. This was not done. Again, at an identification parade a defendant <u>must</u> be told of his rights, especially the right he has to request his lawyer to be present. This again was not done and what is outrageous is that the defendant requested that Mr. Ressler, who was present, be present at the identification parade held in regard to his identification. The defendant's request for Counsel to be present at the Identification Parade line- up was DENIED. What was the reason?

The MIRANDA CASE is an outstanding case. It is the high level of United States Jurisprudence. The reasoning and the dicta have been approved and adopted by Courts in England, Canada, Australia and many other countries where the Common Law Jurisdiction is firmly entrenched. See: <u>Miranda –v- Arizona.</u> (June 13, 1966 per C.J. WARREN – 384 U.S.). On page 492 of the Miranda decision, Chief Justice Warren of the U.S. Supreme Court set out clearly the reasons for reversing the decision handed down by the Supreme Court of Arizona.

I think I have established enough to show that the State's case here lacks credibility and is plagued by severe violations of established principles of law and practice. The manner in which the investigation was carried out, infringes the standards set out by the U.S. Supreme Court. The vital parts of the evidence on which the State relied, were inadmissible.

I ended my letter to Mr. Ressler with the reminder, that in keeping with established practice and traditions of the Bar, "we must do everything in our power to protect our client."

(Left) My client, Kasodatt Chand of New York.
(Top) Kasodatt, his wife, Alicia and daughter, Felicia.
(Below) Shakoor shares a joyous moment with Kasodatt and daughter.

Still very happy, Shakoor returns to New York in 2003 and visits the Chand family.

On August 17, 2001, Mr. Ressler phoned me. He was in receipt of my letter of August 14, 2001 and was very lavish with his kind remarks regarding my full, adequate and correct principles stated therein. He agreed that the State's case was weak and could not survive legal submissions to have it dismissed. He agreed that the matter can be ended by a simple ACD (Adjournment in Contemplation of a Dismissal).

I had the pleasure of meeting Miss Valerie Batista, at the time, Assistant District Attorney (ADA). She is a very charming and efficient ADA and I admired her for her ready grasp of difficult legal concepts. You will recall that very early in this chapter, I mentioned that my client admitted being involved in a disorderly encounter with the "Bouncer." He was prepared to enter a plea of guilty to the Disorderly Conduct taking place at the bar earlier in the evening in question. He did so on September 28, 2001 in open Court. Mr. Ressler and I were present in Court. Kasodatt was ordered to perform forty hours of Community Service. This was the tame and unspectacular end to what appeared on paper to be a cause *célèbre*. I am happy to say that my client went on to become the owner of a successful and vibrant trucking company in his favourite New York. We see each other whenever I am in New York.

When I originally came to Florida from Canada, I met an American Attorney, Mr. Nashid Sabir. He and I became very much associated in legal matters. Mr. Sabir is a very devoted practitioner and a very competent lawyer. I became attached to his office as a legal consultant and adviser. We have together worked in some interesting matters in and out of Court. In Court, he is focussed and with deliberate and studied rhetoric, gets his points across successfully. I have appeared with him in Court in several matters and he knows how to marshal his arguments. He is well respected at the Bar and since we became associated with each other, I always refer all matters to him for our collaboration. In his office, he has a very short, but effective quotation from Abraham Lincoln: "A lawyer's time and advice are his stock in trade." This is a truism. If we allow the ever present and sometimes unnecessary invasion of our time, busy practitioners will never have any time left for themselves. It is a pleasure to be associated with Mr. Nashid Sabir.

Sometimes it is not always big matters in Court. One would be surprised to know how retainers flow into the Office. Several years ago, four U.S. Investors contacted me. They were interested in the lumber industry in Guyana. As the reader already knows, Guyana does not only export sugar, rice, bauxite, gold and diamonds and a number of reputable brands of beer and rum but also greenheart, (very hard) mahogany (for furniture) and other lumber. These four U.S. Citizens wanted my advice and guidance. The first question I asked them was how they were able to make contact with me. I was interested. Really, it was simple.

They had contacted the Guyana Consulate. My name was given to them as one who was very familiar with the timber and lumber potential of Guyana, as I was once legal adviser to a large lumber exporting company. In addition, they looked up some reference books and found all the information about me which influenced their decision to consult me. In "Personalities Caribbean," (5th Edition), they saw I was a Director of two large timber companies namely, "Timber Development (Guyana) Ltd." and "Project Investments (Guyana) Ltd." (a company with large holdings of timber lands). They also told me that the fact that I was a student at Lincoln University, Pennsylvania and Columbia University in New York did convince them that they should come to me.

Their research amazed me. I never knew that there was so much relevant information on me in the other reference books they consulted, namely "Dictionary of International Biography (1970)," "Dictionary of International Biography (1975)," and "Men of Achievement, (1977)." There is an old saying that goes this way, "The things that you do are never hidden under a bushel." I was amazed at the meticulous, searching and scrupulous efforts of these four businessmen. If this is how they do business, they were destined to be successful in the business plans they had involving the investment of twenty millions dollars in the thriving lumber industry in Guyana which would have done well at that time, with this welcome "shot in the arm" investment. My clients were particularly interested in the greenheart lumber which is the hardest and most durable lumber used in the construction of harbours, moorings and buildings exposed to sea water.

I was very happy with these American investors. They knew what they were doing. My duty was to guide them and prepare a contract they had to have executed with the two large lumber exporters. This I did. They were completely satisfied with the advice given to them and the draft documents I prepared for them. They discharged their obligations. I told them how best to take care of their money in Guyana and in their presence, I phoned the Manager of one of the leading Banks in Guyana with whom I do business and asked him to give special attention to my clients.

He thanked me for recommending his Bank to them and the resulting sizeable deposit of US Funds in his bank. My clients were very pleased and to my surprise, when they were leaving, they presented me with a very impressive-looking black brief case, which I value very much and which I have in my possession to this day. That was not the end of my professional relationship with them. They invested their money. Things are still going well and I have been retained as their legal adviser for this special investment in Guyana.

One or more of these fine U.S. Citizens would regularly visit Guyana. I recommended to them the Hotel where I book in, whenever I go to Guyana. They maintain that I am not only their lawyer, but a good and sincere friend. This is a recommendation par excellence.

One can earn a good reputation not only as a successful Criminal Defence Attorney, a competent civil lawyer and an excellent advocate in Court, but also as one who deals fairly and effectively with people. There is the human side to every relationship. The success of it all is simple: Give of your best always and treat everyone with respect. That kind of behaviour is very infectious. It is amazing how the recipients of your fair, understanding and courteous treatment react with a similar response. Justice is not found only in the Halls of the Majestic Court-rooms. Justice is where fair play, good and upright relationship are extended to all with whom we come into contact. It never fails.

Chapter 16

Administration of the Law

Leads to Attainment of Justice

Judges, Magistrates, Justices of the Peace and all those who are entrusted with the onerous responsibility of administering Justice, have a sacred trust to see that at all times Justice has been attained and done. Any shelving of this responsibility results sometimes in a multiplicity of proceedings to right the wrong that resulted from the dereliction of the duties imposed on those who are there to hold the scales evenly. Certain basic principles must always be uppermost in the minds of all Judges and others who are there to see that Justice is done.

Since my student days in Law School I can remember how well it was put to us, that there are two fundamental principles to consider when one has to consider what is the basis of Justice that we expect from our Courts. Firstly, there is the principle known as the *"audi alteram partem"* rule – "Let the other side be heard" or put another way, "every man has a right to be heard." The second basic rule is *"nemo indux in propia sua causa,"* meaning "No man should be a judge in his own cause," clearly indicating that a Judge in any cause or matter must be free from bias. All things considered, the conscience of man underscores the attainment of Justice.

Let me consider now, dear readers, two cases, one to illustrate how Justice suffers and is denied when those who administer legal Justice do not grasp fully the impact and scope of the law and embark upon their own erroneous interpretation of the law, despite ample warning and advice not to do so. Justice is also compromised when Judges conveniently forget or overlook the second basic rule that "no man should be a judge in his own cause." The second case illustrates so well how Justice is preserved and protected by those who know their responsibility.

A young chauffeur was charged with the offence of causing death by dangerous driving. The preliminary investigation was held and he was committed to stand trial in the Supreme Court Criminal Sessions. I appeared for him when the matter came up before a Judge and Jury. The Judge before ascending the Judicial Bench was a Magistrate for many years and had a wide experience in traffic violations. He came on the Supreme Court Bench and one expected great things from him. Unfortunately those great expectations were not fully realized.

A Judge must, in his summing-up to the jury, instruct the jury and give them directions on the law relating to the offence before them. The facts are for the jury and as I always tell the jury, no one can usurp that function. They are the sole judges of the facts of the case and the jury, though they are told over and over how the Judge sees the facts and what is his opinion, he cannot foist his views upon the jury. Judges who are called "Prosecution Judges" take advantage of this "shelter" and sometimes canvass their views ad nauseam to the jury who are laymen. They sometimes feel that if that is how the Judge sees it, perhaps they, the Jurors, would be wrong if they found otherwise.

I have always been opposed to this practice of the Judge extolling his views to the jury. It is one thing for the Judge to make a comment on a particular piece of evidence, but quite a different thing to tell the jury how he sees the evidence and that that view is the only reasonable one that makes sense. I have also always been opposed to Judges expressing their own personal views, whether properly perceived or not, to the jury. I have heard Jurors complain time and time again that they felt they had to accept the views which the Judge canvassed to them in his summing up.

The law is very clearly stated. The jury arc the judges of the facts. They make the findings of fact. The jury take their directions of law from the Judge. The jurors are not lawyers. They rely, especially in difficult offences, upon the Judge for directions of law on the offence. The Judge must tell the jurors what are the essential ingredients of the offence before them and what are the legal principles governing the proof by the State or Crown, of the offence engaging their attention. The Judge must also give directions in law of the alternative verdicts they, the jurors, can consider and eventually come to their verdict.

The Judge cannot just tell the jury that, as in this case under review, the offence is causing death by dangerous driving and that is the case they have to consider in their deliberations and return a verdict on that charge. This is bad law. Any Judge must know that this is not permitted and cannot be done. How can the trial Judge sum up on the law if he himself does not understand or know the law? Or were there extraneous matters in the mind of the Judge, to which he was addressing his views?

The Judge is bound to tell the jury what are the alternative offences on which they can properly return a verdict. For example, in an indictment before the jury for "causing death by dangerous driving," the jury could properly return the following verdict: "We find the defendant not guilty of causing death by dangerous driving but guilty of dangerous driving."

The trial Judge must direct the jury not only on "causing death by dangerous driving." He must direct the jury on the alternative offence of "dangerous driving" and give them the directions of law relating to this offence. In short, he must sum up to the jury fully. Not only must he give them directions on the law relating to the offence on the indictment, but he must go on to tell the jury that, if they find the accused guilty of dangerous driving *simpliciter*, they are permitted in law to do so and must return a verdict in keeping with their finding.

What the Judge is not permitted to do, is for him to make up his mind that the only offence before the jury is "causing death by dangerous driving" and that in his mind, this is the only offence they must consider and he then proceeds to give them directions in law on this offence only. For there to be a proper summing up, the Judge must direct the jury on the alternative offence or offences and instruct them on the law applicable to all the various verdicts they could return on the indictment. Of course, the accused cannot be guilty of "causing death by dangerous driving" and the alternative offence of "dangerous driving." It has to be one or the other, not both.

I sat there somewhat perplexed at the summing up of the Judge, who, as I am writing, is no longer with us. Off the Bench, Mr. Justice Sydney Miller, was quite a pleasant man and an omnivorous reader. Several times, he and I had some healthy and illuminating discussions on questions of law and social reform. He could be amusing in his discussions. When he was finished with his summing up, he did what is so often done by the best Judges.

Judge:	"Mr. Manraj, is there anything you would like me to tell the Jury?"
Mr. Manraj:	"There is one area where I know you must give directions to the Jury, but I cannot properly and ethically inform you of this in the presence of the Jury."
Judge:	"But I have concluded my summing-up and I am about to direct the Jury to retire to consider their verdict."
Mr. Manraj:	"My Lord, I know that is the stage you have reached. You have asked me a question. There is one aspect of the case on which it is necessary for you to give directions to the jury. I do not feel that I would be acting in the best professional conduct at the Bar, if I advert your attention to what I have in

	mind to say, in the presence of the Jury."
Judge:	"This is rather strange, Mr. Manraj. What do you suggest?"
Mr. Manraj:	"My Lord, you can do one of several things. You can either let the Jury retire or have them sequestered for a few minutes, while I answer your original question or you can adjourn the Court for a short while, placing the Jury in the charge of the Marshal and the Orderly of the Court, while my learned friend, Counsel for the Crown and I, see you in your Chambers."
Judge:	"That is the practical solution to the problem. Thank you, Mr. Manraj."

The learned Judge then placed the Jury in the charge of the Marshal of the Court and the Orderly of the Court and adjourned the Court for half an hour while the Prosecutor and I saw him in his Chambers.

We all met as directed, in the Judge's Chambers. I came straight to the point and told the Judge in the presence of the Prosecutor, that he had not addressed the Jury at all on the alternative offence of Dangerous Driving. He was very concerned. He asked the Crown Attorney what he had to say and he unhesitatingly stated that he agrees with me. The Judge, however, was of a different view. He said that as the trial Judge, he had to make up his mind what offence was made out on the evidence adduced and sum up to the Jury on the law relevant to that established offence. I told the Judge that his remarks were rather novel to the established practice and he was usurping the functions of the Prosecutor and the Jury. He was set in his erroneous view of the law.

A Distinguished group celebrates Mr. B. O Adams' attainment of Queen's honour.

From left: Justice Keith Gordon, Sir Eustace Woolford, Q. C., Mr. E. A. Adams, Town Clerk, Mr. Joseph Gonsalves and Mr. A. Shakoor Manraj, Q.C.

Delegation from the Guiana All Indian League headed to discussions with Governor. From left: Dr. Balwant Singh, Mr. S. Manraj, Mrs. M. Persaud, Mr. G. Khan and Mr. D. Hetram.

The 21st Anniversary Picture of the then British Guiana Dramatic Society. Shakoor often participated in many of their productions.

We debated the matter for the full half-hour. The Prosecutor asked him to give the Jury some directions on law on the alternative offence of dangerous driving. The Judge thought that was not necessary. He concluded by saying that if he is wrong, "Mr. Manraj would know what is to be done." We ended on a pleasant note.

We returned to open Court. The Jury was re-sworn and the learned Judge told them to retire to consider their verdict. It was not a long deliberation. Within an hour the Jury returned with a verdict of guilty of causing death by dangerous driving. This was an open assault on the fair name of Justice. The accused had a clean record. There is provision in the law for a fine, but the Judge thought that there was too much of this type of offence before the Court and sentenced my client to eighteen months imprisonment. My client was in shock and his elderly mother was very upset. I told her to go over to my Chambers and I will speak to her there.

I do not usually give guarantees on cases involving facts as the trier of facts could think in so many different ways and could make findings of fact in favour of one side to the detriment of the other. But when it comes to Appeals on the law, I do not have any reservations. I told my client and his elderly mother not to worry. I would succeed in the Court of Appeal. I did not charge any more fees for the Appeal as I felt in my heart that I should not let my client or his elderly mother pay for the lack of learning and consequent error of the trial Judge. My client and his mother appreciated this consideration shown to them.

I filed the relevant Appeal papers. In the column where Counsel for the Appellant is usually asked to give an estimate of the time that the Appeal should last, I put half an hour. The matter came up very early before the Federal Court of Appeal of the Caribbean, (the Caribbean Court of Appeal) presided over by the President, Sir Clyde Archer with Sir Donald Jackson and Justice Adrian Date as Appeal Court Judges.

I went straight to the point. I argued before the Court of Appeal that the learned trial Judge usurped the functions of the Jury in holding that the evidence disclosed only the offence of causing death by dangerous driving. The Jury were never given any directions on the alternative verdict of dangerous driving, even though I adverted the Judge's attention to this fact in the presence of the Crown Prosecutor, before the Jury retired to consider their verdict. I cited several cogent and relevant authorities on the law that dealt squarely and forcefully with the point I was arguing. Copies of all my authorities were laid over with the Court.

The Appeal Court agreed with my submissions that no mention was made by the trial Judge on the alternative verdict. Their Lordships allowed the Appeal and substituted a verdict of guilty of dangerous driving. Justice was vindicated. This I felt was my mission – to fight and strive to see that Justice is done. I felt very happy. The lawyers at the Bar table all nodded their acquiescence of the decision of the Court. The next day, the Appeal Court fined my client for the offence of Dangerous Driving. My client and his mother expressed their thanks very movingly and my client told me that he did not intend to pursue the means of his livelihood by driving motor vehicles.

Now let me turn to the second case that I want to bring to your attention. This was in Toronto, Ontario, Canada. Apparently, the Appellant in the Provincial Appeals Court had some difficulty with a Traders Breach of Contract case. He appeared before the Magistrates Court and his matter was heard. He lost his case and had to pay some money as fine as well as by way of restitution to the owners of the property.

At the time of the hearing of this Appeal, I was Counsel appearing on behalf of the Crown, in the Provincial Appeals Court. I read the transcript of the proceedings in the Magistrate's Court. I myself did not know who were the shareholders or owners or directors of the Company involved. The learned Magistrate found that the Appellant was guilty of a Breach of his Traders Contract and proceeded to fine him and make certain orders regarding restitution to the owners of the property.

The Appellant appealed the Magistrate's finding, albeit that the decision was based upon findings of fact made by the Magistrate. Everyone involved in the law knows that appeals on questions of fact are not usually very successful. An Appellate Court is reluctant to interfere with the findings of fact made by a Magistrate on the ground that the Magistrate was the trier of the facts of the case and his decision was the result of the findings of fact.

If the findings of fact are perverse or so unreasonable or are not supported by the facts adduced in evidence before the Magistrate, then the Appeal Court usually sets aside the Magistrate's findings and properly give a decision based on the facts of the case disclosed by the evidence adduced before the Magistrate. The Judge sitting in the Provincial Appeals Court was a brilliant Judge and he and I worked very hard to get this new Appeal Court, functioning out of Old City Hall, established.

It is this reluctance to interfere with findings of fact that makes Appeals from the findings of fact, made by a jury so difficult. Appeals on questions of law are usually what takes up most of the time in Appeal Courts. When one is going to argue an Appeal based on the findings of fact by the jury, then he has an uphill task. The rationale is simple. The Appeal Court has not seen the witnesses, has not had an opportunity to observe the demeanour of the witnesses and observe the appearance and attitude of the witness or witnesses. The Court of first instance is in a far better position than an Appeal Court, to judge and assess credibility of the witnesses.

Whereas the Court of first instance has these physical advantages of seeing and observing the witnesses, the Appeal Court has before it only the impersonal, lifeless transcript of the evidence adduced before the Court of first instance. Many Magistrates and triers of fact in summary trials take full advantage of this and always resort to the established language used by them and perfected in this formula:

> *"I have had the opportunity of observing the demeanour and conduct of the witness (or witnesses) and he (or they) did not impress me as being truthful with the Court."*

Then as if to justify their findings and make an Appeal against their findings of fact almost impossible, they add this punch line:

> *"Whenever the evidence of the witnesses for the defence was in conflict with the evidence adduced by the prosecution, I found in favour of the prosecution and rejected the evidence of the defendant."*

The wording of the formula is changed depending on the nature of the case. If it is a Civil Action, which the Magistrate is trying, the parties would be the Plaintiff and the Defendant and not the Prosecution and the Defendant. So much for a picture of how the Court of First Instance functions.

It appears that the Appellant before the Appeal Court had some information that I was not privy to. When the Appeal was eventually reached, the Appellant, appearing unrepresented by Counsel, addressed the Court stating, "Your Honour, I must respectfully ask that you do not hear this Appeal as I have information to the fact that you are very much a part of the Company that owns the property in question and as such, I do not think that Your Honour should hear this Appeal."

The learned Judge, the late Robert Dnieper, was a brilliant Judge. He and I together had built up a reputation of putting the comparatively new Provincial Appeals Court in orbit. His Honour's knowledge was deep and he knew his law. He was always very kind and always announced to the Court that he is privileged to have in his Court, representing the Crown, a British Queen's Counsel, appointed by Her Majesty the Queen. He was always very kind to me. On the Bench, he was respected, was tolerant to the public and appreciated good legal arguments.

When the Appellant made his request in open Court, Judge Dnieper stated to the Appellant: "You are so correct in your representation. I want to assure you that on my reading of the transcript, I realized that I have an interest in the Company and I decided to recuse myself and decline to hear your Appeal on the ground of conflict of interest. Mr. Manraj, have you anything you would like to say."

This was always Judge Dnieper's attitude. He never left me out of any decision he had to make pertaining to the conduct of a case or the Jurisdiction of the Court.

I told His Honour that his statement is so replete with the appreciation of his responsibility of his standing as a respected Judge and continued my statement,

Mr. Manraj:	"...Justice embodies two important principles. The first, Your Honour, is so aptly expressed in the Latin maxim: "Audi alteram partem" and the second and to my mind, the more important of the two, is also set out in impeccable Latin: *"Nemo indux in propria sua causa"* – "No man should be a Judge in his own cause." It embraces situations such as the one which is presently engaging Your Honour's attention. *Fiat Justitiae.* Your Honour, I respectfully suggest that this Appeal be set down for hearing before the next sitting of

this Appeal Court which will be presided over by another Judge."

Justice was done.

Judge: "I thank you, Mr. Manraj. Your Latin maxims and references are reminiscent of Cicero's orations which you and I have had the privilege of studying."

Mr. Manraj: "For the record, this matter is to come up for hearing before the next sitting of this Appeal Court presided over by another Judge."

I go back to the title of this Chapter. Justice triumphs and is done when there is "unfailing application of the rules, by those who are appointed to see that Justice is done." The Judge knew what his responsibility in the circumstances was and he stated very early his intention in open Court.

Epilogue

The Evolution Of Justice:

The Past Fifty Years And The Expectations Of Justice For The Next Fifty Years

I would not be so egoistic as to conclude that I have satisfied the interests of everyone, who so kindly decided to read this book. What I do state is that I have sincerely and conscientiously studied the varied and wide practice I conducted for over fifty years and I then tried to evaluate the interests of the reader of a book of this type. The choice of material used in these Chapters is solely mine.

No one dictated to me how I should express myself, what material I should cover, which of the three hundred and thirty murder cases in which I appeared should be the subject matter of my book, or what types of cases I should write on. The selection was purely subjective and I wrote on matters and cases that I feel would find a place in the hearts of all those who would really like to follow what I did in my fifty years at the Bar and read the reviews of the cases that remind me vividly of the struggle and determination to attain Justice.

I am thinking as I write, of the lovely and simple words used by Prospero in the Epilogue of "The Tempest" by William Shakespeare. Here is how "Prospero" expressed his inner feelings about the acceptance by the audience of the play:

> *"With the help of your good hands, (1) Gentle breath (2) of yours my sails must fill, or else my project fails, Which was to please ...."*

The footnotes to the Epilogue give as the meaning to (1) "Good hands" as "applause" and the meaning of (2)

"Gentle Breath," as "favourable comment." Like Prospero, I sincerely hope that my efforts will receive your approval and appreciation.

Now for my views and insight of the evolution of Justice in the next fifty years. We, as Defence Counsel, go into the Courts each day inspired by the deep-rooted feeling that we are there to see that rights and privileges are protected. Even today, it seems commonplace and normal that the invasion of rights and privileges of individuals continues with unremitting regularity and intensity. It is a matter of concern.

Everyday our life is becoming more and more circumscribed by regulations, by-laws, rules and legislation setting out and sometimes, re-defining our behaviour, conduct and relationship with the country or state. The modern legislative assembly is so focused on the political stability of the government in power, that incursions on the rights of citizens seem acceptable and necessary.

Little by little, it seems that established rights, even the enshrined rights, are being eroded. Although definitions have been assigned to certain types of behaviour and status, yet we find that there are misapplications and incursions of those established rights by the Courts presided over by Judges who do not sit on the Bench to protect those rights and privileges. It appears to them that is not really their function.

As Criminal Defence Counsel, I am concerned about the maxim that "one is innocent until proven guilty by the prosecution." This has been the established procedure for centuries. It is the inheritance from the Common Law. In the forthcoming years I feel very uneasy about the course of a criminal trial and the presumption of innocence. It could very well develop into a situation that "a man is guilty until he proves himself innocent." The prosecution presents the facts, true or false, without any regard for the doctrine of "reasonable doubt" or a scaled down version of some semblance of justification and necessity and the defendant must then rebut the allegations and in so doing, shoulder the responsibility of proving that he is innocent and not guilty.

Governments are becoming more and more powerful and it is becoming increasingly difficult for Defence Counsel to continue his role as the protector of all those rights and privileges that we inherited and on which we grew up to accept as immutable. It is conceded that changing situations necessitate changing procedures and laws, but the "rights of redress" must never be withheld or denied. The Courts reflect the education, the training and the ability of the Judges who preside over them. There is a trend to put insufficiently trained, inexperienced and unsuitable persons on the Bench.

This causes a lamentable deterioration in the administration of Justice. Justice is steadily moving away from established principles of fair-play and that which is morally right. The old, well-tested and accepted maxim of: "JUSTICE DELAYED IS JUSTICE DENIED" (see Chapter 13) will almost certainly be completely guillotined, as trials will become more speedy and procedurally short-circuited at the expense of established constitutional safeguards of what is right, moral and fair.

Democracy is a good thing. It is more easily preached than practised. Our lives are becoming more difficult by an over effective control of the authorities and all those concerned with individual liberty and all its related features. Poor people are suffering and I can see their plight getting worse. Monopolistic control of basic necessities and services will become more frightening. Mergers have gone off into a direction that can lead to grave hardships for the ordinary man in the street.

A very important development causes me some concern. Courts costs are on the rise. Disbursements and service charges are in no way reflective of the benefits that are sought. It seems that in the next fifty years, Justice will not be in the hearts and minds of individuals who aspire to hold the scales evenly, but will be codified. What is Justice will be found in the pages of a book – a text book – not what is found in the hearts and conscience of men. The principles of Equity were mentioned earlier in my Chapter on "What is Justice?" Chapter 1, will become, if this trend continues, nothing more than a set of Statutory enactments.

The world is moving fast – too fast and since human behavioural patterns are being outstripped by developing rubber-stamp laws, I feel that the whole of the Equitable Jurisdiction of the Courts will be merged completely in the establishment of Civil Rules of Procedures, administered by the Courts of Civil Jurisdiction. What is "unconscionable and unjust" will no longer reside in the Courts of Conscience, but rather in the mind or feeling or understanding of a Judge who is not even on "nodding acquaintance" with the time-honoured and recognized principles of Equity and the Maxims of Equity.

I make no comments on accepted social behaviour, respect for elders by young people, the old, established and respectable institution of marriage. Common law relationships seem to be the accepted norm in today's social standards. No one raises an eye-brow anymore over the common law relationship between man and woman. Will there be a complete turn-around of the behaviour, mind-set and thinking-processes of our young generation fifty years hence? Perhaps, in time not too far distant, anyone over sixty-five might be regarded as an anachronism or a redundant misfit.

Criminal Defence Counsel will be a different type of lawyer, more concerned with the lessons of History, Economics, Politics and Genocide, than with Miranda rights and *voire dires*. How far Criminal Defence Attorneys will be able to prevail in the Courts in the defence of the rights and privileges of their clients, is an area that causes me much concern. I was present in the Criminal Court about two months ago to observe how the current Court functions. Counsel for the Defence was submitting that the statement alleged to have been made by the defendant is not admissible and advanced sound legal arguments. The Judge, very anxious to get on with the list said, "Counsel, I hear that all the time. Don't you really think that the Police by now know all about taking statements?" This caused me some serious concern as in the matter in which I was involved in New York, the statement taken by the Police was taken without the rights of the defendant being told to him. Worst of all, at the identification parade held by the Police, conducted without Counsel for the defendant being present, proceeded although the defendant had requested that his Counsel be present and Counsel was there and agreed to be present at the Identification parade. Fortunately, in that matter, my colleague and I appearing for the defendant were successful in getting the prosecution to withdraw the charges.

The law is a noble profession. Reading jurisprudence, legal history and the subjects incorporated in present-day legal studies, is a rewarding exercise. The syllabuses of Law Schools may undergo radical surgery resulting in many important limbs of the study of law being removed and replaced by more so-called "pragmatic" syllabuses incorporating more social and economic subjects. I am very concerned about the continued juristic evolution of Private International Law. Already, one sees that serious incursions are being made in that area of jurisprudence. The world is in turmoil and so are the governing principles relating to Private International Law.

The 9/11 incident of 2001 has changed the whole world and the freedom of movement of citizens of other countries, to emigrate to the U.S.A. and many other countries. More stringent safeguards have been and are being implemented and freedom of travel has already become very restricted. Generally speaking, Immigration Laws have become and will become much tougher.

One hesitates and ponders over the development of AVIATION LAW. Air travel will be the way to go. Perhaps space travel would become the accepted holiday travel for people in the high income bracket. If recent developments are of any significance or indication, it is clear that there will be faster, much bigger and more powerful and sophisticated passenger aircrafts and space-crafts. One only hopes that the necessary safeguards would keep pace with the developing technology. Crashes and space-accidents prevention techniques will have to be drastically updated and developed. Ejection procedures will have a new meaning at supersonic speeds. In the next fifty years, the whole aviation industry will be run on completely new procedures and techniques. Flight crews will have to undergo an entirely different type of training to cope with the advanced machines on which they will be working.

The Substantive Law and Subsidiary Legislation relating to bars, cafes and night clubs and other places of entertainment where alcohol is served, will have to be drastically reviewed and perhaps replaced, to keep abreast of the growing and sometimes strange and unorthodox behaviour and demands of people who go to such places for a casual drink or relaxation. The bars and clubs will hardly be the place where one would go to have a drink and play a game of darts or meet with friends. These places under discussion will become places of strange types of entertainment demanded and supported by a new breed of club patrons.

Ecclesiastical Law and established traditions of the Church will have to be drastically reviewed and revised to accommodate the new trends in the Church, involving disturbing changing patterns of social and domestic behaviour and the religious precepts and practices that are presently infiltrating into the established Church and the ordained clergy.

Road Traffic Law and Traffic Regulations will undergo drastic reforms. The Law on Speeding and Parking Regulations will have to undergo intensive surgery to bring them in line with the state of affairs and existing conditions fifty years hence. The general road traffic law will have to be updated and revised to accommodate the invasion of new concepts relating to much faster and more powerful motor vehicles and the role they will play in establishing a new standard of motoring. More and more, people are intent on bringing their living room into their expensive, fancy and fast-moving motor vehicles.

Concentration when driving will be a matter of grave concern and the use today of the cellular phone when driving, will become a harmful accepted practice and more distracting gadgetry would distract drivers even more. If the telephone in the car is to be used, then legislation must provide that drivers must pull over, stop and make or take the call. If effective and necessary checks are not implemented, then I dread to think of the carnage that would be caused on our roadways and highways traversed by the speedier and highly powerful cars and other motor vehicles. The cockpits of these cars and other vehicles of the future would greatly contribute and facilitate distractions when driving.

The Law and the administration of the Law will change drastically and what is more disturbing, is the fact that the Judges who are now administering the Law and those who will continue to administer the law, seem to feel that the preservation of rights and liberties should not occupy the place of prominence they now hold. Civil rights and liberties will have to be vigilantly advocated in order to survive in our established system of Justice. Justice may not be as illusory as was once thought. Efforts to codify the essentials of Justice and reduce them to substantive or procedural law will annihilate all that *Themis*, the perfection of Justice, stood for since the early days of Greek mythology.

All the statues of the blindfolded lady with scales in one hand and sword in the other, erected in and over the Courts of Justice will have lost their symbolism. *Themis* still stands on top of the Central Criminal Court ("Old Bailey") in London, England. Justice may no longer have a blindfold over her eyes to denote impartiality and unbiased application of the two fundamental concepts of Justice as set out in Chapter 1 of my book. The two fundamental concepts are: (i) every man has a right to a fair hearing and (ii) no man should be a judge in his own cause or matter. As Justice is compromised, so more and more emerging difficulties to protect the rights of society, will result in serious problems engaging the attention of the Courts already pre-occupied by an overflow of criminal, civil and domestic litigation.

Index